THE GREAT AMERICAN MAKEOVER

TELEVISION, HISTORY, NATION

EDITED AND INTRODUCED BY
DANA HELLER

THE GREAT AMERICAN MAKEOVER
© Dana Heller, 2006.

First published in 2006 by
PALGRAVE MACMILLAN™
175 Fifth Avenue, New York, N.Y. 10010 and
Houndmills, Basingstoke, Hampshire, England RG21 6XS
Companies and representatives throughout the world.

PALGRAVE MACMILLAN is the global academic imprint of the Palgrave Macmillan division of St. Martin's Press, LLC and of Palgrave Macmillan Ltd. Macmillan® is a registered trademark in the United States, United Kingdom and other countries. Palgrave is a registered trademark in the European Union and other countries.

ISBN-13: 978–1–4039–7483–9 (hardcover)
ISBN-10: 1–4039–7483–7 (hardcover)
ISBN-13: 978–1–4039–7484–6 (paperback)
ISBN-10: 1–4039–7484–5 (paperback)

Library of Congress Cataloging-in-Publication Data

The great American makeover : television, history, nation / edited and with an introduction by Dana Heller.
    p. cm.
    Includes bibliographical references and index.
    ISBN 1–4039–7483–7 (alk. paper)—ISBN 1–4039–7484–5 (alk. paper)
    1. United States—Civilization—1970– 2. United States—Civilization. 3. National characteristics, American. 4. Popular culture—United States. 5. Self-realization—Social aspects—United States. 6. Self-perception— Social aspects—United States. 7. Makeover television programs—United States. 8. Television—Social aspects—United States. I. Heller, Dana A. (Dana Alice), 1959–

E169.12.G7 2006
302.23'450973—dc22   2006045410

A catalogue record for this book is available from the British Library.

Design by Newgen Imaging Systems (P) Ltd., Chennai, India.

First edition: December 2006

10 9 8 7 6 5 4 3 2 1

Printed in the United States of America.

Again, for G. T., makeover artist extraordinaire

CONTENTS

Part II   Makeover Television Formats, 1950–Today

LIST OF FIGURES

Acknowledgments

THIS BOOK IS A PRODUCT OF THE PLEASURE that I take in watching, thinking, and talking about television in its historical and national contexts. However it never would have progressed beyond the dinner conversation phase if not for the dedicated colleagues, friends, students, and fellow fans who share this pleasure with me and who take it as seriously as I do. Above all, I would like to express my appreciation to the contributors to this volume, who together constitute the most venturesome and energetic lot I've had the pleasure to make a book with. I would also like to thank the editorial and production staff at Palgrave Macmillan, and in particular Farideh Koohi-Kamali who took a risk with my quirky idea for a collection, and the anonymous reviewers whose sage guidance brought cohesion and balance to the blueprint—they know who they are.

I am most fortunate to have a job that nurtures my indiscriminate critical impulses and places no limits on the interdisciplinary imagination. I am deeply grateful to all those who support and sustain the well-being of Old Dominion University's Humanities Institute and Graduate Program, as I cannot imagine another academic environment that would have so readily and faithfully embraced the idea of a book on makeovers. And I am enormously grateful to my Research Assistants, Ashley Graham Kennedy (2005–2006) and Wendy Creekmore (2004–2005), whose perseverance and precision was, and continues to be, nothing short of staggering.

Finally, I must acknowledge the following for their assistance and gracious permission to reprint:

Portions of Dana Heller's introduction to this volume first appeared in her review piece, "Taking the Nation 'from Drab to Fab': *Queer Eye For the Straightguy*," which was published in *Feminist Media Studies* 4.3 (Fall 2004): 347–50.

Portions of June Deery's chapter in this volume first appeared in her essay, "Trading Faces: the Makeover Show as Prime-time Infomercial," which was published in *Feminist Media Studies* 4.2 (Summer 2004): 211–14.

The photos of John Brown in chapter 2 appear courtesy of the Library of Congress, the Boston Athenaeum, and the Kansas State Historical Society.

The photo of Joel Handler Harris in chapter 3 appears courtesy of the Hargrett Rare Book and Manuscript Library, University of Georgia Libraries.

Dana Heller
Norfolk, Virginia

CHAPTER 1

BEFORE: "THINGS JUST KEEP GETTING BETTER . . ."

DANA HELLER

A DISTINCTIVE SUBGENRE OF REALITY TELEVISION, contemporary makeover shows invite us to participate in fantasies of individual as well as national transformation and advancement. Consider, for example, ABC's successful series, *The Biggest Loser*, a show dedicated to the dangerous "pathology of fatness" and its threat not only to the overweight contestants who compete throughout the season to lose weight and attain the strength and confidence associated with "hard bodies," but also to the United States and its ability to function as a healthy, unassailable nation.[1] A thinner citizenry is a more desirable citizenry, the series suggests, and contestants must demonstrate fierce discipline, motivational team-spirit, and theatrical emotional candor in order to realize their makeover from fat to fit, or from object of ridicule to agent of self-control. The national ramifications of this metamorphosis are plainly expressed in one fitness coach's reference to himself as "America's trainer." *The Biggest Loser*, from this perspective, conveys a double meaning: not only does it refer to the contestant who sheds the most flab, but also to all nonparticipants in the nation's collective boot camp, those who are marked by the bodily and psychological stigma of national nonbelonging—excessive fat being one such obvious stigma. Interestingly, what American makeover shows often tell us is that self-realization and conformity to cultural ideals are twin virtues founded on one's unrealized desire for belonging: in this sense, makeover shows promise to make subjects more truly themselves by making them look, dress, decorate, and desire as others ostensibly do.

Increasingly we witness reality television's preference for programming arranged around the theme of self-transformation. We see it in makeover shows that annex and transform the private space of the home (e.g., *Extreme Makeover: Home Edition, Design on a Dime, Trading Spaces, While You Were Out*), in shows that arbitrate and surgically transform the body (e.g., *Extreme Makeover, The Swan, I Want a Famous Face*), in shows that transform the dynamics of the intimate familial relations (*Supernanny, Wife Swap, Nanny 911*), in shows that promise to transform ordinary persons into celebrities and celebrities into ordinary persons (e.g., *American Idol, I Want to Be a Hilton, The Osbournes, Simple Life*), and in shows that perform a total overhaul of consumer lifestyle (*Queer Eye For the Straight Guy, Queer Eye for the Straight Girl, Pimp My Ride*). Some of these shows have proved controversial, eliciting both protest and praise from audiences and critics; however, few if any television commentators have noted the striking congruity between makeover as contemporary televisual format and makeover as a distinctive national historical myth. Indeed, in the United States, where ratings for shows such as *Extreme Makeover: Home Edition* have posted higher than popular scripted dramas, gaining audiences in a surge that has stunned industry executives, the complex cultural origins of makeover narrative can be broadly traced to myths of American expansionism, evangelicalism, and immigration. Robert Thompson, Director of the Center for the Study of Popular Television at Syracuse University, summarizes these connections:

> If you had to describe the American mythos in one single word, "reinvention" really would not be a bad choice. One could argue that from the time of the Pilgrims' arriving at Plymouth Rock, a lot of at least the European settlement story of America has been about reinvention, leaving the Old World for the New. It's American culture as the annihilation of history, of the past. . . . *In a very real sort of way, the history of the United States is one big fat makeover show.*[2]

Here Thompson points to the historical currents, practices, and precedents that shape the production and reception of contemporary makeover television in the United States, opening the way toward a genealogy of a national makeover mythos. However, what Thompson's commentary does not explicitly account for are the gendered, racialized, and sexualized notions of self-realization, consumption, power, and pleasure that inform the "big fat makeover," otherwise known as American cultural history. Makeover industries that address white, middle-class women as their principal subjects and offer feminine instruction and advice in physical appearance, deportment, and lifestyle remained staples of nineteenth- and twentieth-century popular culture, from magazines such as *Ladies Home Journal*, to 1950s "misery shows" such as *Glamour Girl* (1953–1954) and *Queen for a Day* (1956–1964) to fitness, well-being, and lifestyle gurus such as Jane Fonda, Oprah Winfrey, and Martha Stewart. However, contrary to the assumption of a natural correspondence between white bourgeois femininity and U.S. consumerism's transformational rituals, American history reveals countless examples of the makeover myth's wider social, cultural, and political relevance. This is evident in the popularity of nineteenth-century advice manuals for boys on how to reinvent oneself for success in the business world, as well as in the frequent refashioning of racial self-image performed in American literature and folklore, as seen in the plantation tales of Joel Chandler Harris, and in the political agitations by reformers such as the abolitionist John Brown. In the twentieth century, the makeover impulse continues to reverberate through the scholarly Adamic myth of R.W.B. Lewis, the commercial celebrity of "Charles Atlas" (born Angelo Siciliano, an Italian immigrant) and the men's body-building culture he helped spawn, the popularity of African American lifestyle magazines such as *Ebony*, and the indeterminate number of people, both men and women, gay and straight, who have enjoyed exercising with Richard Simmons.

Thus, the interdisciplinary essays that comprise this book will seek to identify, interrogate, and historicize the American makeover and explore its relation to national myths that have circulated throughout the cultural history of the United States, up to the current television "makeover takeover" (to use the phrase coined by Rachel Moseley, in an essay examining the format's ubiquitous presence on British television).[3] In this way, this book considers makeover television formats as backward-glancing, or as descended from earlier national myths and practices of reinvention and transformation. At the same time, writers for this volume are committed to the analysis of contemporary makeover culture as forward-looking insofar as it registers faith in myths of perpetual progress and upward mobility. In other words, this collection will demonstrate that the makeover is a crucial link between earlier and emergent forms and processes of engagement with the national imaginary.

As a case in point, we might consider the July 2003 premiere of Bravo's lifestyle makeover series, *Queer Eye for the Straight Guy*. When that show began setting new records for ratings at the cable network (reaching 3.35 million viewers by the third episode), media critics scrambled to account for the phenomena. Certainly, historically the moment seemed right. The euphoric "summer of love," inspired largely by Canada's recognition of same-sex marriage rights and the U.S. Supreme Court's landmark ruling in "Lawrence versus Texas," appeared to foreshadow the unprecedented extent of incorporation of gays and lesbians into mainstream social, civic, and cultural life. At the same time, figures released in July 2003 by the Consumer Research Center's Index of Consumer Confidence suggested a gloomy economic picture of the nation, as numbers for June 2003 took a sharp, unexpected downturn from levels already notably low.[4] In the midst of these controversial and uneven developments, television viewers were treated to yet another reality show, *Queer Eye for the Straight Guy*, this one featuring a posse of five witty, well-groomed gay men with a mission "to transform a style-deficient and culture-deprived straight man from drab to fab in each of their respective categories: fashion, food & wine, interior design, grooming and culture."[5]

Queer Eye's meteoric rise to popularity prompted Bravo's parent company, NBC, to announce that it would rebroadcast a modified version of the show's premiere during its prestigious Thursday night lineup. When asked whether a major network was ready to embrace the *Queer Eye* concept, Jeff Zucker, president of NBC Entertainment admitted, "The sensational ratings speak for themselves."[6] But how might we make sense of these ratings? To begin with, *Queer Eye* conveys a message very similar to its nineteenth and twentieth-century cultural predecessors: self-realization, romance, and success are attainable through the acquisition of services and durable goods for the self and the home. *Queer Eye* demonstrates, within the time-honored framework of "before and after" juxtaposition, that our shortcomings and self-doubts are not necessarily the result of who we are, but of what we buy, how we present ourselves, and how we are consequently perceived. A classic loafer from Pink, a Zirh exfoliant, and some Pottery Barn sectionals can all add up, from this perspective, to a new sense of our inner worth and an improved standing in the outer world. The upwardly mobile, can-do optimism that guides *Queer Eye* is a key component of U.S. makeover culture insofar as it satisfies the wish-fulfillment longings of viewers (presumably the female partners of the straight guys who need training) and provides endless opportunities for product endorsements. At the same time, this makeover spirit is a key element of a deeply power-stratified society that regards the middle-class (and, as on *Queer Eye*, often ethnically marked) body as protean and in need of supervision by administrators well-versed in the manipulation of consumer technologies designed to secure consensual belief in our perpetual personal—and, by extension, national—progress. In mid-summer 2003, there was no better community to assign this administrative function to than the gay community, one of the few segments of American society that seemed to be making any progress at all.

At the same time, *Queer Eye* shows American audiences something that they have not been accustomed to seeing on network television: nonviolent, mutually respectful, cooperative relations between openly homosexual and heterosexual men, in situations where the latter are outnumbered by the former. In this sense, the progress narrative generated by *Queer Eye* gestures beyond the individual consumer subject and addresses viewers as citizen subjects by suggesting through its weekly narratives the progress of liberal democratic society's widening embrace of social diversity and tolerance. This is well summed up in the final moments of an episode in which straight guy Chris Lim expresses his gratitude to the Fab Five: "You've really shown me what it *means* to be a man."

As Joanne DiMattia observes of this scene, which recalls the early twentieth century ad campaigns of Charles Atlas, the ironic "lessons learned, are not lost on the Fab 5 or their audience."[7] This optimistic narrative is belied, however, by the show's adherence to media stereotypes of gay men, the most pernicious of which is that there are no gay men of color. The fact that James Hannaham, the sole African American cast member, was dropped from the series as the "Culture Vulture" and replaced with the lighter-skinned Jai Rodriguez demonstrates *Queer Eye*'s blindness to racial differences in the very process of its marketing of "culture" as the readily tradable property of the racially or ethnically marked other, himself apparently equally exchangeable.

Moreover, as queer caricatures, the so-called "Fab Five" are often shrill and cruel in their assessments of the lifestyles and behaviors of the men they tutor. Viewers receive no information whatsoever about their lives and histories. Watching *Queer Eye*, one would have to assume that gay men live in splendid isolation from emotion and desire, spending their days in upscale shops and salons, meditating over color-coordinated bath towels, and finally relaxing with a fluorescent-colored cocktail as they wryly observe straight men conduct the messy business of "real" life from behind the safety and insularity of their television monitors. On the other hand, straight guys do not fare much better, appearing for the most part a sorry lot of unkempt dimwits, still wearing t-shirts from the Reagan era and furnishing their apartments with castaway items pilfered from their mother's basements. Thus it comes as no surprise that the straight guy whose looks and environment are transformed in the space of an hour ritually expresses profound gratitude to the Fab Five as he prepares for his appointed task, be it a consequential dinner party, job interview, or marriage proposal. The point is this: more than accepting gay men as part of the rich, colorful tapestry of American life, the straight guys of *Queer Eye* must finally admit that they *need* gay men in order to realize their completion and, perhaps more importantly, to receive their compensation for the bankrupt pieties of classic heterosexual masculinity, a masculinity that the series suggests is inadequate, deficient, and in crisis. As the Fab Five heroically intervene to save the day, the strategic, well-executed consumer arts that they entrust to their straight charges cannot be thought apart from the larger cultural effort to sustain confidence in American masculinity, consumerist ideology, and the coherence of the national body in times of deepening anxiety over what the nation is becoming and uncertainty over who, ultimately, will bear the cost.

* * *

The premise of this collection—as briefly demonstrated above and as explicitly stated in the subtitle of this volume—is that television, history, and nation come together under the banner of the American makeover mythos. As a means of organizing this assertion, readers will note that this book consists of two parts. The first part includes chapters on what we are calling the "makeover mythos," or the historical currents, practices, and precedents that inform contemporary makeover television programs. These chapters emphasize connections between past myths and the national imaginary, with an eye toward understanding how the current conjunction of makeover television shows is distinct and yet reasonably a part of this tradition. The second section includes discussions of particular popular makeover television programs of the last 50 years and their mediated social messages and functions. These chapters address the questions of why these shows matter and, perhaps more importantly for our purposes, why they matter in very particular historical contexts. In keeping with the makeover theme, readers will further note that the entire collection is framed by this introduction, the "Before," and an "After," written by television historian, Lynn Spigel, which considers the art of American pop culture icon Andy Warhol as a critique of the makeover's darker national significance.

There is little question that further research is called for: Indeed, while much has been written and published in the last few years on the global phenomena of Reality Television (RTV) and its hybrid formats, this is the first book to examine the makeover television phenomena, its origins and its pervasive influence in modern American cultural life.[8] If critical attention has not kept pace with the recent resurgence of makeover television formats, it is my hope, as editor of this volume, that *The Great American Makeover* will inspire others to take up and further analyze the genre of makeover television programming and its long-standing cultural precedents. Clearly, more work is needed to extend scholarship on global televisual formats, nationally rooted myths, and the relationship of television viewing practices to diverse, local cultural idioms and constructions of national identity and belonging. The writers for this volume agree that makeover television offers fertile ground for the cultivation of such discussion. If their task was initially to demonstrate the tenacity of the makeover mythos—its enduring ability to speak to our shifting national desires and anxieties—they have succeeded and have in the process revealed American television's own enduring ability to reinvent itself.

NOTES

1. Elaine Hanson Cardenas, "Dubious Moniker: Review of *The Biggest Loser*," PopMatters, September 13, 2005, Available at: http://www.popmatters.com/tv/reviews/b/biggest-loser-050913.shtml (Accessed on January 5, 2006).

2. Robert Thompson, "Finding Happiness Between Commercials," *The Chronicle of Higher Education* 17 (October 2003): B4.

3. Rachel Moseley, "Makeover Takeover on British Television," *Screen* 41, no. 3 (2000): 299–314.

4. The Conference Board (2003) "U.S. leading economic indicators and related composite indexes for June 2003," released July 21, 2003. Available at: http://www.conference-board.org/economics/ (Accessed on November 4, 2004).

5. *Bravo* (2003), "Queer Eye for the Straight Guy." Available at: http://www.bravotv.com/Queer_Eye_for_the_Straight_Guy/About.shtml (Accessed on October 31, 2003).

6. Steve Rogers, "NBC to Broadcast condensed version of Bravo's *Queer Eye for the Straight Guy* premiere on Thursday, July 24." *Reality TV World*. Available at: http://www.bravotv.com/Queer_Eye_for_the_Straight_Guy/About.shtml (Accessed on October 31, 2003).

7. Joanna L. DiMattia, "The Gentle Art of Manscaping: Lessons in Hetero-Masculinity From the "*Queer Eye* Guys," in *Makeover Television: Realities Remodeled*, ed. Dana Heller (London I.B. Tauris, 2007).

8. Those works include, but by no means are limited to, Mark Andrejevic, *Reality TV: The Work of Being Watched* (Lanham, MS: Rowman & Littlefield, 2004); *Reality Squared: Televisual Discourses on the Real*, ed. James Friedman (New Brunswick, NJ, and London: Rutgers University Press, 2002); Annette Hill, *Reality TV: Audiences and Popular Factual Television* (London and New York: Routledge, 2005); *Understanding Reality Television*, ed. Su Holmes and Deborah Jermyn (London and New York: Routledge, 2004); *Reality TV: Remaking, Television Culture*, ed. Susan Murray and Laurie Ouellette (New York: New York University Press, 2004).

PART I

THE MAKEOVER MYTHOS, PAST TO PRESENT

A THEATRICAL MANAGER: JOHN BROWN AND THE RADICAL POLITICS OF THE AMERICAN MAKEOVER MYTHOS

ZOE TRODD

> no theatrical manager could have arranged things so wisely to give effect to his behavior and words
>
> Henry David Thoreau, 1860

"DOES ANYONE EVEN STUDY HISTORY ANYMORE?" So enquired Timothy McVeigh, soon to become the Oklahoma City bomber, in a 1994 letter to the American Legion. *He* apparently studied history, for after his attack on federal buildings he told reporters that he hoped America would remember him as kin to John Brown, the original American freedom fighter. "If I am going to hell," he added, "I'm gonna have a lot of company." According to one newspaper, he cited Brown as an inspiration, though "conveniently forgot or downplayed the fact that his militia philosophy has its repressive roots in a reactionary, rightwing agenda of racism, sexism, and cultish religious fundamentalism."[1]

Brown was as conscious and manipulative of historical and mythic precedents as McVeigh. His life and death have been reimagined and remade across history, by McVeigh and others, in part because Brown himself cultivated the American makeover mythos: his various self-representational strategies were models for the discourse that came after his death. Brown made himself, to use his own phrase, "a mere blank" upon which new faces could be sketched, but he was the first to make over his face. He was a self-made man in the more literal sense of the expression, for he made and remade himself during his lifetime, with a keen eye for his own mythology; from business-man to Indian warrior, from black man to martyr. After his capture at Harper's Ferry, the national press used various images that Brown himself had projected—prophet, patriot, messiah, terrorist. Abolitionists were able to feed the myths and remake Brown because he had begun the makeover process. To examine Brown is to come face-to-face with a man who wrote himself into myth and saw the radical potential of the American makeover mythos.[2]

Called an enigma by several who knew him personally, and notoriously difficult for biographers and historians to understand, Brown relied on his self-constructed public image because he had no identity through a career, little education, and an unimpressive history of bankruptcy. To be an insider he needed a public persona, and power and influence came with the construction of legends, during his life as well as after his death. He used the chronic social upheaval of his times and the instability of his life as oppor-tunities to constantly redefine himself, and this self-definition was complex, multivalent, and fluid. The perfect subject for the philosopher of biography, Brown resisted the "myth of coherent personality" and played multiple roles consciously, purposefully, and with great skill. He loved disguise and indulged his romantic streak, embracing such roles as the Job-like loser, the philosophical Mayflower descendent, the simple farmer, the brutal Kansas terrorist. He wrote his autobiography in the third-person, read John Foxe's *Book of Martyrs* repeatedly, and used a variety of stage names, for logistical reasons but perhaps also to express his shifting selfhood: in April 1857 he was Nelson Hawkins; in May 1857, James Smith; in June 1858, Shubel Morgan (complete with long white beard); and in May 1859, Isaac Smith. He played in particular on the expectations and self-conceptions of New England abolitionists, invoking their self-fashioned Puritan heritage.[3]

His public self-fashioning involved mythic self-description. William Phillips recalled an occasion on which Brown invoked Spartacus:

[Brown told] me of Spartacus and his servile war, and was evidently familiar with every step in the career of the great gladiator. I reminded him that Spartacus and Roman slaves were warlike people in the countries from which they were taken . . . [that] the negroes were a peaceful, domestic, inoffensive race. In all their sufferings they seemed to be incapable of resentment or reprisal. "You have not studied them right," he said, "and you have not studied them long enough. Human nature is the same everywhere." He then went on in a very elaborate way to explain the mistakes of Spartacus, and tried to show me how he could easily have overthrown the Roman empire.

In his letter to Franklin Sanborn in 1858, Brown likened himself to Samson as well, for example, he observed: "God has honored but comparatively a very small part of mankind with any possible chance for such mighty and soul-satisfying rewards . . . I expect to effect a mighty conquest even though it be like the last victory of Samson." Samson-like, Brown toppled the pillars of slavery upon which the South rested, and was crushed as they fell.[4]

Drawing on such mythic examples for his own self-construction, Brown also knew that his own life could be used as an example. In 1857, two years before his execution, he wrote an autobiographical sketch and sent it to the twelve-year-old son of George Stearns, an abolitionist and benefactor. Here he narrated his history as a morality tale, a story of "follies and errors," but also as a success story "calculated to encourage any young person to persevering effort." He carefully reinvented himself so that his business failings vanished behind a trajectory of determination and success. Pain and disappointment were rarely his own fault; since his birth in 1800, he always found himself simply "placed in the School of adversity." He infused the account with a sense of self-division: it was difficult to represent his white past from the vantage point of his black present, for by 1857 he had integrated with African Americans and defined himself as a black man. The short autobiography reveals Brown's lifelong ability to sense counterworlds and to empathize with the otherness of a slave existence. He had employed his growing racial empathy and made himself over as early as 1848, when he contributed the essay "Sambo's Mistakes" to *The Ram's Horn*, a black abolitionist journal based in New York. In the essay he posed as a black moralist offering constructive criticism by way of autobiographical example, affecting an apologetic, garrulous style. He created a self-effacing and nervous narrator, different to the real Brown. As an exercise in creative autobiography, the essay marked the early stages of his self-transformation to a white man with a black heart.[5]

Brown was learning how to perform. By the 1850s he was acutely aware of his double audience or readership: young Stearns (the recipient of his autobiographical letter of 1857) *and* the boy's father (Brown's sponsor); the courtroom *and* the slaveholding South; his family *and* the newspaper-reading public in the North who read his prison letters. He understood the importance of symbolism in performance. At Harper's Ferry in 1859, he sent his men to capture Colonel Lewis W. Washington, the great-grandnephew of George Washington, telling the hostage, "I wanted you particularly for the moral effect it would give our cause having one of your name as a prisoner." To complete the symbolism Brown then sent more men to seize the Colonel's sword that Frederick the Great had given to George Washington, a sword that Brown wore until overpowered by Lee's marines. The sword took valuable time to seize but had great symbolic value, indicating that Brown was a patriot and a revolutionary hero, and that the mission at Harper's Ferry was historically important. Undoubtedly aware of the powerful legend of the gallant and compassionate slaveholder, Brown challenged this legend with a performative one of his own, working as a nineteenth-century spin-doctor for the abolitionist image. His receptive audience responded to his rhetoric and understood the excessive theatrics of his eventual transformation into Christ during his imprisonment, trial, and execution.

According to Oswold Villard, his first biographer, in preparing for his Harper's Ferry raid Brown "pictured himself a modern crusader as much empowered to remove the unbeliever as any armored researcher after the Grail," and underwent a "metamorphosis" from "staid, somber merchant and patriarchal family-head" to "John Brown of Osawatomie," a warrior with an Indian name. He fashioned himself as a Western hero in the tradition of the novelist James Fennimore Cooper's Leatherstocking tales, in which a virtuous white man blurs the boundaries between savagery and civilization in his quest for justice. After the Kansas warfare of 1856, during which he relied on the fighting tactics of the Kansas Indians, with whom he associated himself, he began referring to himself as Osawatomie Brown. He had fixed his background, upbringing, and self-conception to the symbol of the savage Indian for a long time, telling the white abolitionist Gerrit Smith on April 8, 1848, "I am something of a pioneer. I grew up among the woods and wild Indians of Ohio," and noting in a third-person passage of his autobiographical letter, "After getting to Ohio in 1805 he was for some time rather afraid of the Indians, & of their Rifles; but this soon wore off: & he used to hang about them quite as much as was consistent with good manners; & learned a trifle of their talk."[6]

Reinvented as an Indian warrior, he entered the proslavery settlement at Pottawatomie Creek on May 24, 1856 with seven others and hacked to death five unarmed settlers. In him it seemed like rhetoric became violence, a human literalization of politics, when Frederick Douglass proclaimed that liberty "must either cut the throat of slavery or slavery would cut the throat of liberty"; unbeknownst to him and his audience, Brown and his men had cut the throats of the five proslavery settlers just four days earlier. Then, with his death, he turned actions back to words. His deeds became myth and symbol, message and document: "his forty days in prison . . . all in all made the mightiest Abolition document that America has known," noted W.E.B. Du Bois.[7]

After the attack at Pottawatomie, the proslavery press compared Brown to Indian "barbarians," but he was already looking ahead to his Harper's Ferry raid. He shifted from Indian Warrior to Cromwellian hero, often in military dress, to thrill Boston ladies in their parlors and to fill the expedition coffers. This increasing sense of theater, while making him politically effective and historically enigmatic, had deeper implications: his most authentic role, the one he remained committed to in thought, word, and deed, was that of an

African American. His various self-conscious metamorphoses displayed an understanding of the self as something that is continually in flux. When whiteness as a superior category was tied to the idea that "character" was determined by heredity and social hierarchy, rather than chosen or self-fashioned, Brown sought to become black. He identified so closely with blacks that he chose to live among them and was willing to sacrifice his life for their cause, and in 1849 he moved into the black community in the wilderness of Timbucto, in the Adirondacks, on land given to blacks by Gerrit Smith in 1846. He considered it his permanent home and final resting place. Brown was able to stand apart from widespread racism and white supremacy in part *because* of his ability to make himself over, and his perception that identity was subjective and ever-changing.

He broke down racial hierarchies and envisaged an egalitarian society in which everyone, men and women, black and white, was free, equal, and judged not on the basis of sex, skin color, wealth, or family and heredity, but rather on their adherence to the Declaration of Independence and the Golden Rule as sacred texts. Douglass recognized this as a genuine process in Brown, and after their first meeting in late 1847, described him in the *North Star* as someone who "though a white gentleman, is in sympathy a black man, and as deeply interested in our cause, as though his own soul had been pierced with the iron of slavery." The editor of the *Ram's Horn*, Willis Hodges, published Brown's "Sambo's Mistakes" and preserved Brown's black identity by publishing anonymously, because, like Douglass, he believed Brown's black persona to be authentic rather than a parody or caricature like blackface minstrelsy. And Du Bois commented later that Brown "worked not simply for Black Men—he worked with them; and he was a companion of their daily life, knew their faults and virtues and felt, as few white Americans have felt, the bitter tragedy of their lot." Throughout the twentieth century, many acknowledged Brown's sincere attempt at blurring racial categories.[8]

Brown's desire to blur racial categories and reshape the world was well answered by daguerreotypes. Pictures allowed him to remake himself, and remaking himself seemed one step closer to remaking the world. He crossed racial lines visually, and established a black performative self, proving correct Douglass's statement in his article "Pictures": "Poets, prophets, and reformers are all picture-makers—and this ability is the secret of their power and of their achievements. They see what ought to be by the reflection of what is, and endeavor to remove the contradiction." The 1856 daguerreotype by John Bowles, one of numerous portraits taken while Brown was in Kansas, is perhaps deliberately underexposed, rendering Brown's tanned skin even darker and thus blurring the line between black and white [figure 2.1].[9]

Figure 2.1 John Bowles, "John Brown," daguerreotype, 1856. (*Courtesy Boston Atheneum*)

Like other abolitionists, Brown had his picture taken often. Modern visual culture emerged at a time when the slavery crisis accelerated, and image-making enhanced the abolitionists' sense of the contrast between the ideal and the real. It spoke to their desire to transform the world and themselves. Brown, always willing to exchange past identities for new ones, recognized that he could remake himself through pictures. The period's new emphasis on present and future, and the fragmentation of past identities that Brown experienced throughout his tumultuous career, both reflected and furthered

Figure 2.2   "John Brown," daguerreotype, 1857. (*Courtesy Library of Congress*)

the visual culture of the mid to late nineteenth century that asked the question "Who am I?" Brown seemed able to answer this question in several different ways with daguerreotypes, and others used these images to answer the same question: the so-called mad photograph of 1857 (where the right side of Brown's face is blurred, his features are asymmetrical, and his right lip sagging) was either distorted by the daguerreotypist or else the lens or plate were damaged [figure 2.2]. Repeatedly cited as evidence that Brown was mad,

Figure 2.3   Frontispiece, engraving, in James Redpath, *The Public Life of Capt. John Brown*, 1860. (*Courtesy Boston Athenaeum*)

the grotesque image made its way into mainstream literature on Brown when engraved as the frontispiece to James Redpath's biography. The frontispiece rebalances his face somewhat, though the influence of the distortion is still evident in the curved lip and asymmetrical eyes, features absent in all other daguerreotypes of Brown [figure 2.3].

Figure 2.4   Augustus Washington, "John Brown," daguerreotype, 1847. (*Courtesy Kansas State Historical Society*)

When capable of answering the question "Who am I?" for himself, how-ever, Brown did so with gusto. Like Douglass, Brown not only wrote himself into public existence and redefined himself continuously through language, he also updated his persona through photography. An early image of 1847 records Brown taking an oath and connects him to the flag held by his side, just at his height, its triangle shape also that of his shirt-front. Brown is one with his oath, starting out along the path that would lead to Harper's Ferry [figure 2.4]. The daguerreotypes of 1856 to 1858 are uncompromisingly that of a warrior: in all of these images Brown stares intensely into the lens, disre-garding portrait conventions of the time with his challenging and penetrating gaze. The overriding impression is one of boldness, with an emphasis on physicality. His hands often grip his elbows, in a classic posture of defiance, and his arms are forcefully crossed whenever in shot, his brow is furrowed

JOHN BROWN.

FROM A DAGUERREOTYPE TAKEN ABOUT 1850, IN POSSESSION OF FRANK B. SANBORN.

Figure 2.5   "John Brown," daguerreotype, Boston, 1857. (*Courtesy Boston Athenaeum*)

dramatically, his lips are tight. He rarely smiles, and his occasional half-smile is more knowing than warm [figure 2.5].

In 1859, however, he adopted a different visual persona. In J. W. Black's Boston photograph of May 1859, a bearded Brown affects a different posture: less aggressive, more statesman-like, his body more open and relaxed,

Figure 2.6   J.W. Black, "John Brown," May 1859. (*Courtesy Library of Congress*)

although his gaze remains direct and challenging [figure 2.6]. The warrior has become a prophet. By the last months before Harper's Ferry, he likely felt more comfortable in his authority, less driven to impose a visual authority through an impression of force and defiance. Painters of the nineteenth and

Figure 2.7   Nahum B. Onthank, "John Brown," painting from photograph by J.W. Black, 1860. (*Courtesy Boston A thenaeum*)

twentieth centuries based their representations of Brown on this late metamorphosis far more than on any of the earlier daguerreotypes: Nahum B. Onthank's painting of 1860, the frontispiece to Villard's biography, is one example [figure 2.7].

Brown perhaps enjoyed the image-making process because he envisioned an alternate reality that was more compelling to him than his material world, although of course he tried to make over that material world and even extemporized a new government and constitution on May 6, 1858. A dreamer and a visionary, he was able to construct alternate versions of himself in photographs, letters, essays, his autobiography, and in person. In a reminiscence that resonates powerfully with all the meteor and sky imagery in the John Brown literature, William Phillips recounts the occasion on which he realized that Brown was, in addition to a visionary, also "a very thorough astronomer": "he enlightened me on a good many matters in the starry firmament above us. He pointed out the different constellations and their movements. 'Now,' he said, 'it is midnight,' and he pointed to the finger marks of his great clock in the sky." As his own scriptwriter, director, mythographer, and interpreter, Brown knew the constellations and movements of that metaphorical canvas for American history, the sky. A meteor himself, he was also an observer and philosopher of meteors. He planned and executed his entrance onto the stage, an entry that he managed, and, with perfect timing, seemed to blaze his own trajectory across the "great clock in the sky."[10]

In 1984, the popular rock band Kansas used as the cover illustration for their album *The Best of Kansas* an adaptation of John Steuart Curry's mural of Brown, a mural that shows him standing as a stage manager, in charge of the stage set, curtains, and lighting, and pointing at the stage. The back cover to the album shows an inkwell and quill, presumably used by Brown to write the script for the performance. Brown stands between drama and audience, the mediator of his own story. For Brown's vocation was that of actor, his world was a stage. He especially understood the media theater of his trial and execution, although his trial was the first event in American history covered widely and on a daily basis by the national media, and he used to his advantage his earlier courtroom experience fighting charges of bankruptcy. By the time of his execution, Henry David Thoreau could say of Brown's expert stagecraft that "no theatrical manager could have arranged things so wisely to give effect to his behavior and words."[11]

And what of that execution, the moment when Brown finally handed over control of the makeover process to others? Dawn broke on December 2, 1859. Aware of the potential symbolism of his death, Brown woke determined to do the occasion justice and to manage the day's theater. He wrote his last letter, a mere two sentences, which resounds, "I John Brown am now quite *certain* that the crimes of this *guilty land: will* never be purged *away*; but with Blood. I had as *I now think; vainly* flattered myself that without *verry much* bloodshed; it might be done." Legend has it that on his way out of the prison he then bent to kiss a slave child, though this is unlikely, for no civilians were allowed near him. John Wilkes Booth, actor and soon-to-be assassin of Lincoln, did slip in, however, to watch and appreciate the drama. There was no minister present. Brown had requested "to be spared from having any mock or hypocritical prayers made over me." He asked that his "only religious attendants be poor little, dirty, ragged, bare headed, & barefooted Slave boys & Girls; led by some old grey headed Slave Mother." Though denied this request for slave "attendants," he was spared the presence of proslavery ministers.[12]

Arriving at the scaffold, Brown looked at the view. He commented to the undertaker, "This is a beautiful country. I never had the pleasure of seeing it before." There was a painfully long interval between blindfolding and swinging out. Brown stood erect and still. Some thought the protracted moment was deliberate, and Brown's calm response a victory. No one was allowed within hearing distance; any words spoken would, for once, go unheard. Then he swung out. The body hung for thirty-seven minutes. Just as he had taken a long time to find his best identity, slowly ripening during decades of bankruptcy and self-doubt into the fruit that now swung in the breeze, so Brown took his time dying. Church bells tolled across the North. In Massachusetts Thoreau announced, "This morning, Captain Brown was hung. He is not Old Brown any longer; he is an angel of light."[13]

Immediately after Brown's death, artists, speechmakers, and commentators saw him as variously as angel, Christ-figure, frontier hero, transcendental force, and nineteenth-century Cromwell. To George Luther Stearns, he was simply "the representative man of this century, as Washington was of the last" or, as Douglass repeatedly put it, "the man of this nineteenth century." Douglass resented the charges of insanity levelled at Brown and—like some of McVeigh's commentators—sought to place him in the American revolutionary tradition, writing in November 1859, "It is an appalling fact in the history of the American people, that they have so far forgotten their own heroic age, as readily to accept the charge of insanity against a man who has imitated the heroes of Lexington, Concord, and Bunker Hill." He continued, "It is an effeminate and cowardly age, which calls a man a lunatic because he rises to such self-forgetful heroism." But he trusted that that "[p]osterity will owe everlasting thanks to John Brown for lifting up once more to the gaze of a nation grown fat and flabby on the garbage of lust and oppression, a true standard of heroic philanthropy, and each coming generation will pay its installment of the debt," and concluded, "This age is too gross and sensual to appreciate his deeds, and so calls him mad; but the future will write his epitaph upon the hearts of a people freed from slavery, because he struck the first effectual blow."[14]

However, in his address at Storer College in 1881, Douglass explained that he was *still* unable to fit Brown correctly into the "age," for the "age" could not yet see Brown for what he was. Here he discussed Brown's memory and set him in the context of legend and ancient history, twice comparing him to Moses: "The beating of a Hebrew bondsman, by an Egyptian, created a Moses," he pointed out, "and the infliction of a similar outrage on a helpless slave boy in our own land may have caused, forty years afterwards, a John Brown and a Harper's Ferry Raid." He linked the life-stories of Moses and Brown later in the speech:

> forty years passed between [Brown's] thought and his act . . . this man was struggling with this one idea; like Moses he was forty years in the wilderness . . . this one thought, like the angel in the burning bush, had confronted him with its blazing light, bidding him on to his work. Like Moses he had made excuses, and as with Moses his excuses were overruled.

But the distance was not enough.

> We yet stand too near the days of slavery and the life and times of John Brown, to see clearly the true martyr and hero that he was and rightly to estimate the value of the man and his works," he deduced. "Like the great and good of all ages, the men born in advance of their times, the men whose bleeding footprints attest the immense cost of reform, and show us the long and dreary spaces, between the luminous points in the progress of mankind, this our noblest American hero must wait the polishing wheels of after-coming centuries to make his glory more manifest, and his worth more generally acknowledged.

Douglass's own wheels of judgment had turned several times to accommodate his various attitudes toward Brown, but only the "the polishing wheels of after-coming centuries" would reveal Brown's true worth.[15]

Sure enough, these wheels turned during the twentieth century. Through the rhetoric of twentieth-century writers and speakers of the United States, England, and continental Europe, Brown morphed into Socrates, Ironsides, Spartacus, Martin Luther, John Milton, William Tell, Sir Walter Raleigh, Washington, Garibaldi, Marquis de Lafayette, Longfellow, Moses, David, and Saint Paul. In an article for the *New York Tribune* on July 29, 1906, Sanborn predicted that Brown would join King Arthur and Joan of Arc. And protestors began to call on Brown. From Eugene Debs and Michael Gold, to Langston Hughes and Countee Cullen, radical writers used elements of the John Brown myth to make over their own protest movements into an American tradition. Building on the past, protest artists chose and reshaped their ancestry and emphasized an American tradition of patriotic protest. Their attempts to make over America with reference to Brown, debunked the myth of American history as a series of fresh starts, of America as a perpetual New World. Excavating and reconstructing, protest artists fought attempts to stamp out the country's radical past. They refused to discard history or participate in the "sloughing of the old skin, towards a new youth," which D.H. Lawrence identified as the "myth of America." This is the frontier myth, explained by Frederick Jackson Turner in 1893: "American social development has been continually beginning over again on the frontier," said Turner. "This perennial rebirth, this fluidity of American life, this expansion westward with its new opportunities[. . .] furnish[es] the forces dominating American character." But although they sought and found new countries and then set sail for better ones, the artists carried along fragments. They disproved the particularly pervasive idea that writing on the Left is without memory, never putting down roots. Part of the radical politics of the makeover mythos was an insistence that this was no makeover from scratch.[16]

And so, amid centennial commemorations of the 1859 Harper's Ferry raid, civil rights groups reclaimed Brown as a hero to blacks. As debates unfolded on the role of the white man in black America's struggle for equal rights, it seemed that another civil war loomed—unless white America could follow in Brown's ever-marching footsteps. Malcolm X looked back to John Brown, as did many 1960s radicals. In 1968, Truman Nelson claimed that there was a "John Brown in every man's conscience" and referenced Malcolm X's call: "If you are for me and my problem[. . .]then you have to be willing to do as old John Brown did." Lerone Bennett, Jr., pointed to Brown's "complete identification with the oppressed": it was "his wife who was being raped in the gin house," he wrote, "John Brown *was* a Negro, and it was in this aspect that he suffered." After Malcolm's death, Ossie Davis explained that Malcolm stood in relation to the " 'responsible' civil rights leaders, just about where John Brown stood in relation to the 'responsible' abolitionist in the fight against slavery." Davis added, "Almost all disagreed with Brown's mad and fanatical tactics [. . .]Yet, today the world, and especially the Negro people, proclaim Brown not a traitor, but a hero and a martyr in a noble cause. So in future, I will not be surprised if men come to see that Malcolm X was [. . .] also a martyr in that cause." Brown "marched on," as the song "John Brown's Body" had observed during the Civil War.[17]

Brown was also made over by 1970s guerilla groups. In each issue of its 1970s journal, the Weather Underground printed a picture of Brown. Underneath the picture, they explained that the publication was called *Osawatomie* because "in 1856, at the Battle of Osawatomie, Kansas, John Brown and 30 other abolitionists, using guerrilla tactics, beat back an armed attack by 250 slavery supporters, who were trying to make Kansas a slave state. This was a turning point in the fight against slavery." In a 1975 article for *Osawatomie*, Joe Reed claimed Brown as "a[n] heroic American revolutionary, a brilliant military tactician and guerrilla fighter, an uncompromising swordsman in the great fight to end slavery." He called for "fireworks" at the "official Bicentennial" that would expose "the truth of U.S. history," like Brown's "dazzling flash of light." Later issues of the journal published letters from a John Brown Book Club.[18]

Then, in 1978, a now-forgotten white antiracist group with connections to the Weather Underground began a national campaign against white supremacists and the racist violence of the Ku Klux Klan. In the late 1970s, working to support incarcerated Black Panthers and Black Liberation Army members, activist Lisa Roth and others heard rumors that the KKK was organizing itself in New York State prisons. They could not believe it at first—"we were fundamentally skeptical Northern intellectuals," Roth recalled in a interview of August 2005. They drove to Albany, examined the New York State Klan incorporation papers, and discovered that the man who had incorporated the state chapter was the head of the guard unit at Napanoch prison. All those listed in the Klan incorporation were guards there. They began to protest this, calling themselves the John Brown Anti-Klan Committee. They explained in their newspaper, "We take our name from John Brown, the nineteenth-century white abolitionist who gave his life fighting for Black people's freedom from slavery. In this tradition we build solidarity with the Black Liberation Movement and support all its struggles for human rights and self-determination [. . .] We believe all people have the right to defend themselves against racist, sexist or homophobic violence by any means necessary." Roth, who worked with the Committee until its end in the 1990s, added in an interview,

> We named ourselves after John Brown because we felt like he was a white man who made fighting racism the center of his life. Brown's willingness to fight for his principles are part of what made him so compelling for us. For most white anti-racists making the leap from ideas to action is a bit of a challenge . . . Brown was someone who really understood white privilege. He understood that this is nothing to feel guilty about, nobody chooses how they're born. But the way you relinquish your privilege is by fighting for those who have no privilege. Ultimately, he made the ultimate sacrifice of privilege.[19]

In 1988, committee member Terry Bisson retraced Brown's path through Lawrence, Osawatomie, and Harper's Ferry and then wrote the novel *Fire on the Mountain*. He had been a member since the first days of the committee and edited its newspaper with Roth. He took as epigraphs to his novel David Walker's line from *Appeal to the Coloured Citizens* (1829), "America is our country, more than it is the whites' . . . we have enriched it with our blood and tears," and Brown's statement "My love to all who love their neighbors." One character explains that if Harriet Tubman is "the Mother of Our Country and Frederick Douglass the Father . . . then bloody old Shenandoah Brown . . . is some kind of Godfather. Blood may be thicker than water, but politics is thicker than either." The novel is a counterfactual history—"a story of what might have happened if John Brown's raid had succeeded," as the preface explains. In a sense, however, the committee replaced counterfactuals with a *new* attempt to succeed. As the music band Eek-A-Mouse observed in a track on their 1983 album, *Mouse and the Man*, "John Brown him dead and gone / Jah know that him history still a go on / As him dead more John Brown born."[20]

In 1994, McVeigh saw himself as another "John Brown born"—keen to know if others studied history. Gore Vidal, who attended McVeigh's execution by invitation of the condemned man, could have answered "yes" to McVeigh's question. Telling the American press that "McVeigh saw himself as John Brown of Kansas" and was "reacting to something that is going on in the country, as John Brown reacted against slavery." Vidal added ominously, "one year after [Brown] was executed, we had a Civil War. I trust we don't have one; but we might . . ."

Journalists writing in the wake of McVeigh's bombing could also have responded to his question about the study of history. *The Gully* online magazine noted on June 17, 2001 that Brown's shadow hung over the Oklahoma City bombing and insisted that "one of McVeigh's heroes was America's own John Brown." The article went on to explain that McVeigh saw himself as catalyst and teacher, "a patriot holding the U.S. government accountable," and that McVeigh was a mirror held up to American faces, although "we pretended it wasn't there." It concluded that McVeigh was part of an American tradition—not a "self-made anomaly." "Our opinion shapers' refusal to consider that America runs on the same moral and cultural batteries that propelled McVeigh, means they had to turn him into a self-made monster [. . .] to try very hard to reassure their readers that McVeigh was an anomaly, and that his reading of American history as a history of righteous violence rewarded was wrong."

Numerous other journalists emphasized and explored the connections between Brown and McVeigh. The magazine *Race Traitor* said of McVeigh in its Fall 2001 issue, "He might even have become the John Brown of our day. It's a shame he didn't." On December 3, 1998, the online magazine *Salon* noted, "Brown's vision is reminiscent of the logic behind Timothy McVeigh's bombing of the Murrah building in Oklahoma City—the sight of a federal building in rubble was supposed to rally the militia around the country to rise and overthrow Washington." The article went on to differentiate McVeigh from Brown, however: "This might have actually happened had McVeigh let God do the planning. The Lord was ostensibly the one responsible for John Brown's acts of righteous terrorism." The online magazine *The Reporter* saw McVeigh through a similarly historical lens, writing on May 6, 2001 that

McVeigh's many contemporary missives [. . .] take great pains to say that Oklahoma City was a planned, measured act of war against a totalitarian government whose own violence had grown intolerable. Does this sound familiar? [. . .] [John Brown] sought to free slaves and arm them for violent revolution against white oppressors [. . .] Oklahoma City was the final desperate chapter [. . .] of the so-called modern "patriot" movement in America.

Ironically, after Brown's long history within the left-wing American protest tradition, the polishing wheels described by Douglass had turned again, seemingly to let McVeigh and the far-right wing complete the John Brown story.

As David Blight said in 2000, Brown's execution "provokes us to think about the meaning and uses of martyrdom. His story is a template for our understanding of revolutionary violence in any age [. . .] he represents some of our deepest political ambivalences, standing as he does for high ideals and ruthless deeds." Blight asked how we might "weigh John Brown's body at the turn of the twenty-first century, a time when our notions of violence in a righteous cause are troubled by a litany of terrorism committed by individuals, religious groups, and governments?" He posed the pivotal question: "Can John Brown remain an authentic American hero in an age of Timothy McVeigh, Osama Bin Laden, and the bombers of abortion clinics?" More than ever, Brown's words merit a close reading, his role in American myth and history a fresh attention. Confronting Brown afresh brings the whole weight of nineteenth-century history to bear on our contemporary global politics of the early twenty-first century. We might use Brown's "template" to remind ourselves that American culture sanctions violence in the name of a cause, and to deepen the ongoing debate about principled violence, the emblematic concept in American history and culture.[21]

America after McVeigh, and now 9/11, is making over John Brown. As American notions about idealistic politics and national identity shift and change, and as America's makeover of the Middle East is increasingly viewed as a projection of its own ideological makeover as an empire, journalists and scholars are returning to the John Brown story. As the Bush administration's "global war on terror" becomes a "struggle against violent extremism," as Bush's own makeover from compassionate conservative to tough-talking wartime president continues, and as makeover television programs ascend to unprecedented levels of popularity, we are seeking the source of Brown's continuing symbolic value within the American narrative of redemptive makeover.

The polishing wheels might continue to turn and make Brown a madman and villain, with the same aspect he bore during Jim Crow and McCarthy years. A feeling of horror for the violence at Pottawatomie and Harper's Ferry may supersede any admiration for Brown's humanity toward blacks. We may regret that Brown shifted the antislavery movement from an era of New Testament love and peace to one of Old Testament vengeance and apocalypse, that America abolished slavery the John Brown way. In a later time he might again provide patriotic juice for the heroic American makeover process, but during America's current war on "terror," Brown might seem antidemocratic and un-American, perhaps responsible for all the self-made terrorists that came after him. Twenty-first-century freedom-fighters might change shape when held up to Brown's light, but equally we might reinterpret Brown.

On the morning that Brown went to the gallows, a Boston journalist predicted that the execution would "reproduce other attempts like that of Brown." Four days later, on December 6, 1859, the *Christian Mirror* claimed that Brown wanted "to put a premium on such measures in the future, and to move a host of reckless aspirants to power and fame, to attempt the same thing." Examining the makeover mythos raises a question: when does a "reckless aspirant" become the "hero" Thoreau anticipated, when he said of Brown's execution that "when you plant, or bury, a hero in his field, a crop of heroes is sure to spring up?" On December 12, 1859, the abolitionist George William Curtis insisted that Brown was "not buried but planted" and that he would spring up "a hundred-fold." Brown planted no church with his martyr's seeds of blood, tears, and ink, but rather a self-made crop of division, provocation, and change. It has been a riotous harvest.[22]

NOTES

1. Timothy McVeigh, cited in "History and Timothy McVeigh," *New York Times*, June 11, 2001; *Courier-Journal*, Louisville, Kentucky, Sunday, June 10, 2001.

2. John Brown, "Sambo's Mistakes" (for *The Ram's Horn*, 1848), in Zoe Trodd and John Stauffer, *Meteor of War: The John Brown Story* (New York: Brandywine, 2004), p. 56.

3. James Clifford, " 'Hanging up Looking Glasses at Odd Corners': Ethnobiographical Prospects," in *Studies in Biography*, ed. Daniel Aaron (Cambridge, MA: Harvard University Press, 1978), p. 44.

4. William Phillips, "Three Interviews with Old John Brown," December 1879, in Trodd and Stauffer, *Meteor of War*, p. 187.

5. "Autobiographical Letter of John Brown (To Henry L. Stearns, July 15, 1857)," in Trodd and Stauffer, *Meteor of War*, pp. 37–38; "Sambo's Mistakes," pp. 55–58.

6. Oswald Garrison Villard, *John Brown, 1800–1859: A Biography Fifty Years After* (Boston: Houghton Mifflin Company, 1910), p. 77; Brown, in Franklin B. Sanborn, *The Life and Letters of John Brown, Liberator of Kansas, and Martyr of Virginia* (Boston: Roberts Brothers, 1885), p. 97; Brown, "Autobiographical Letter," in Trodd and Stauffer, *Meteor of War*, p. 38.

7. Frederick Douglass, in John Stauffer, *The Black Hearts of Men* (Cambridge, MA: Harvard University Press, 2002), p. 21; W.E.B. Du Bois, *John Brown* (Philadelphia: G.W. Jacobs & Company, 1909), p. 365.

8. Du Bois, *John Brown*, preface.

9. Douglass, "Pictures," holograph, n.d. [ca. late 1864], Frederick Douglass Papers, Library of Congress, unpaginated.

10. Phillips, "Three Interviews," in Trodd and Stauffer, p. 193.

11. Henry David Thoreau, "The Last Days of John Brown," July 4, 1860, in Trodd and Stauffer, *Meteor of War*, p. 234.

12. Brown, prison letters, in Trodd and Stauffer, *Meteor of War*, pp. 156–157, 159.

13. Henry David Thoreau, "A Plea for Captain John Brown," October 30, 1859, in Trodd and Stauffer, *Meteor of War*, p. 232.

14. George Luther Stearns, *The Mason Report: Harper's Ferry Invasion* (June 15, 1860), in Trodd and Stauffer, *Meteor of War*, p. 122; Frederick Douglass, "Capt John Brown Not Insane," *Douglass' Monthly*, November 1859, in Trodd and Stauffer, *Meteor of War*, pp. 203–204.

15. Douglass, "John Brown: An Address at the Fourteenth Anniversary of Storer College" (1881), in Trodd and Stauffer, *Meteor of War*, p. 206.

16. D.H. Lawrence, *Studies in Classic American Literature*, 1923 (Garden City: Doubleday, 1953), p. 64; Frederick Jackson Turner, "The Significance of the Frontier in American History, 1893, in *The Significance of the Frontier in American History*, ed. Harold P. Simonson (New York: Ungar, 1963), pp. 2–3; see Oscar Wilde, "The Soul of Man Under Socialism,": "A map of the world that does not include Utopia is not worth glancing at, for it leaves out the one country at which humanity is always landing. And when humanity lands there, it looks out, and seeing a better country, sets sail. Progress is the realization of Utopias," *The Fortnightly Review* (February 1891): 290.

17. Truman Nelson, *The Right of Revolution* (Boston: Beacon Press, 1968), pp. 3, 6; Lerone Bennett, Jr., "Tea and Sympathy," in *The Negro Mood and Other Essays* (Chicago: Johnson, 1964), pp. 100–101; Ossie Davis, "Grump, 1965," in *For Malcolm*, ed. Dudley Randall and Margaret Burrough (Detroit: Broadside, 1969), p. xxvi. Originally published in *Grump* (1965).

18. Joe Reed, "Fireworks," *Osawatomie* 4 (Weather Underground Organization, Winter 1975–1976): 14–15.

19. Lisa Roth, interview with Zoe Trodd (August 20, 2005). All comments by Roth are from this source; "What We Stand For," *No KKK— No Fascist USA!* (San Francisco: JBAKC, 1989), p. 16.

20. Terry Bisson, *Fire on the Mountain* (New York: Avon, 1988), p. 4, and preface, n.p.

21. David W. Blight, "John Brown: Triumphant Failure," *The American Prospect*, March 13, 2000.

22. Editorial, *Boston Daily Advertiser*, December 2, 1859; George William Curtis, lecture in Worcester, December 12, reported in the Ohio *Sentinel*, December 15, 1859; Thoreau, "A Plea for Captain John Brown," p. 227.

CHAPTER 3

PLANTATION MAKEOVER: JOEL CHANDLER HARRIS'S MYTHS AND VIOLATIONS

CLAIRE PAMPLIN

JOEL CHANDLER HARRIS (figure 3.1) enjoyed popularity in his day as an American writer who was second only to his contemporary Samuel L. Clemens. Harris, who worked for a quarter-century as editorial page editor at *The Atlanta Constitution*, authored 36 books that included collections of short stories and novels, but his fame and importance as an author is secured by his first: *Uncle Remus: His Songs and His Sayings*, published in 1880. This, along with *Nights with Uncle Remus: Myths and Legends of the Old Plantation* (1883) and several other collections, retold traditional African American animal folktales. Importantly, these books also utilized his original invention, the elderly former slave, Uncle Remus, as narrator in short framing stories in which Remus tells the fables to a little white boy (figure 3.2).

The Uncle Remus tales were best sellers around the world, translated into nearly every language, and quoted in Parliament, Congress, and from church pulpits and politicians' stumps.[1]

Reviewers at the time praised Harris for preserving the animal tales, and many cited Uncle Remus as an immortal addition to American literature. Clemens, upon reading the first collection of stories, recognized Remus's significance and acknowledged it quickly. He wrote a letter to Harris in the summer of 1881: "Uncle Remus is most deftly drawn, & is a lovable & delightful creation; he, & the little boy, & their relations with each other, are bright fine literature, & worthy to live, for their own sakes."

Figure 3.1   Joel Chandler Harris in the 1890s

Uncle Remus and the little boy

Figure 3.2   "Uncle Remus and the Little Boy"

Clemens valued Uncle Remus so much that he went on to say that the stories themselves "are only alligator pears [avocados]—one merely eats them for the sake of the salad-dressing."[2]

Harris's work fell precipitously from critical favor in the mid-twentieth century, however. In an influential essay published in *Commentary* in 1949, Bernard Wolfe wonders whether Brer Rabbit is a symbol of "the Negro slave's festering hatred of the white man" and stated that while, for Harris, the Negro and the artist were synonymous, the Southern author virulently hated blacks, even as he identified with them.[3] Later, critical disfavor increased, particularly during the Civil Rights era, when Harris's depiction of black people angered many who were searching for strong, updated images to serve as role models for children and icons for the movement. Harris and his body of work were easy targets, and Remus was readily dismissed—he looked too much like Uncle Tom.

In recent years, the critical public-opinion pendulum has begun to swing in Harris's favor again, because readers have acknowledged the complexity of both the folktales and the Uncle Remus framing narratives, and also because, as Jennifer Ritterhouse observes, "Harris himself deserves more credit for his relatively progressive racial views than he has generally gotten in the last thirty or forty years."[4] Harris the journalist was no radical, anti-Jim Crow, pro-Negro rights activist, but rather a political moderate, whom we would today call a liberal, on the most important issue of his day, race relations; he wrote newspaper and magazine editorials denouncing lynching and praised achievements by blacks since emancipation. Harris the creative writer and Harris the man, on the other hand, shared an important trait with Uncle Remus, and with Brer Rabbit: tricksterism.

This chapter examines how Harris, a New South journalist, politically moderate and personally modest, who served at *The Atlanta Constitution* in the last decades of the nineteenth century, worked as a trickster and a makeover artist in his creative writing. Without ever openly admitting to doing it, he embraced the idea of inventing and reinventing oneself and applied it to his racial identity, to Southern plantation culture and even to American race relations, and he did it in trickster fashion, subversively, from behind a verbal mask of dialect and from within African American animal fables. The language is an important aspect of the Africanist quality of the Brer Rabbit tales: not true dialect, but a new invention that seamlessly melded black language and white language the way Harris longed to meld the world of blacks and the world of whites. By virtue of the language mask, the reader could infer multiple meanings, and the author—the trickster—would be safe from punishment.

Numerous critics until recently speculated that Harris could not possibly have consciously understood the subversive qualities of the animal fables or deliberately fashioned Uncle Remus as a multilayered agent of social criticism. After all, Harris never acknowledged anything countercultural in his work, and his journalism, again, was that of a white moderate. However, Robert Cochran writes,

> It's high time, then, to at least consider the possibility that Harris constructed his tales and their framing narratives with consummate skill and deliberate cunning, that multiple ironies were not only not lost upon him but were in fact something of his stock-in-trade, and that he was, in short, something of a Brer Rabbit among authors. Uncle Remus, by such an approach, is revealed as a secret hero of Harris's work, a figure wholly worthy of comparison with Brer Rabbit himself. In creating him, Harris put forward, covertly, by extraordinarily oblique means, a vision that would have shocked and horrified the great majority of his readers, had they understood him.[5]

By extraordinarily oblique means, Harris also became a curious but important agent of the American makeover ethos. His shocking vision was one that unveiled grim realities of black life in America, one that revealed a desire for an impossible racial unity between black and white on a national and on a personal level. His vision connects him, curiously, to the current television makeover fervor, for whether the pursuit is for racial unity or for dramatic weight loss, a transformative beauty treatment or a complete home remodeling job, the intention is the same: to release the grip of the past and to create a self-determined future.

Harris, to all surface appearances, was a tolerant, open-minded New South journalist and humor writer. What lay behind his mask was something quite different. Further clouding the issue of his subversive undercurrents was the fact that the character Uncle Remus and the author himself merged in the minds of the reading public. Just three years after the publication of the first collection, even reviewers had begun referring to the author as Uncle Remus. Samuel L. Clemens published *Life on the Mississippi* in 1883 and included a short chapter titled "Uncle Remus and Mr. Cable," an anecdote written to illustrate Harris's shyness (his reticence when around strangers and in public was pathological). The story also reveals how closely connected Harris and his creation were.

Twain and George Washington Cable received Harris at Cable's home in New Orleans. Twain writes,

> He deeply disappointed a number of children who had flocked eagerly to Mr. Cable's house to get a glimpse of the illustrious sage and oracle of the nation's nurseries. They said:—
> "Why, he's white!"

They were grieved about it. So, to console them, the book was brought out, that they might hear Uncle Remus's Tar-Baby story from the lips of Uncle Remus himself—or what, in their outraged eyes, was left of him.[6]

But Harris refused to read.

Harris for many years was credited with launching the plantation revival of the 1880s, when in fact he violated the conventions of plantation fiction. He did so by remaking the three essential elements of plantation literature[7]: first, he replaced the estate's great house with the slave cabin as center stage for the story's action. This differentiates him from Thomas Nelson Page, a popular plantation revivalist with whom Harris is often compared, who published *In Ole Virginia* in 1887, and John Pendleton Kennedy, whose *Swallow Barn* (1832) is generally acknowledged as the fountainhead of plantation literature[8]. Kennedy's novel both satirizes and pays homage to the Southern plantation and also establishes the big house's status in the opening sentence: "Swallow Barn is an aristocratical old edifice which sits, like a brooding hen, on the southern bank of the James River."[9] The house is the heart of the plantation, and in Old South myth, the plantation is the symbol of and model for Southern society. There is no such description of the big house in the Remus tales.[10]

In his second violation of the conventions of plantation fiction, Harris diminishes, if not eliminates, the image of the white Southern gentleman. The remaining requisite is the "old time" black slave or servant, and Harris provides Remus. But Remus functions differently from his counterparts in conventional plantation fiction. Remus and the dialect that he speaks function as Harris's mask. If, as a journalist, he could write only moderate political statements in favor of black progress and the recognition of black humanity, then as a creative writer he could make over Southern society and race relations, and, indeed, his own racial identity, through Uncle Remus. Through Uncle Remus, black struggles were acknowledged and validated; black people's lives, histories, and stories were situated in a place of high honor. Through Remus, Harris could go as far as saying that racial differences were insignificant and that, in fact, a time once existed when everyone was black.

A story called "Why the Negro is Black" spells out the reasons for differences in skin color, but it expresses implicitly and explicitly a longing for racial unity that few Southern whites would have dared to utter, especially in a time when the gap between black and white was widening and Jim Crow laws were growing in stringency.

The little boy watches Remus twist and wax shoe thread, and "he made what appeared to him to be a very curious discovery. He discovered that the palms of the old man's hands were as white as his own [. . .] Uncle Remus says, "[. . .] dey wuz a time w'en all de w'ite folks uz black." He says that the desire to become white was overwhelmingly strong and led to a situation in which some were washed "clean" of their blackness, others became partially clean and became mulattoes, and the rest remained black. Remus's meaning is veiled by dialect, and further disguised by the idea that blacks *wanted* to be white and sought to be cleaned of the their blackness. He adds a couple of sentences and one crucial word that allows an opening for interpretation for those wise enough to see it. He adds, "Yasser. Folks dunner w'at bin yit, let 'lone w'at gwineter be. Niggers is niggers now, but de time wuz w'en we 'uz all niggers tergedder."[11] The key word is "tergedder"—together. The tale serves as a nimble satire of plantation nostalgia, taking one of its staples—the desire for the good old days when blacks and whites lived together in harmony on idyllic estates—and pushing it to what has to be its logical end: complete unity.

Many critical interpretations of the Uncle Remus character have held that, as complex as he is, Remus is ultimately "white," a blackface, disguised mouthpiece for Harris's moderate segregationist views, and that the utopia he makes is one based on white superiority and dominance over blacks who are subservient, although not actual slaves. Indeed, Harris's characters and settings are stereotypes. Uncle Remus is on the surface a contented old "darky" with no resentment of slavery, and the plantation as Harris presents it is a Southern paradise—a safe, secure home where a community of blacks and whites live in harmony. In fact, Ritterhouse believes that

> It is fruitless to attempt to sort out what Harris wanted to say, what he said to appeal to a white audience, and what he said to be true to the folklore. Cultural admixture—"love and theft," as Eric Lott describes it in a different context— is what the Uncle Remus stories were all about.[12]

However, Harris was a trickster, and like all tricksters, what he says and what he does are often two very different things. And while Ritterhouse sees little value in seeking authorial intention, she does acknowledge his layering of meaning:

> The important question, then, is not whether or to what extent Joel Chandler Harris was a racist, but why and how he, as a white southern author apparently committed to a nostalgic image of the old plantation, was able to capture such a multiplicity of racial views.[13]

Harris is able to capture a multiplicity of racial views, in part through the language he invents for Remus. This invention is a mask and robe of dialect, a disguise that allows the author to express what he cannot say in his own voice: that black people were human, that he craved some sort of racial and social unity instead of the soul-killing Jim Crow.

While he never overtly explored any such motives, he did unveil, in a letter to one of his children, the strong sense of creative double-consciousness or dual identity that he felt. Harris seems to anticipate a theme repeated in television makeover programs: that the true self is hidden, but it can be unveiled, revealed, or set free—with help. An otherwise vibrant existence is smothered by poverty, obesity, or plain bad taste. New home design, a diet regimen, or the refreshing presence of a fashion advisor who shows you what not to wear releases the real you. Harris's other identity is released through his creative writing:

> As for myself—though you could hardly call me a real, sure enough author—I never have anything but the vaguest ideas of what I am going to write; but when I take my pen in my hand, the rust clears away and the "other fellow" takes charge. You know all of us have two entities, or personalities. That is the reason you see and hear persons "talking to themselves." They are talking to the "other fellow." I have often asked my "other fellow" where he gets all his information, and how he can remember, in the nick of time, things that I have forgotten long ago; but he never satisfies my curiosity. He is simply a spectator of my folly until I seize a pen, and then he comes forward and takes charge. [. . .] it is not my writing at all; it is my "other fellow" doing the work and I am getting all the credit for it. Now, I'll admit that I write the editorials for the paper. The "other fellow" has nothing to do with them, and, so far as I am able to get his views on the subject, he regards them with scorn and contempt; though there are rare occasions when he helps me out on a Sunday editorial. He is a creature hard to understand, but, so far as I can understand him, he's a very sour, surly fellow until I give him an opportunity to guide my pen in subjects congenial to him; whereas, I am, as you know, jolly, good-natured, and entirely harmless.
>
> Now, my "other fellow," I am convinced, would do some damage if I didn't give him an opportunity to work off his energy in the way he delights.[14]

The dialect stories and the narrative frames allow Harris—actually, his "other fellow"—to describe the richness, complexity, and the difficulty of black life in late nineteenth-century America, because the tales are trickster tales, pure expressions of rage, frustration, liberation, and prophesy: the last shall be first and the one that appears weakest now will become the strongest.

READING THE SIGNS

In the first story in the first collection Harris uses Miss Sally, the little boy's mother, as a stand-in for white readers, most of whom never heard the tales first-hand as he had done. Miss Sally gazes through the window at Remus and the boy, just as the reader gazes through the story-windows created by Harris. The original story, as it appeared in *The Atlanta Constitution*, was titled "The Story of Mr. Rabbit and Mr. Fox." For publication in book form, Harris changed the title to "Uncle Remus Initiates the Little Boy," moved the setting from the piazza of the big house to the interior of Remus's cabin, and changed the age of the boy from six to seven. With each of the revisions, Harris added a degree of ritual and exclusion to the tales, which strengthened his inversion of plantation power—the scene moves from the white world to the black world, and the boy's age becomes the age of reason, at which a child is ready for apprenticeship, or *initiation*. Harris sets the scene as one of teacher and apprentice. Raymond Hedin explores this idea: "In the sanctuary of Remus's cabin, Remus becomes a shaman, and the tales become instruments of initiation into a world the boy can learn from only to the extent that he leaves his own world behind."[15] Unlike his readers, however, Miss Sally will never join Remus and the boy, never listen to the animal tales first-hand, and never be "initiated" into the secret world of the stories.

Eric Sundquist cites two examples in *Nights with Uncle Remus*, in which the boy's questions probe deeper, lifting the veil of allegory. In these examples, Brer Rabbit pits himself against Mr. Man rather than another animal, "representing a more marked intrusion of the world of the masters into the dream world of the animal tales."[16] Brer Rabbit tricks Mr. Man and steals his money and, on another occasion, takes his meat. The boy questions Remus about the theft and he replies, "In dem days de creeturs bleedz ter look out fer deyse'f, mo' speshually dem w'at ain't got hawn en huff." Later, Remus comments, "Dat little chap gittin' too much fer ole Remus—dat he is!"[17] Sundquist observes that the old man is spelling out the allegory of slavery in the stories, and the boy is getting " too close" to recognizing the underlying truth of the tales. "Paradoxically, of course, this is just what he is supposed to do—or what Harris's readers are supposed to do."[18] In the secret language of folktales in dialect, Harris warned his readers to read the signs carefully.

In the strange world of the folktales, religion is reinterpreted, conventional society is subverted, convention itself overturned, and morality flouted. Harris reverses the "civilizing" effect of white culture on black slaves: it is not ex-slave Uncle Remus who needs to learn anything, or to be civilized; it is the little white boy who must learn, and what he learns, in addition to the fact of Africanness as both center and backdrop in his world, often contradicts the established white justice system, Christian teaching, and any sense of a universal moral code. The only way Harris/Remus could teach such a lesson is through a dialect tale: a white reading audience in the late nineteenth century would not have tolerated such an unadulterated presentation, for the dialect allowed the audience to ascribe its own meaning to the story and left open as to how and where it found it.

Remus tells of a time " 'fo' enny un us wuz borned" when the creatures "had lots mo' sense dan dey got now; let 'lone dat, day had sense same like folks" in "The Story of the Deluge." The great flood comes about when the Elephant steps on several crawfish, making them angry. They bore deep into the earth and, in retaliation, "dey onloost de fountains er de earf," causing the earth to be flooded and all the creatures to be drowned. This being the story of *the* flood, the little boy asks about the ark. "W'ich ark's dat?" Remus replies.[19] "Noah's ark," the boy answers, but Remus replies that there is no ark in the story of the crawfishes' flood. Remus's story is from a parallel history, a second secret history shrouded in mystery. Even the authenticity of this parallel history is a secret: "Dey mouter bin two deloojes, en den agin dey moutent," the old man says. He warns his young charge to protect their secret shared knowledge: "Don't you bodder longer dat ark, 'ceppin' your mammy fetches it up."[20] In other words, when spoken to by an outsider, speak the language of the outsider. The story undermines conventional Christian teaching, but the dialect allowed the nineteenth-century reader the necessary distance to read the story as simply another Negro animal tale.

"The Wonderful Tar-Baby Story" is often regarded as the most important of Harris's tales. This and its companion piece, which contains the tale's conclusion and the famous brier patch scene, "How Mr. Rabbit Was Too Sharp for Mr. Fox," lampoon whites' rage at black insolence, reflecting the satiric mimicry that slaves indulged in among themselves.[21] Brer Rabbit attempts to exchange polite conversation with the Tar-Baby that Fox has made and set beside the road as a trap for Rabbit.

> "Mawnin'!" sez Brer Rabbit, sezee—"nice wedder dis mawnin'," sezee.
> Tar-Baby ain't sayin' nothing', en Brer Fox, he lay low.
> "How duz yo' sym'tums seem ter segashuate?" sez Brer Rabbit, sezee.
> Brer Fox, he wink his eye slow, en lay low, en de Tar-Baby, she ain't sayin' nothin'.[22]
> Rabbit then becomes angry:
> "I'm gwineter larn you howter talk ter 'specttuble fokes ef hit's de las' ack. Ef you don't take off dat hat en tell me howdy, I'm gwineter bus' you wide open."[23]

The Tar-Baby story hints at violent sexuality. When the Tar-Baby does not answer, Rabbit takes on the role of an abusive man, calling the female Tar-Baby stuck up and threatening to "take care" of her and bust her wide open.

The rest of the story is easily interpreted in terms of racial and sexual allegory: The fox, playing a white man, catches the rabbit "mixed up" with the Tar-Baby and chastises him soundly and threatens to punish him (and the Tar-Baby) by burning the Tar-Baby and therefore "barbecuing" Brer Rabbit, in a humorous, sadistic twist on lynching. Brer Rabbit is a black man playing a white man, and in this lynching, the white man is punished for messing around with a black woman, instead of the usual "crime" of a black man making sexual advances toward a white woman. Fox tries to punish Rabbit for his arrogant capers around the neighborhood and for trying to strike up an acquaintance with the Tar-Baby "widout waitin' fer enny invite." The "white man" threatens to cure the black woman of her silence and her refusal to speak to him or socialize with him, much less cooperate with him. In a reversal of signifiers, now the Fox plays the "white" role to Brer Rabbit's "uppity black." Brer Fox threatens Rabbit with all kinds of grisly deaths: he says he will barbecue him, hang him, drown him, or skin him. "The Wonderful Tar-Baby Story" is many things, but it certainly is a tale of multiple signifiers, and of signifying, and of satirizing white attitudes toward black people. He of course saves himself by uttering his famous words: "I don't keer w'at you do wid me, Brer Fox, so you don't fling me in dat brier-patch."

Brer Rabbit signifies upon Brer Fox magnificently. A few moments after Brer Rabbit hits the bushes, Fox sees him far away on a hillside, "settin' cross-legged on a chinkapin log koamin' de pitch outen his har wid a chip." Remus says, in a perfect example of the language of reversal, "Den Brer Fox know dat he bin swop off mighty bad." Rabbit "fling[s] back some er his sass: 'Bred en bawn in a brier-patch, Brer Fox—bred en bawn in a brier-patch!' "[24] Fox could not read the signifiers. Remus warns of the danger of living life as one who cannot interpret the signs. He tells the little boy a story about witches. Remus explains to the little boy that a witch can change appearance because he has a slit in the back of the neck and can pull his "hide" over the head the way most people pull a shirt off. Those who can read the signs know that they can lie in wait, and when the witch pulls off his skin and flies away in the form of a bat or flees into the night as a black cat, the "hide" can be salted so that the witch will give up his evil practice. Things are not as they appear to be; beware the seeming totality of presence.[25] Remus portrays the witch according to his listener's expectations: the witch is evil and must be caught. But Remus knows that every black person out of necessity must be a "witch," every Negro must be able to slip in and out of disguise. The Negro's full intelligence and power cannot be revealed to the white world, because whites will become threatened and try to take away that power.

BECOMING UNCLE REMUS

The work of Joel Chandler Harris endures, not only as he originally created it, but also in numerous retellings of the tales. Just as Harris slipped into a disguise in the form of Uncle Remus, so have storytellers who have followed him. Harris's invention has become everybody's Uncle Remus, whether the old man is retained as an actual character in the stories, as in Walt Disney's 1946 film "Song of the South," or whether an artist takes on the role of Remus.

Julius Lester regards slavery, the characters of Uncle Remus and the little white boy, and the Jim Crow culture as obstacles to the tales' relevance, and so he removes all references from the stories, leaving a suggestion of the old man in the language and tone of the tales, preserving the name Uncle Remus only in the titles of his four volume retellings: *The Tales of Uncle Remus: The Adventures of Brer Rabbit* (1987); *More Tales of Uncle Remus: Further Adventures of Rabbit, His Friends, Enemies and Others* (1988); *Further Tales of Uncle Remus: The Misadventures of Brer Rabbit, Brer Fox, Brer Wolf, the Doodang, and Other Creatures* (1990); and *The Last Tales of Uncle Remus* (1994)—all of which were gathered into one volume in 1999, *Uncle Remus: The Complete Tales*.

He preserved Uncle Remus as a name, a "voice," and a presence in his retelling of the tales. Lester writes, "I hesitate to call it my voice, because it is also the voice of a people, the black people of Kansas City, Kansas; Pine Bluff, Arkansas; Nashville, Tennessee; and the state of Mississippi." He further explains that he decided against changing the characterization of Remus to avoid distracting those who know and love Harris's Remus.[26]

He lays out a simple mission in retelling the stories: to preserve them but at the same time to divorce them from their association with slavery. "The power of folk tales is that they transcend their social origins, and that is certainly true of these tales," Lester writes in the introduction to the compilation of his four collections.[27] Yet he consistently refers to the stories as "the Uncle Remus stories," giving Harris the credit he deserves for the collecting the stories and creating Uncle Remus. "It is questionable whether the tales would have been so popular if Harris had not created a character named Uncle Remus as storyteller," Lester writes in the foreword to his first collection.

Lester is part of what Mark Schone calls "a final line of defense, an argument about the authenticity and accuracy of the dialect, for the purity of the tales."[28] Schone says most "black Harris-haters" reject the argument out of hand—that Remus is real. Schone cites the evidence that Remus is a composite of three slaves from Turnwold plantation, most specifically "Uncle" George Terrell. More important in relation to Lester, "Remus is realistic," writes Schone.[29] Lester defends the interpretation of Remus as the "faithful darky" when he writes, "There are no inaccuracies in Harris's characterization of Uncle Remus. Even the most cursory reading of the slave narratives collected by the Federal Writer's [sic] Project of the 1930s reveals that there were many slaves who fit the Uncle Remus mold."[30]

Schone concludes,

So despite those who scorn him as "inauthentic," and despite [Walter] Brasch and [Bruce] Bickley's attempt to reshape him, the problem may be that Remus is too authentic. In his lack of rebellion, and in his identification with his master, he is uncomfortably believable. That, more than his politics or the tainted dialect, may be what puts Harris beyond redemption.[31]

But Lester, "Harris's best-known black admirer," as Schone calls him, believes Harris is owed credit for saving the stories, and that Remus cannot be completely extracted from the tales. In the introduction to his collection, Lester offers an explanation for his work: ". . . a question I have been asked often is, 'Why did you keep the name of Uncle Remus?'" His reply is simple. The title of his works, he says, "identifies a particular collection of Afro-American folktales, the largest single body we have."[32] Lester observes that the genius of Joel Chandler Harris was creating Uncle Remus, and Harris made the story and storyteller one. The teller and tales cannot be separated, and the tales would not have survived without Remus.[33]

Though Lester gives a nod of acknowledgment to Remus, he refrains from allowing his presence into the stories because of the association with slavery. David Clark, who is white, performs as Remus but divorces him from slavery completely. In Clark's use of Remus, the stories are not told by an old ex-slave; they are told simply by a wise old black man. A 2002 profile of Clark and his work reveals his attitude toward what he does:

The Uncle Remus stories are not without controversy, including allegations of racism. Nor is Clark unaware of the controversy. But "I always ask how many Uncle Remus stories objectors have heard," he says. "The Uncle Remus stories honor the wisdom of old black folks; the stories honor old folks in general.

"I was taken with the rhythm in the reading of the Uncle Remus stories," he says. "These stories relay an old man's wisdom. There is at least one sentence in each Uncle Remus tale that teaches."[34]

Another Uncle Remus is Van Dyke Parks, who also extracts Jim Crow and the relationship between Uncle Remus and the little boy as barriers to the value of the tales. He places Brer Rabbit front and center. Mississippi-born musician and composer Parks, perhaps better known as a collaborator on Beach Boy Brian Wilson's seminal album, *Smile*, put Joel Chandler Harris's Uncle Remus tales to music in 1984 and followed the unusual album rapidly with three slim volumes of adapted tales that Barry Moser illustrated with rich watercolors. Parks is careful to credit Joel Chandler Harris but to omit Remus. The books present Harris as the author. Below Harris's name on the covers is written "Adapted by Van Dyke Parks/Illustrated by Barry Moser."

Parks sought to reclaim nineteenth-century minstrelsy, according to Timothy White, who described the debut live performance of the album material at a small venue in Santa Monica, California, in 1985. Calling the music "a shimmering, tuneful evocation of *Uncle Remus and Br'er Rabbit*," White writes,

> The subject may seem more than a trifle obscure, even for a quasi-"art-rock" artist noted for an unusually esoteric output. But as a child of the deep South, growing up musically precocious and culturally inquisitive, with the Remus stories, the cakewalk and ragtime for psychic wallpaper, Parks has been building for ten years to a peculiarly wonderful reclamation project: a modern recasting of the popular entertainment in the United States between 1845 and 1900—the minstrelsy.[35]

Parks, then, sees Harris as a blackface entertainer and the stories as a form of minstrelsy. He views minstrel shows as " 'the reigning rock 'n' roll of the nineteenth century' " and believes they have been unjustly maligned and miscomprehended, according to White. "Scholars and sociologists investigating the minstrel show concur that it thrived not when it burlesqued black experience, but when its racial authenticity was most in evidence. The nation got to know itself through the minstrelsy, esteeming the culture of the American black." (If Harris were alive today, he might not approve of Parks's linking him to the minstrel stage. In his introduction to *Uncle Remus: His Songs and His Sayings*, he states "The dialect, it will be observed, is [. . .] different [. . .] from the intolerable misrepresentations of the minstrel stage [. . .].")[36] Parks also sees himself as a "blackface" entertainer, putting the animal fables to music and performing them on stage and planning a theatrical run of the show. (The run never happened, however. Parks was unable to obtain financial backing.)

Eric Lott supports a fresh examination and validation of minstrelsy in order to "reorient the traditions of American Studies by asking questions about the role of culture in the political development of a specific national identity," and to acknowledge that culture, rather than shared work experience, "primarily creates the conditions for social movements."[37] He writes, "If at this juncture we are to understand anything more about popular racial feeling in the United States, we must no longer be satisfied merely to condemn the terrible pleasures of cultural material such as minstrelsy, for their legacy is all around us."[38]

RACIAL MAKEOVER

Harris, undersized as a child, with flaming red hair, struggled his entire life for a feeling of acceptance. He carried a sense of shame over his father's abandonment of his mother without marrying her. He was pathologically shy and spoke with a stammer. In a letter to his friend Georgia Starke in 1870, he wrote that he had an "*absolute horror* of strangers" and that he was morbidly sensitive. He went on to explain in some detail how he felt: "With me is an affliction—a disease—that has cost me more mortification and grief than anything in the world [. . .] It is *worse* than death itself [. . .] My dearest friends have no idea how often they have crucified me."[39]

Yet he reported no horror of the black strangers he met at a railway station in Norcross, Georgia, one evening in 1882. As he stood waiting for a train he noticed some black railroad workers relaxing at the end of their workday. He sat down next to one of them and listened to their stories and jokes for a while, then he told one of them the tar-baby story " 'by way of a feeler.' " His listener was captivated and enthusiastic in his response to him. He told two other stories and then, for two hours, the whole group swapped tales. There were no traces of the painful shyness that caused him, in other circumstances, to flee from conversation with strangers, no traces of the obsessive lack of confidence in his art. As Robert Hemenway observes, Harris's psychological investment in the Remus character is "startlingly revealed" in this anecdote. Harris wanted to think he was one of those workers, "their language shared, their stories mutually possessed."[40] He did not merely imitate black speech, he was fluent. Like Clemens's Roxy in *Pudd'nhead Wilson*, Harris was "as white as anybody," but going by his manner of speech, "a stranger would have expected him to be black."

Enveloped by the darkness of the Georgia evening, masked in dialect, Harris reinvented himself. As night fell on a southern state and a nation increasingly divided by the color line, Harris and the others united black and white through storytelling. He gained the personal acceptance he so fervently desired, and perhaps for a brief time he could also believe that blacks and whites could accept each other.

In that curious moment on the railroad tracks, Harris completely made himself over, and curiously, that moment continues to unfold, as others remake Harris's work again and again.

NOTES

1. Julia Collier Harris, *The Life and Letters of Joel Chandler Harris* (Boston and New York: Houghton Mifflin Co., 1918), p. 145.
2. Quoted in R. Bruce Bickley, Jr., *Joel Chandler Harris: A Biography and Critical Study* (Boston: Twayne Publishers, 1978), p. 41.
3. Bernard Wolfe, "Uncle Remus and the Malevolent Rabbit: 'Takes a Limber-Toe Gemmun fer ter Jump Jim Crow,' " *Commentary* 8 (July 1949). Rpt. in *Critical Essays on Joel Chandler Harris*, ed. R. Bruce Bickley, Jr. (Boston: G.K. Hall, 1981), pp. 72, 83.
4. Jennifer Ritterhouse, "Reading, Intimacy, and the Role of Uncle Remus in White Southern Social Memory," *The Journal of Southern History* 69, no. 3 (August 2003): 590.

5. Robert Cochran, "Black Father: The Subversive Achievement of Joel Chandler Harris," *African American Review* 38 (Spring 2004): 21–34. Available at: http://www.findarticles.com/p/articles/mi_m2838/is_1_38/ai_n6148028/pg_2/ (Accessed on November 6, 2005).

6. Samuel L. Clemens, "Life on the Mississippi," in *Mark Twain: Mississippi Writings* (New York: Literary Classics of the United States, Inc., 1982), p. 503.

7. Lucinda H. Mackethan, "Thomas Nelson Page: The Plantation as Arcady," *Virginia Quaterly Review* 54 (Winter 1978): 317.

8. MacKethan, "Planatation Fiction, 1865–1900" in *The History of Southern Literature*, edited by Mouis D. Rubin, Jr. (Baton Rouge and London: Louisiana State University Press, 1985), p. 210.

9. John Pendleton Kennedy, *Swallow Barn; or, A Sojourn in the Old Dominion* (Revised Edition, 1853) (Baton Rouge: Louisiana State University Press, 1986), p. 27.

10. Harris was not the first to put slaves at center stage, however. By the time he began writing stories, Harriet Beecher Stowe had already forever changed the way writers treated Southern plantations. William R. Taylor observes in *Cavalier and Yankee* that after *Uncle Tom's Cabin*, the slave rather than the master became the center of fictional representations of plantation life (*Cavalier and Yankee: The Old South and American National Character*. 1957. [New York: Oxford University Press, 1993]), p. 307. Stowe was not the only influence pushing the white plantation owners into the background in fiction. After Emancipation the reading public craved local color stories about blacks and black life; Harris was well aware of this demand.)

11. Joel Chandler Harris, "Why the Negro is Black," in *The Complete Tales of Uncle Remus* (New York: D. Appleton & Co., 1880). Comp. Richard Chase (Boston: Houghton Mifflin Co., 1955), p. 102.

12. Ritterhouse, "Reading, Intimacy, and the Role of Uncle Remus in White Southern Social Memory," p. 594.

13. Ibid.

14. Quoted in Julia Collier Harris, *The Life and Letters of Joel Chandler Harris*, pp. 384–386.

15. Raymond Hedin, "Uncle Remus: Puttin' on Ole Massa's Son," *Southern Literary Journal* 15 (Fall 1982): 85.

16. Eric J. Sundquist, *To Wake the Nations: Race in the Making of American Literature* (Cambridge, MA: The Belknap Press of Harvard University Press, 1993), p. 346.

17. Joel Chandler Harris, "Mr. Man Has Some Meat," in *The Complete Tales of Uncle Remus*, p. 195.

18. Sundquist, *To Wake the Nations*, p. 346.

19. Joel Chandler Harris, "The Story of the Deluge and How It Came About," in *The Complete Tales of Uncle Remus*, p. 15.

20. Ibid.

21. Wolfe, "Uncle Remus and the Malevolent Rabbit: 'Takes a Limber-Toe Gemmun fer ter Jump Jim Crow,' " p. 80.

22. Joel Chandler Harris, "How Mr. Rabbit Was Too Sharp for Mr. Fox," in *The Complete Tales of Uncle Remus*, p. 6–7.

23. Ibid.

24. Joel Chandler Harris, "How Mr. Rabbit Was Too Sharp for Mr. Fox," in *The Complete Tales of Uncle Remus*, p. 13.

25. Joel Chandler Harris, "A Plantation Witch," in *The Complete Tales of Uncle Remus*, p. 95.

26. Julius Lester, Foreword. *Uncle Remus: The Complete Tales* (New York: Phyllis Fogelman Books, 1999), p. xvii.

27. Ibid., p. viii.

28. Mark Schone, "Uncle Remus is Dead, Long Live Uncle Remus," *Oxford American* 43 (January/February 2003): 92.

29. Ibid.

30. Lester, Foreword. *Uncle Remus: The Complete Tales*, p. xiv.

31. Schone, "Uncle Remus," p. 92.

32. Lester, Foreword. *Uncle Remus: The Complete Tales*, p. ix.

33. Ibid., pp. x–xi.

34. Vyvyan Lynn, "Greetings from Cochran, Georgia" *Georgia Magazine* (July 2002). Available at: http://www.outofthesky.com/info/gamag.txt (Accessed on January 9, 2006).

35. Timothy White, "Van Dyke Parks and B'rer Rabbit Update the Lost Art of the Minstrelsy." *Musician Magazine* (February 1985) Available at: http://www.songcycler.de (Accessed on October 25, 2003).

36. Joel Chandler Harris, Introduction. *Uncle Remus: His Songs and His Sayings*, 1880 (New York: Penguin Books, 1982), p. 39.

37. Eric Lott, *Love and Theft: Blackface Minstrelsy and the American Working Class* (New York: Oxford University Press Inc., 1995), pp. 11, 12.

38. Ibid., p. 11.

39. Quoted in Julia Collier Harris, pp. 83–84.

40. Robert Hemenway, Introduction. *Uncle Remus: His Songs and His Sayings*. By Joel Chandler Harris (New York: Viking Penguin, 1982), pp. 17–18.

CHAPTER 4

MAKING OVER THE NEW ADAM

MELISSA CRAWLEY

> That is the true myth of America. She starts old, old, wrinkled and writhing
> in an old skin. And there is a gradual sloughing off of the old skin, towards
> a new youth. It is the myth of America.
>
> (D.H. Lawrence, Studies in Classical American Literature)

THROUGHOUT HER TROUBLED MARRIAGE, Laurie Willow turned to food for comfort. When the marriage ended in divorce, she faced life as a 300 pound single mother of four without a high school education. Forced to live in a shelter with her children, Laurie decided to change. She went back to school and eventually earned her masters degree in behavioral psychology. She underwent gastric bypass surgery and shed 186 pounds. With a new husband and a new life, she made one final decision. She went to a plastic surgeon for a full body lift, a procedure that removes pounds of unsightly excess skin from people who have lost large amounts of weight.

Both Laurie's story and her operation were broadcast on Discovery Health's *Plastic Surgery: Before and After*, a program that depicts physical transformations through cosmetic surgery procedures. The series mixes surgical footage with personal profile, documenting the "before and after" of patients' physical and psychological transformations. A hybrid of reality TV and lifestyle program, *Plastic Surgery: Before and After* is one example of several popular shows that have moved makeover from the living room to the operating room.[1] Though the series' emphasis on self-exposure secures its position in our current "post-documentary" culture, its narrative reflects an ideology formed in our nation's past.

This chapter examines the discourse of *Plastic Surgery: Before and After* in relation to both America's founding myths and newly emergent discourses on the "medicalization" of everyday life. It suggests that the mid-nineteenth-century ideas of rebirth and emancipation from history and ancestral inheritance find not only a contemporary parallel in the series' narrative but also converge with new myths that claim the body as a site of psychological change. While the transformations of the participants are often striking visual evidence of their rebirth, the program's narrative also supports this notion as the participants themselves testify to their desires for a new and unique individual history. The participants' choice to undergo surgery is often narrated as a brave step toward a promising future and they are celebrated for both their individual agency and their rejection of a (damaging) physical and emotional past.

THE NEW ADAM

In his 1955 work on the formation of American cultural identity, R.W.B. Lewis argues that a "native" American mythology is found in the collective writings of the mid-nineteenth century. A Yale scholar, critic, and biographer, Lewis made enduring contributions to the study of American culture. In *The American Adam*, he traces the "cultural conversation" of mid–nineteenth century through the writings of Thoreau, Whitman, and others, and suggests that their dialogue created an American identity based on the biblical image of Adam before the fall. In the Adamic myth, Americans found a "figure of heroic innocence and vast potentialities, poised at the start of a new history."[2] Like Adam, the people of the fledgling nation had no past, only a limitless future. They "saw life and history as just beginning."[3] This condition is reflected in literature that stressed unlimited potential and embraced the birth of a new self. For Lewis, Thoreau's emphasis on a completely new life immersed in nature suggests that the past should be discarded so that individuals could "enact the rhythmic death and rebirth" found in the change of seasons.[4] A life determined by nature's renewable cycles reflected the fresh start offered by the new world. Lewis finds a similar project in the work of Walt Whitman where the Adam character is emphasized in the individual self "who is always moving forward."[5] In the hero of *Leaves of Grass*, Lewis sees an innocent in an innocent world who creates himself.[6] This self-made man has forgotten the past and is only responsible for the present and the future. It is a sentiment captured by one newspaper editorial of the time that claimed, "our national birth was the beginning of a new history . . . which separates us from the past and connects us with the future only."[7] In the Adam character, the new Americans found a convincing representation of their personal and social liberation from British rule.

With its offer of a fresh start, the American Revolution gave expression to the Adam character found in nineteenth-century literature. It also created an enduring national myth that valorized the individual.[8] Alfred Kazin argues that the revolution's greatest historical impact was to promote a "secular religion" based on "the free individual."[9] The war "raised the individual and above all the theory of individualism to new heights." Every person became his/her "own revolution."[10] The individual born of this personal revolution rejected elite superiority and replaced it with a strong belief in self-reliance and personal responsibility, what S.M. Lipset would term the "American Creed."[11] The core of this belief system is the idea that every person should be permitted to pursue his/her own desires and interests free from collective constraints.[12] In the "American Creed," individualism shed its past negative connotations and became the foundation for a new American outlook.[13] It is a foundation that many Europeans would depend upon as they immigrated to America, leaving family and social roots to make individual choices and succeed on their own merits.

The search for a new history in the United States, whether by immigrants or citizens, relies on the formative mythology born of the American Revolution. The refusal to unquestioningly obey authority created a unique individualism, "virtually of purely American origin."[14] For R.W.B. Lewis, it was an individualism that first appeared in the characters and themes of early nineteenth-century literature where Emerson, Thoreau, Whitman, and other cultural spokesmen narrated the story of the new American who was an innocent "Adam" in a brave new world. During this time, the individual self emerged from the collective, and the cultural dialogue turned to ideas of self-reliance and disassociation from history. Writing in *Journals*, Emerson captured the zeitgeist: "Here's for the plain old Adam, the simple genuine self against the whole world."[15] Adam's Americans were reborn into a new world of new selves with only the present and the future on their minds.

ART MEETS SCIENCE MEETS SCREEN

The art and science of plastic surgery has a long history.[16] In 600 B.C., a Hindu surgeon remade a nose from a piece of a cheek and in A.D. 1000, rhinoplasty or nose surgery that uses skin from the forehead was known as an Indian technique.[17] In the late nineteenth century, plastic surgery grew in popularity as people sought perfection as a means to happiness. It was a position supported by one doctor of the time who wrote,

> Few patients suffer more of mental discomfort than the unfortunate possessors of some unsightly disfigurement on the face which attracts constant notice, few are more soliticious for any operation which promises relief, and none are more grateful for the slightest improvement in their condition.[18]

By World War I, plastic surgery was routinely performed on soldiers who had suffered facial injuries and disfigurement. Doctors were praised for their efforts to fix the horrific damage suffered by veterans who would now have the chance to return home looking (almost) as they had when they left. However, tension grew between those who believed in surgery as functional and those who saw its aesthetic merits. While actresses such as Fanny Brice were turning to doctors for rhinoplasty, other physicians were promising transformations that are strikingly similar to those offered by today's makeover shows. In 1924, the *New York Daily Mirror* sponsored a contest "to take the homeliest girl in the biggest city in the country and to make a beauty of her."[19] Despite these public tributes to the side of beauty, the fight between the two camps continued into the late 1920s. While both sides argued over the standards to be met, a powerful national value began to inform the debate.

As Feldman notes, the arguments between the need for plastic surgery and the desire for it were complicated by a belief in American ideals that forced one clear question: "Wasn't it subversive to deny an individual the right to self-improvement?"[20] The postwar years quickly answered the question as the demand for cosmetic procedures rose significantly. In these years, choosing self-improvement through surgery became associated with the right of a free and independent individual to pursue personal happiness. In most cases, this individual happened to be a woman. As plastic surgery defined its product, it incorporated the language of domesticity; and the discourse quickly grew to include both the power of individual (female) choice and the necessity of that choice to ensure success in life through beauty. While doctors used words such as "tidying" and "fixing up" to describe surgical procedures,[21] women, including "husband-hunting girls, divorce-aversive wives and even career women" began to feel that they "had to look their best to succeed."[22] Since the postwar years, plastic surgery has become less gender specific as men embrace aesthetic self-improvement, but the rhetoric remains the same.[23] Looking younger equals life success. More importantly, this belief seems to be uniquely American. Patricia Pitts, a clinical psychologist who evaluated participants for both a British and an American makeover show, notes the difference. According to Pitts, the goal for the British participants was to match the exterior with the interior, to look as young on the outside as they felt on the inside. The Americans expressed similar desires but focused more on how their physical appearance could impact their personal and professional success. Their belief was that "if you look younger, you have a better chance of getting ahead in life."[24] In this cultural context, plastic surgery is a "quest for self-realization."[25] It is an expression of self-reliance in a society that equates beauty with success. If nature and ancestry fail to provide you with the right tools, you provide for yourself.

While plastic surgery secured its position in American culture long before it became a screen subject, television has contributed to its normalization and created new debates. Body changes that used to be achieved over months or years are now realized within weeks.[26] For some doctors, the programs create a dangerous distortion that "trivializes and sensationalizes" surgery.[27] Other commentators point to a more complex effect, with one suggesting that "the plastic surgery craze plays to the nation's tendency to favor youth over experience, the immediate over the past . . . To erase the lines of one's face is a way of destroying one's history."[28] More than a philosophical musing, the comment highlights the relationship between medicine and myth. In America, physical change is contextualized within a discourse of affirmation. Plastic surgery is transformation that enables physical and psychological separation from personal history.

MAKING OVER REALITY TV

The medical themes of programs such as *Plastic Surgery: Before and After* first emerged in the reality television formats that began in the United States in the early 1990s. These shows focused on the behind-the-scenes action of emergency services, crime, and accidents, or what Jon Dovey calls "trauma TV."[29] Typically, they were characterized by surveillance or observational footage of crime, eyewitness testimony, reconstructions of events that relied on fictional narrative styles, and news program "studio links" to presenters with expert commentary. Voyeurism was often combined with a moral or public service safety message.[30]

Throughout the 1990s, reality programs substantially increased. Jacobs argues that the genre's rise was partially a response to economic pressure within the television industry "where high-risk drama formats such as *Twin Peaks* and *China Beach* were abandoned in favor of cheaper reality shows."[31] Reality formats evolved in style from the observational footage of crime and home video found in shows such as *Cops, Rescue 911*, and *America's Funniest Home Videos*, to more strategically edited narratives that incorporated game show and melodramatic conventions. As the new millennium began, reality television was all about being a winner—financially (*Survivor*), romantically (*The Bachelor*), and professionally (*The Apprentice*)—and body image was often a key ingredient for success. Popular culture entertained various debates surrounding the sexual power of reality television contestants. Did Amber really love Rob or was she using her sexuality purely to make an advantageous *Survivor* alliance? Was Ivana's skirt-dropping sales stunt unbecoming conduct for *The Apprentice* of the Trump organization? Could a beautiful woman look past her cultural conditioning and fall in love with an *Average Joe*? As Americans pondered these questions, reality television turned to aesthetics and proclaimed that body image did not have to hinder your success in life or love. Programs hosted by a team of experts could help average people transform themselves with easy to master lessons on style and personal grooming. However, fashion advice and skin care tutorials offer only temporary solutions. True body transformation demands a deeper commitment and reality television soon turned to surgical intervention.

Reality television's thematic progression from the quick fix makeover to radical surgical change reflects recent discourse about the body. In her work on the spectacle of bodily trauma in media and social space, Anita Biressi suggests that "the climate of the 1990s onward has been one in which body management, in all its manifestations, has become a central preoccupation."[32] Jason Jacobs argues that the decade saw "an unprecedented intensification of the medicalization of everyday life" that was characterized by "regular health scares, the theorization of the 'risk society,' [and] the promotion of 'healthy living' . . . as a moral as much as a medical imperative."[33] The impact, for Jacobs, is an increase in popular engagement with medical dramas. Yet, these issues are also relevant to plastic surgery shows where viewers are witness to the "medicalization" of real people's everyday lives. Foregrounding the thematic developments of current plastic surgery programs, the decade of the 1990s saw the body become an important site of self-expression. During this time, the body became "the privileged site where anxieties, hopes and fear were projected . . . the available sphere of action and intervention in the public sphere became radically contracted to the limits of the human body itself."[34] If people feel that they are socially ineffective, that social change is beyond their reach, their focus will turn to the body. As Michael Fitzpatrick argues, "if you cannot do much about society or your place in it, at least you can mould your own body according to your own inclinations."[35] The increase in programs that feature personal makeovers since the late 1990s to date suggests that this discourse continues to have an impact as the body is still being contextualized as a limited space for change.[36] Underlying this notion of change is the idea of choice. Individuals, seemingly ineffective in changing society, make a decision to change themselves. In makeover and plastic surgery narratives, choice typically involves discarding the past, be it an old sofa or, as in the case of cosmetic procedures, an "old" face. This shedding of personal history expresses the self through the body, but it also exists within a discursive context of individualism that has become part of an American mythology.

PLASTIC SURGERY: BEFORE AND AFTER

The tag line for Discovery Health Channel is: "Real Life. Medicine." Miracles. If read as an equation, real life + medicine = miracles, the line neatly summarizes the channel's themes. Real people, whether they are giving birth, losing weight, or surviving cancer, often experience "miracle" outcomes through medicine (and self-discipline and determination). In turn, the programs on Discovery Health inspire as much as they inform, and they empower as much as they educate. This focus on both physical and psychological change is perhaps most evident in *Plastic Surgery: Before and After*, the only U.S.-based program to focus on the effects of cosmetic surgery procedures. Every episode profiles several patients who have chosen surgery in the hopes of improving their life.

Each broadcast of *Plastic Surgery: Before and After* begins with a warning. On a green background featuring scenes of surgeons in an operating room, white text declares that the show contains graphic scenes of surgical operations that may be disturbing to some viewers. The warning serves as a signal to the program's authenticity and establishes its claim to reality, while it also cautiously welcomes the audience as voyeur. Following the warning, the title sequence begins. A male narrator introduces the program's themes that are then visually matched with scenes from the upcoming episode. In this introduction, plastic surgery is typically represented as an active agent. It "reverses the signs of aging" or "repairs the scars of trauma" ("Life Lift"). Using active verbs the introduction treats plastic surgery as if it is a character in the narrative, a subject with agency and will. It becomes a healer, a worker of "miracles."

After a fast edit of preview scenes, the action cuts to a split screen in which two contrasting head shots of a patient from the upcoming episode, one in each screen, revolve 180 degrees to face the viewer. This is the teaser shot, a preview of the before and after of transformation. The sequence cuts to the episode title that floats onto the screen in white text over a black and white moving image of an operating room. Accompanying the sequence is the sound of high pitched tones that pulse over lower notes produced by a synthesizer. The effect is futuristic and suggests computers, technology, and medical equipment, as the pulse of the notes imitates the pulse of heartbeats. The music fades to low background, and the sequence cuts to pictures of torsos lying next to one another in a long row. The faceless bodies slowly move across the screen. Arms, legs, and hands are positioned so that they cover breasts and genitalia. The bodies touch and sometimes overlap in ways that suggest a deliberate, artistic placement. It is a sculpture of flesh, individual yet anonymous. The "art" of the body screen is then joined by "science" as the host, Beverly Hills plastic surgeon Dr. Jan Adams appears and introduces himself. Dressed in a suit, his address to the viewer is upbeat and friendly rather than authoritarian. His brief introductions are often punctuated with plural pronouns ("in this episode we will see") that invite the viewer to participate in the journey that is plastic surgery.

As the show progresses, Adams also makes occasional appearances to offer brief medical commentary. Now dressed in scrubs, he is featured in a hospital setting. His comments range from statistics: ("Did you know that last year more than 280,000 women received implants in the United States?") to short tutorials on procedures. In these lessons, his descriptions of surgical incisions and methods are accompanied by simple computer graphics. The animation comfortably shifts the viewer's subject position. They are now "surgeon" minus the blood. This absence of body trauma is also evident in the surgical procedures themselves. Doctors, first depicted as preoperation consultants, are later filmed in the operating room, however, the invasive techniques themselves are shown in long shot. The result is a sanitized version of transformation where the "body horror and visceral explicitness" of fictional medical dramas or horror films (or real procedures) is absent.[37] The mastery of the surgeons is unchallenged and every operation is a success. Weeks of painful healing are not documented. As Biressi suggests, "pain is essentially a private matter" and revealing it "unmakes the subject, reducing and objectifying him/her in the eyes of others."[38] Avoiding this outcome, the series' narrative focuses on the celebratory "reveal" where the newly transformed patient gives a postoperative interview and testifies to the merits of his/her life-changing experience. The patients thus maintain their emotional suffering without being reduced by their physical pain, and surgery is exalted for its triumph over psychological trauma.

The personal stories that form the foundation of the narrative structure of *Plastic Surgery: Before and After* reflect what Leland suggests is one of "America's official scripts."[39] That is, each patient's life success is narrated as the result of hard work for which he/she has been rewarded. This is commonly depicted through voice-overs that give viewers an account of a patient's "active lifestyle." For example, in one of the episodes breast-reduction patient Peggy is described as an "energetic wife, mother, and grandmother" who lives "an active life riding motorcycles, waterskiing and raising six children" ("Extreme Fix"). In another episode, facelift patient Tony's professional achievements afford him larger pleasures in life, as evidenced by shots of him on luxury yachts and driving race cars. In this context, the choice to have surgery is associated with individual achievement. It is a hard-earned reward that recognizes the patient's commitment to self-reliance and celebrates his/her freedom to move forward. Like the American Adam character, each patient is characterized as a "hero" embarking on a new adventure.[40] Having already met domestic and professional goals, participants turn to surgery as yet another way to successfully express themselves. As one 24-year-old female liposuction patient notes, "Now I can think for me a little bit" ("Destination Rejuvenation"). All patients profiled on the series reflect similar desires. Whether their surgery is the "culmination of a fantasy" ("Destination

Rejuvenation") or a means to gain a competitive edge in business ("The Skin Game"), their choice is a way to realize the self more fully.

While the series' emphasis on self-expressive activity recalls an Emersonian ethic,[41] it also suggests a search for truth. In her work on ethics and television, media scholar Gay Hawkins argues that "growing amounts of television programming now involve examinations of ways to live: . . . quests for the truth of the self."[42] For many of the patients on the series, self-truth is found in achieving harmony between the physical and the psychological. In one episode, Michelle, a breast-augmentation patient, notes, "I don't think my exterior is as sexy as I feel inside" ("Extreme Fix"). Robin, a rhinoplasty patient, comments after her surgery, "Now I feel like I fit into my body" ("Skin Deep"). After a face lift, Kathy expresses a similar feeling: "I'm reflecting on the outside how I feel on the inside" ("Extreme Fix"). The comments suggest that an authentic self is made possible through surgery. However, the idea of authenticity being achieved through an adherence to cultural norms of beauty is a troubling one. Feldman questions whether surgical trends are "a move toward individuality or merely adherence to a new stereotype."[43] Others suggest that plastic surgery programs "seem to signal that the herd mentality has reached alarming new levels."[44] The program's narratives circumvent this argument by framing cosmetic procedures as positive expressions of self-agency that in fact allow people to realize their true and better selves. Tracy, a college student undergoing breast implants, notes, "I just looked in the mirror one day and I thought this isn't who I am. This is not me. I can be better than this" ("Operation Reconstruction"). In this context, surgery enhances individuality rather than undermines it. After her facial procedure Susan comments, "When I look in the mirror, I still see me" ("Skin Deep"), a view echoed by a male patient, Brian, who claims, "To me, I'm just new and improved" ("Beneath the Skin"). Because the narrative continually emphasizes the acceptability of personal fulfillment over a self-indulgent desire to meet societal expectations, individuality is not lost through surgery, it is rather discovered and even celebrated.[45]

On *Plastic Surgery: Before and After*, the idea of discovering one's "true" self through plastic surgery is also facilitated by framing the past as damaging. The damage is either physical (traumatic accident, disease, birth defect) or mental (painful childhood). In both cases, surgery is constructed as the means to release and the path to a better future. As with the Adamic myth, personal history is disavowed and the patient becomes "an individual emancipated from history."[46] This message is voiced by both the host and the patients themselves. In his introduction to the episode "Surgical Healing," Adams comments that viewers will "meet a man who hopes his reconstructive surgery will put an end to his painful past." The patient is Daniel, a college student who suffered severe facial deformities from a car accident two years before the broadcast. In the episode, Daniel consults with a surgeon who offers to correct his past medical procedures and further reconstruct his damaged face. The surgery improves his appearance but does not erase the evidence of the accident. Yet, Daniel's viewpoint expresses a commitment to a future that surgery has provided for him: "I know what I have to work with so I'm going to start fresh—see what I can make with my life" ("Surgical Healing"). Daniel's tone is echoed by Holly, a journalist and a mother of two, who survived breast cancer twice and now hopes several facial procedures will help her "look the best" she can. Setting the tone, the narrator notes that "Holly arrives ready to reverse her past" ("Surgical Healing"). After her surgery, Holly repeats the theme: "I have wiped out so much of my past . . ." ("Surgical Healing"). Some patients even offer the viewers advice about moving beyond painful history. Having lost one breast to cancer, Anita suggests that women "need to get past losing the breast and look forward to what life has to offer" ("Beneath the Skin"). She chooses to do this by undergoing a breast reconstruction, a procedure that the narrator notes will "shed a positive light on her future" ("Beneath the Skin").

In the Adamic myth, Lewis argues that the biblical figure symbolizes an American who is "happily bereft of ancestry . . . untouched and undefiled by the usual inheritances of family and race."[47] Several episodes of *Plastic Surgery: Before and After* focus on patients who have suffered from painful childhoods. While their stories suggest that they are not unaffected by a damaging "ancestry," the Adamic myth remains valid because surgery is constructed as the only way to truly free them from the confines of their inherited past. Choosing full facial "restoration," Shelly notes that her current feelings of being the "ugly duckling" began at the age of six when she became aware that she "wasn't a beauty" ("Operation Reconstruction"). Unhappy most of her life, Shelly comments that her results finally made her "feel liberated" ("Operation Reconstruction"). For Laurie, "a carefree childhood changed abruptly when she was six" ("Skin Deep"). A series of events including her parents' divorce and her mother's remarriage to an abusive man left her with "emotional weight" that began to show physically. Laurie's surgery is framed as a step toward future happiness. She comments, "In a year or two I would like to see myself in a relationship, just enjoying life on a larger scale than I have up until now" ("Beneath the Skin"). Both Shelly's and Laurie's stories are supported by old photographs from childhood. Used often on the series, the technique juxtaposes the child self with shots of the present (preoperative) and future (postoperative) adult self. The archival quality of the old photographs lends credibility to the narrative, but it also adds to the power of transformation. When the patients are revealed in the "after" segment of the story, their history is firmly displaced.

The series' narrative focus on the future also incorporates elements found in the Adamic notion of rebirth. For one patient whose face was severely burned in a car accident, her procedure "was about letting go of the scarred young girl" ("The Skin Game"). Another expresses her presurgery feelings this way:

> This Camille is gone. She's bye-bye. A lot of things about this Camille are leaving. It's all about pressing forward with the new body, the new look and just new beginning.

Post surgery, the theme continues, as she adds,

> When I look at pictures, I'm like that wasn't me, that's not me. She's gone. This is a whole new person. I feel like a whole new person. I think differently, I'm not self-conscious . . . ("The Skin Game")

This idea is repeated by patients and doctors alike. Commenting on his patient's upcoming procedure, one doctor suggests, "You can come out like the butterfly who used to be a caterpillar" ("Skin Deep"). Physically and mentally leaving the past behind is not only admired but also encouraged. Like the biblical Adam, patients emerge "fundamentally innocent" in their "very newness."[48] Through surgery they are born again.

POST-OP

A rare birth defect left 15-year-old Daniel Demby with multiple facial deformities. For Daniel, "life [had] been a struggle from the start" ("Beneath the Skin"). Born in Poland, he was abandoned at birth and raised in an orphanage. When Daniel was nine years old, he was granted a medical visa for treatment in the United States. He was soon adopted by a couple who were volunteers at the foster home where he lived. Settled into his new home, Daniel is now "flourishing and discovering new talents" ("Beneath the Skin"). He plays several musical instruments, enjoys baseball, and attends weekly church services with his family. Daniel is not seeking perfection, but instead he hopes that his surgery will make him "normal" ("Beneath the Skin").

In his introduction to the Daniel episode of *Plastic Surgery: Before and After*, Dr. Adams notes that the patient's journey to the United States was not only for surgery, but also for "a chance at a normal life" ("Beneath the Skin"). Perhaps more than any other narrative, Daniel's story most clearly contextualizes the program's mythic discourse. An immigrant child comes to the United States, seeking a new life. Plastic surgery helps him to transcend his physical and psychological origins. With the fresh start provided by his surgical reconstruction, Daniel is able to escape his past and is free to make of himself whatever he wishes. In Daniel's narrative, the American dream *is* plastic surgery and his rebirth is just beginning.

In Daniel's narrative, the American dream as plastic surgery is also televised. Viewers are voyeurs to the transformative experience. Their participation is not only safe from unsightly expressions of physical pain but is also welcomed for its emotional support. The patients on *Plastic Surgery: Before and After* invite viewers on their surgical journey and viewers accept the invitation, in part, because the resulting transformation is restorative, that is, it strengthens their faith in America's mythological foundations. America, as Gregory Rodriguez notes, is "addicted to a sense of new beginnings."[49] It is an optimism ignited by the revolutionary war and promoted by early cultural critics who saw a new America free from the past, an optimism that is renewed in every private and public effort to advance. The cultural conversation started by Emerson, Thoreau, and others continues within the context of television.

At the end of every episode of *Plastic Surgery: Before and After*, Dr. Adams reassures the viewer that "we the doctors will continue to find ways to improve procedures and make our patients' requests a reality." He ends by cheerfully proclaiming, "I want the patient to be happy. That's the bottom line." Happiness in this case is exercising individual choice to erase the lines of the past. In the series, surgery is physical transformation that in turn enables psychological change, and each patient is reborn as a new American Adam, free from personal history, "self-reliant and self-propelling."[50] As one patient suggests, "Life doesn't have to be what you have. Nothing has to stay the same. You can always change" ("Life Lift").

NOTES

1. Other programs include ABC's *Extreme Makeover*, Fox's *The Swan* and MTV's *I Want a Famous Face*.
2. R.W.B. Lewis. *The American Adam: Innocence, Tragedy, and Tradition in the Nineteenth Century* (Chicago: The University of Chicago Press, 1955), p. i.
3. Ibid., p. 5.
4. Ibid., pp. 21–22. Lewis goes on to suggest that the past should be "cast off like dead skin."
5. Ibid., p. 44. See also *Song of Myself Verse*, p. 32.
6. Ibid., p. 44.
7. Ibid., p. 5.
8. The myth also evolved and found expression in the frontier myth of rugged individuals prevailing in the wilderness and the Horatio Alger myth of self-made men achieving upward mobility.
9. Eric C. Mount, "American Individualism Reconsidered," *Review of Religious Research* 22, no. 4 (June 1981), Available at: <http://0-search.epnet.com. innopac. ln.edu.hk/login.aspx?direct=true&db=aph&an=10826537> (Accessed on September 13, 2005).
10. Ibid.

11. Seymour Martin Lipset, *American Exceptionalism: A Double-Edged* Sword (New York: W.W. Norton, 1996), pp. 19–23, 31.

12. Edward Grabb et al., "The Origins of American Individualism: Reconsidering the Historical Evidence," *Canadian Journal of Sociology* 24, no. 4 (Fall 1999): 511–513 <http://0-search.epnet.com.innopac.ln.edu.hk/login.aspx? direct=true&db=aph&an=5483657> (September 13, 2005).

13. The term had negative associations when it was coined in nineteenth-century Europe as opposed to the positive associations given to socialism. See Robert Bellah, *The Broken Covenant* (New York: Seabury Press, 1975), p. 113.

14. Yehoshua Arieli, *Individualism and Nationalism in American Ideology* (Baltimore: Penguin Books, 1964), p. 189.

15. Lewis, *The American Adam*, p. 1.

16. Throughout this essay, plastic surgery will be used to refer to both cosmetic and reconstructive surgery. While there has often been tension in the field between these two areas, the plastic surgery depicted in *Plastic Surgery: Before and After* includes both reconstruction and cosmetic procedures.

17. Ellen Feldman, "Before and After," *American Heritage* 55, no.1 (March 2004), <http://0-search.epnet.com.innopac.ln.edu.hk/login.aspx?direct=true&db=aph&an=12399761> (September 13, 2005).

18. Ibid.

19. Ibid.

20. Ibid.

21. One doctor even told a popular women's magazine that the experience was similar to fitting a garment. See Feldman.

22. Feldman, "Before and After."

23. Since 1997 procedures performed on men have tripled, although this still only represents 15 percent of operations. See Feldman.

24. Lynn Elber, "Makeovers Show U.S., European Differences," *Associated Press*, August 24, 2005, http://web.lexis-nexis.com/universe/document?_m=5c9b2e887c9fc1faa0bfa388a1d43e02&_docnum=2&wchp=dGLbVlb-zSkVA&_md5=02076aea65a24b0734fd77701bf1533f> (September 30, 2005).

25. Feldman, "Before and After."

26. Programs such as ABC's *Extreme Makeover* and Fox's *The Swan* deliver radical transformation through multiple procedures in as little as six weeks.

27. Graham Lawton, "Extreme Surgery," *New Scientist* 184, no. 2471 (October 30, 2004), <http://0-search.epnet.com.innopac.ln.edu.hk/ login.aspx?direct=true&db=aph&an=15347694> (September 13, 2005).

28. Alex Kuczynski, "A Lovelier You, With Off-The-Shelf Parts," *New York Times*, May 2, 2004, http://0-search.epnet.com.innopac.ln.edu.hk/login.aspx?direct=true&db=aph&an=13207223> (September 13, 2005).

29. John Dovey, "Reality TV," in *The Television Genre Book*, edited by Glen Creeber (London: BFI, 2001), p. 135.

30. Jason Jacobs, *Body Trauma TV: The New Hospital Dramas* (London: BFI, 2003), p. 55.

31. Ibid.

32. Anita Biressi, "Above the Below: Body Trauma as Spectacle in Social/Media Space," *Journal for Cultural Research* 8, no. 3 (July 2004), <http://0-search.epnet.com.innopac.ln.edu.hk/login.aspx?direct=true&db=aph&an=14910662> (September 13, 2005).

33. Jacobs, *Body Trauma TV*, p. 12.

34. Ibid., p. 44.

35. Michael Fitzpatrick, *The Tyranny of Health: Doctors and the Regulation of Lifestyle* (London: Routledge, 2001), p. 160.

36. It can also be argued that the events of 9/11 and the war on terror have increased feelings of social stagnation or diminished expectations for the future that have in turn increased the interest in personal change, particularly when that change involves a disavowal of history.

37. Jacobs, *Body Trauma TV*, p. 67.

38. Biressi, "Above the Below."

39. John Leland, "Why America Sees the Silver Lining," *New York Times*, 13 June 2004, <http://0-search.epnet.com.innopac.ln.edu.hk/login.aspx?direct=true&db=aph&an=13722695> (September 13, 2005).

40. Lewis, *The American Adam*, p. 5.

41. James Albrecht, "Saying Yes and Saying No: Individualist Ethics in Ellison, Burke and Emerson," *PMLA. Publication of the Modern Language Association of America* 114, no. 1 (January 1999), <http://0 search.epnet.com.innopac.ln.edu.hk/login.aspx?direct=true&db=aph&an=1422743> (September 13, 2005).

42. Gay Hawkins, "The Ethics of Television," *International Journal of Cultural Studies* 4, no. 4 (December 2001), <http://0-ejournals.ebsco.com.innopac.ln.edu.hk:80/direct.asp?ArticleID=B2HBL5U49RLKP2WF5ECG> (October 7, 2005).

43. Feldman, "Before and After."

44. Kuczynski, "A Lovelier You."

45. In one episode a patient's choice is even defended by Adams who tells the audience: "For some men like Tony, a face lift makes them feel refreshed and gives them an extra edge in a world obsessed with youth" ("Extreme Fix"). By transferring responsibility to society, Adams dilutes any impression the viewer may have that Tony's choice is vain.

46. Lewis, *The American Adam*, p. 5.

47. Ibid.

48. Ibid.

49. Leland, "Why America Sees."

50. Lewis, *The American Adam*, p. 5.

CHAPTER 5

WHAT PARIS REVEALS: THE SARTORIAL AND SENSUAL TRANSFORMATION OF AMERICAN GIRLS

ALISIA G. CHASE

IN EPISODE SIX FROM THE FIRST SEASON of *America's Next Top Model*, the remaining young women who "are still in the running" are sent by their guru to Paris, France. There, in a glamorous little bistro, Tyra Banks tells her enthralled, gazelle-limbed charges, "This city is responsible for the success of my career." As she reminisces about her "bittersweet memories" of go-sees at 17, the camera shows viewers a much younger Tyra posing on the streets of Paris. In one photograph, she wears the clichéd black beret, in another she stands in front of a *Paris-Match* covered newsstand, and in yet another she looks pensively across the Seine. Here, in the City of Light, like countless other American girls who spend months, if not years, slouching down the catwalk of Gallic designers with the hope of becoming the next face to grace the cover of *Vogue*, Tyra metamorphosed from this earnest, straight backed black girl to her present incarnation as a sexy, mocha-skinned, *Sports Illustrated* swimsuit model. For nearly all of the competitors, this is their first journey abroad, and by the end, each will have invariably tasted champagne, climbed a narrow little flight of stairs only to open the door of an even smaller hotel bedroom, and been transformed, as Tyra was, into a haute couture clad mannequin. But not without being subjected to a series of tests that not only reveal the young women's ability to literally embody whatever the French fashion world desires or demands they be, but which also disclose their moral and cultural attitudes toward illicit love affairs, exotic food, and the nude body; ergo, what is pejoratively assumed by many Americans to be the French way of life.

That the budding supermodels return from Paris sensually and sartorially transformed is a given, as even a cursory examination of feminine culture would suggest that Paris, its citizens, or even its signifiers have a magical power to make over American women's lives. Carrie from *Sex and the City* seeks more *amour* in Paris, *French Women Don't Get Fat: The Secret of Eating For Pleasure* surges to the top of the bestseller list, and Pottery Barn and Target both sell lamps in the shape of the Eiffel Tower. Undoubtedly it is a notion reminiscent of Daisy Miller's exclamation that a dress from Paris was like "a wishing cap" that had the power to transport her across the continent.[1] But this moneyed Victorian was a fictional exception and not the rule, for in the decades preceding, during, and, most surely, immediately following Henry James' era, it was also a given that the transformed American was male. Benjamin Franklin's letters about pretty French ladies who proffered their necks to be kissed, and the Lost Generation's decadent literature were among popular narratives that underscored the city as a locus associated with an American man's loss of innocence.[2] In the American imaginary, Paris "[was] the flesh pot and romance capital of the world," a transformative site of sensual indulgence where the puritanical traveler was tested in regards to his opinions about eating snails and public displays of affection.[3] My intention in this chapter is to illustrate how the narrative of the Parisian makeover has itself been made over, in this instance, within visual narratives from the mid-twentieth century to the present, to both suit and reflect the gendered and nationalist aims of history. Specifically, I want to argue that it is the discursive shifts regarding gender in the mythos of the continental education that destabilize the once dominant masculine narrative, in turn facilitating and further cementing our image of France as a feminized, and thus politically insignificant, site of effete pleasures and consumption.

Although scholars have long recognized the Parisian transformation as a literary trope, its visual counterpart has remained largely unexamined despite the fact that it appears as early as 1904 and has probably contributed as much, if not more, to the literal "image" of Paris in the national imaginary.[4] Film pioneer Edwin S. Porter initially equated the City of Light with the sensual in his short film titled, *Doing Paris*, which shows an American tourist drinking wine in a café. When he persuades two coquettes to Can-can, their skirts fly up and the man (and viewers) is privileged to the naughty sight of lacy French lingerie. After the debauchery, they all pour champagne upon each other—*et voilà*—an early cinematic trope is born. They were not yet dancing on the Pont Neuf, but there was an American man having a scandalous fête with sexy French women; these few elements began to reify the visual image of Paris in the minds of early cinemagoers. Musicals made between the wars, many of them penned by Cole Porter, furthered the myth of Paris as a place of hedonistic indulgence, and his lyrical query "Paree, Paree, What Did You Do To Me?" from *Fifty Million Frenchmen* was typical of the belief that the lascivious atmosphere of Paris transformed "a respectable [American]" into a champagne sodden playboy. The visual conventions— love scenes on top of the Eiffel Tower, singing peasants gathered around ging- ham café tables, and artists' costume balls with bottles of bubbly—continued into the post–World War II period with MGM's enormously popular musical of 1951, *An American in Paris.* The film was a postwar fantasy attempting to recreate the glory days of the roaring twenties, albeit in Technicolor, and for many years it lingered in the American imaginary as the most memorable example of romantic expatriate life.

But despite the success of *An American in Paris*, Hollywood could not repeat the formula, for this is when the expatriate mythos begins to trans- form, and the subplots in that film provide a clue as to how it changes.[5] Although the title suggests a singular American in Paris, there are actually three other U.S. citizens, that is, in addition to Gene Kelly's piano playing sidekick: the slumming heiress, the perfume-indulgent tourist, and the sassy "third-year girl," most likely meant to be a coed from one of the Seven Sisters' schools. Their pejorative treatment could purportedly be considered comic relief, as in the matronly vacationer, or integral to the plotline, as in the heiress whom Kelly rejects, effectively choosing orphaned postwar France over patrician prewar America. But the film's disparaging portrayal of these women suggests that the only Americans allowed to be in Paris were hetero- sexual white males, certainly a fiction that attempted to negate, even at that time, the cultural awareness of the multitudes of "other" types of Americans who had their own unique narratives about life in the City of Light.

Printed media in the 1950s betrayed the nostalgic fiction of MGM's lone GI abroad. One such article, "American Girl in Paris: The Intimate Story of a Girl Living Precariously in Paris—Her Private Life, Her Romance, Her Search for Happiness," detailed the life of a coed who had come to Europe on a bicycling trip and then stayed on, working odd jobs to make ends meet. The writer opened with a romantic assessment of the real-life counterparts of Kelly's character who write "rapturous books about her quaint little quartiers" or paint "the most soft-eyed watercolors." But he then went on to propose that, recently, it was not only young men who sought their sentimental education in Paris:

> The most dedicated expatriates . . . are the American girls, a few years past college age, who have flocked here by the hundreds since the War.
>   . . . it is they who carry the most tarnishproof (sic), preconceived picture of Paris, and who find the finest justifications for these preconceptions

everywhere they go—in the meanest hotel and the mangiest restaurant and the most feeble lover's arms.

It is about one such expatriate girl I'd like tell you . . . She had agreed to show me her Paris—the peculiarly American Paris of the girl expatriate—which has so far escaped notice of the guidebook writers and the moviemakers and is never written about in letters back home.[6]

"The Girl Expatriate" was not journalistic fiction. Employment in various postwar reconstruction organizations under the auspices of the Marshall Plan and study abroad programs implemented as early as 1938 offered young women from a much greater segment of the United States the chance to go overseas. Travel statistics cite that more women than men visited France in the immediate postwar era.[7] Additionally, a journey that once took ten days by ocean liner now took one night by jet, making it possible for the average secretary to spend her two-week vacation on the continent. Paris was quickly becoming the place where American women of the middle classes went, often unaccompanied (not just sans chaperone, but completely alone), in order to maximize their chances of meeting men. That their activities abroad were socially objectionable with respect to 1950s strictures regarding premarital sex is underscored within the *Holiday* article: letters back home never told the truth. But interviews with young women abroad in this era repeatedly bear witness to the theme of being remade anew, an idea that is borne out in such exclamations as "How can I tell them that I've learned to live [in Paris], that I've discovered my self as a woman?"[8]

Their experiences did not escape the moviemakers for long, however, and Hollywood began to produce dozens of films in response to this explosion in travel. Many of these movies could be considered quest romances, with female protagonists literally departing for adventure in new lands, setting off on an inward journey that they hope would change them irrevocably.[9] Yet these films are also cinematic evidence of the period's cultural anxiety regarding unmarried female sexuality, in particular, regarding ideas about female sexuality that were believed to be coming from France. As such, in Cold War America and Production Code Hollywood, the journeys had to be truncated, usually via marriage or an implied proposal. Following Jameson, the films are concurrently an attempt to give female audiences the narratives they desired—narratives that showed beautiful, intelligent, and independent young women transformed by their travels on the continent—as well as an attempt to "manage" (or for this essay's purposes, "make over") the less overt but no less pressing desires of real American women "to live" while they were abroad.[10] "To live" meant to experience the sensual world, not only in regards to becoming familiar with *petit fours*, or being able to discern a Cezanne from a Picasso, but also to seeking physical pleasure on one's own terms without fear of reprisal.[11] Given the period's stress on virginity, experiences gained by these women were not to be divulged upon one's return, and they were certainly not encouraged to be shown on-screen, and I would argue that this is why the transformative evidence of one's trip becomes so culturally significant. A *savoir-faire* in dress, firsthand knowledge of French cuisine, and a command of modern art were part of what one learned on the continent, but these were merely the external components of the more significant transformation that occurred within. They are literally, for many women, the polite "reveal."

These films simultaneously attempt to make over a politically whimsical Paris (and France) that seemed incapable of swearing allegiance to the pleasures of American capitalism. By proffering a cinematic bon-bon of a city filled with chartreuse poodles, perfumeries, and the delectable goodies of couturiers' salons, Hollywood remade the image of Paris in the national imaginary on two levels. Within the white, heterosexual realm, it changed in regards to gender, as a site that was once visually associated with macho GIs sweeping grateful French girls off of their feet became a frivolous locus of female desire, its talismanic stand-in epitomized by silken throw pillows with "I'd Rather Be In Paris" emblazoned on them. Within the realm of women, it makes a more subtle and divalent shift in both economic status and sexual identity—metamorphosing from a rarefied world of heiresses and elegant Sapphists to these same heterosexual bourgeoisies. The result was a sanitized playground of couture, cuisine, and art meant to be consumed by the primarily female audiences and potential tourists at whom these productions were aimed.

The film that most likely established the visual conventions of a young woman's Parisian transformation, and belied the significant reasons that female multitudes were going overseas, was *Sabrina*, the 1954 Paramount Pictures romantic comedy starring Audrey Hepburn. Loosely based on a Broadway play titled *Sabrina Fair, Woman of the World*, the narrative followed a young woman who leaves the United States as a lovesick, ponytailed teenager and returns as the epitome of European chic and feminine knowing. That upon her homecoming she manages to seduce her childhood crush who once spurned her, as well as his older brother, only served to prove what a girl could learn on the continent, but film censorship made it difficult to represent this explicitly. Director Billy Wilder, frustrated by American prudery and the punitive constraints of the code, cleverly insinuated Sabrina's coming of age with a spectacular wardrobe created by French designer Hubert de Givenchy.[12] As befits the period, Sabrina also comes home with a haute couture hairstyle and a command of French cuisine, but most significantly, for this was the part of the Parisian transformation that remained the same despite the shifts in gender, class, and sexual identity, well-schooled in the ways of amour.

To use the language of makeover reality television, Sabrina has three incrementally significant "reveals" within the film. Wilder chose to show little of Sabrina's actual transformation, that is, we do not see her in the hairstylist's or couturier's salons. Rather, through voice-over, we understand from her letters that the cosmopolitan Baron St. Fontanelle and the atmosphere of Paris are turning her from a shy, coltish girl into a self-confident woman who attends the races, visits the opera, and wears dresses that have "yards of skirt and [are] way off the shoulder." On-screen, this is particularly effective, and similar to the interstices in shows such as *Extreme Makeover*, when the waiting husband back in Biloxi is shown going about his daily life, wondering just what his "new wife" will look like, as during Sabrina's voiceovers only the homely Long Island servants are shown on-screen. When the viewer next sees Sabrina, she is seated in her *petite atelier*, and although she wears a modest robe, her once childlike locks are elegantly shorn, and the extent of her change is apparent in the words of the letter she is writing to her father:

> [Here, one learns] so many things . . . not just how to make vichyssoise or calf's head with sauce vinaigrette, but a much more important recipe. I have learned how to live. How to be in the world and of the world. And not just to stand aside and watch. I will never never run away from life again, or from love either.

Audiences accustomed to reading between the lines of censored material, or in this case, reading between the letters, began to understand that the Baron was her entry into the world of sensual pleasures, and Sabrina's Parisian metamorphosis is indicated by her suggestion that "If you should have any difficulty recognizing your daughter, I shall be the most sophisticated woman at the Glen Cove station." On this note, the second reveal occurs, as Wilder cuts immediately to the sight of a miniature French poodle wearing a rhinestone collar, and the camera moves up the dog's leash to find an equally magnificent Sabrina at the end of his lead. Clad in a strikingly tailored suit, Sabrina's newly cultivated poise, gained over the two years she has spent in the City of Light, is visually reinforced by the manicured, bejeweled beast by her side, while the lack of extraneous dialogue and characters further underscore her remarkable change.[13] Spectator-consumers who were familiar with the cultural meanings behind her Parisian accoutrements and remembered the film's tagline—"the chauffeur's daughter who's learned her stuff in Paris"— immediately understood just what it was she had learned, and it was a lot more than how to make vichyssoise.

Aside from the transformation of the filmic Sabrina from gawky teen to sophisticated woman, I would argue that changes made to the play's script are further evidence of the popular media makeover that was occurring in regards to the activities of female Americans abroad, for the alterations suggest that the original Sabrina, a "Woman of the World," was far too sexually and intellectually independent to let stand. As written by Samuel Taylor, Sabrina is nothing less than a self-actualized feminist when she returns from Paris, asking such relatively profound questions as "Isn't it strange of the English language, and typical, that there is no feminine analogue of 'hero worship?' " and refuting the then commonplace idea that "men have the exclusive right to run from domestication."[14] Paramount was most likely aware that the script changes would be abhorred by young audiences who had already seen or read about the popular play, as one month prior to the film's release they ran a promotional article in *Seventeen* magazine, an article that unequivocally underscored that "No two actors play the same role in the same way," a transparent attempt to excuse the drastic revisions to Sabrina's righteous defiance of American mores in the original script.[15] Although the film is an archetypal Cinderella story, in which the ill-clad but potentially dazzling immigrant's daughter learns how to infiltrate the upper-class ball, the theatrical Sabrina vehemently exposes the blatant sexism behind such fairy-tale thinking. In the play, when David Larrabee "arranges" their marriage with his parents, prior even to seeking *her* consent, Sabrina upbraids him for being so presumptuous:

> And that's what's always been wrong with the story. Everyone takes it for granted that Cinderella will marry Prince Charming when he comes knocking on her door with that diamond-studded slipper. Nobody considers Cinderella. What if she thinks Prince Charming is a great big oaf?[16]

Additionally, she outright denies the various proposals made to her throughout the narrative, even those proposals that promised her financial security. Marriage, as Sabrina sees it, is a way of closing herself off to the world, rather than opening up to it. Most probably, Taylor's characterization came in part from the public's understanding that Simone de Beauvoir's *The Second Sex*, which had been published stateside in 1949, was becoming extremely popular.[17] The lengthy work explored the history of women and their consistent representation as "the other," and what was more, in the last section, "Toward Liberation: The Independent Woman," De Beauvoir encouraged women in their attempts to take charge of their own financial life and sexuality, citing the illustrious French author Colette and her fictional heroines as examples of liberated yet fully sensual womanhood. What was coming from France was dangerous, and in the cinematic *Sabrina*, all evidence of her burgeoning feminism and refusal of the American nation's ideal notions of conjugal bliss are obliterated.

The film also revises the reason Sabrina initially goes abroad. As written by Taylor, after graduating from college "Sabrina went to Paris to be a file clerk in one of those world-saving American projects called NATO," not to master the perfect soufflé at cooking school. Most likely, she is meant to be one of what James Agee disparagingly referred to as "one of those Bryn Mawr girls out to police postwar Europe," and the film, like *An American in Paris*, is an attempt to mask the fact that young women in the early fifties, with the first two female U.S. ambassadors as their inspiration, were increasingly seeing themselves as integral participants in world affairs. The revisions thus functioned to remind female audiences that they were better suited for domestic pursuits; on stage, Sabrina succeeds in her job as a "quick, bright and efficient" private secretary to the "Assistant Economic Commissioner," advancing so far up the ladder that she even has her own secretary, whereas on-screen Sabrina repeatedly fails at such simple tasks as cracking an egg. Inarguably, the play's narrative is more progressive in regards to its attitude toward young women's intellectual capabilities than the film's, but even the theatrical script insinuates that this new generation and economic class of young women were only succeeding on the continent because of their sexual willingness. Despite Sabrina's exceptional fluency and intelligence, the Larrabee matriarch remains unconvinced that these attributes are why Sabrina flourished. As she acridly remarks, "No girl moves in the circles she did, and gets to know the people she knew, by being an excellent typist." Her snobbish distaste for the sense of entitlement Sabrina has acquired through her experiences abroad is rooted in her belief that there are certain people who belong in Paris, and a chauffeur's daughter, college educated or not, is not one of them.

Sabrina's final reveal is the visual denouement of the film, and it occurs when Sabrina enters the Larrabee ball through the backyard, her Givenchy gown voluminously floating behind her.[18] While Hepburn's strapless bust is similar to those of the other female guests, the dress's embroidered butterfly train varies dramatically and is an obvious visual innuendo to the sartorial and sensual transformation that Sabrina's stay in Paris has evoked—she has emerged from her virginal cocoon and is ready to fly. Additionally, instead of the full bell shape that suggests a fortress of impenetrable undergarments below, Sabrina's tight skirt emphasizes her shapely hips, and the part of her body that Paris helped her discover. That within the feminine realm, a visual transformation indicated a change that decorum prevented one from explicitly voicing is evident when David Larrabee excitedly informs his mother, "[You see] It's Sabrina. She's been to Paris, you know . . ." The older woman's sardonic tone as she answers "Yes, I *know* . . ." indicates that she sees something her besotted son cannot.

Sabrina's new look was also reminiscent of the 1950s mania for the "New Look" of Christian Dior, whose designs resurrected the severely corseted silhouette of Belle Époque Paris and were thus perfectly suited to a generation of women who desired to experience the demi-monde as described by

Colette. Postwar, her short stories were being republished for a new American readership, and in 1959, *Gigi* was visually immortalized in MGM's frothy musical. By then, the majority of American women were thoroughly inculcated in the fantasy that a Parisian gown could transform one's figure and one's spirit. Margaret Halsey narrated her own couture makeover from suburban spouse to Maxim's courtesan in *This Demi-Paradise: A Westchester Diary*: "[The dress made] me look properly carnal . . . as if I had my mind on lower things . . ." Another 1950s housewife who believed that a Paris gown would turn her into a chic sophisticate was Lucy Ricardo.[19] Given that the televised situation comedy *I Love Lucy* played to a more general audience, the episode *Lucy Gets a Paris Gown* lacks much of the reverence of *Sabrina*, but Lucy and Ethel's desire for "A Paris Original" is just as exemplary of the era's obsession with the transformative power of a dress from Paris. After hounding their husbands for a "Jacques Marcel" gown proves unsuccessful, they ultimately resort to going on a hunger strike. When Ricky and Fred discover their ruse, the men make their own "Paris Originals" out of potato sacks and use horse feed bags for chapeaux. Ethel and Lucy unwittingly wear them out to dinner, where they run into the couturier, who promptly assures them that they are not his designs. But the broader butt of the joke was made by American men of American women who believed that anything created by a French designer would change their lives, as Marcel co-opts their sack and makes it the latest style in Paris.[20] Parisians' preoccupation with *le dernier cri* (the latest thing) was thought to be characteristic of French mutability, and more evidence that "Frogs" could not be trusted in political matters; like their implacable wives, they were subject to fashion's whims and, therefore, needed to be controlled.

Another makeover sequence in which a Parisian gown subdues a freethinking female occurs in *Funny Face*, directed by Stanley Donen and released by Paramount in 1957. It was not accidental that this film also starred the physically waifish Hepburn. After winning over American audiences in *Roman Holiday*, the actress's simultaneously elegant and raffish persona affixed her in the public image as the archetypal young woman on the continent, and, akin to the formulaic narrative of *Sabrina*, it is once more the site of Paris that is responsible for the change of her character.[21] As a Greenwich Village bookstore clerk, Jo Stockton favors no-nonsense black turtlenecks and smocks in dull colors over the *de trop* fashions dictated by Paris, remarking, "[People like me do not] approve of fashion magazines . . . [they are] an unrealistic approach to self-impressions as well as economics." But her resistance to the world of fashion's pleasures is the first clue that she is about to be remade by it, and her reinvention occurs on two levels; not only is she physically revealed to be a beauty, but she is ultimately forced to admit that there can be a "functional advantage in a marvelous mouth," as she falls in love with the Pygmalion photographer, Dick Avery, who initiates her transformation. Although Maggie Prescott, the editorial doyenne who takes Stockton to Paris is far more despotic in her approach than Tyra Banks, the "before" appraisal of the future mannequin's physical attributes and potential follows the same conventions as those of *America's Next Top Model*. What *can* be changed (hair, eyebrows, makeup) *should* be changed, as it makes the final reveal exponentially more stunning, and what is de rigueur in the profession (adequate height, good bone structure, and a rail thin physique) must already exist. When Stockton arrives at the Quality office to deliver books, her hair is covered by a black babushka and she wears the same tweedy jumper and brown loafers that establish her as an aspiring Left Bank *philosophe*. Hepburn's extracinematic resonance from appearing on the real covers of *Harper's Bazaar*, however, demarcated her as couture material, so when Prescott barked out her assessment, stating, "The bones are good!" viewers knew that Hepburn was "in the running."[22]

Her reveal occurs approximately midway through the film, via the mastery of couturier Paul Duval, who has designed his entire spring collection around Stockton. As they wait, Prescott and Avery pace nervously and banter about their initial choice of model, one countering the other's exclamation of "They've been in there for hours!" with "There was a lot to be done!" Finally, Duval comes out and proclaims, "My friends, you saw it here a waif, a gamine, a lowly caterpillar—we opened the cocoon but it is not a butterfly that emerges, it is—A BIRD OF PARADISE!" When he commands, "LIGHTS—CURTAIN!" and the spotlight shines on the center of the catwalk, Stockton slowly advances, the picture of soignée poise. Her once lank hair is pulled into a sleek chignon, the diamond chain draped along her forehead highlights her doe-eyed beauty, and her iridescent shell pink jacket over a white sheath gown is sublime in its modesty. Everyone is speechless; the editor's eyes glisten as she gasps in pleasure, and the designer and photographer nod approvingly. Similar to the reveals in *The Swan* or *Extreme Makeover*, this change in visual appearance is immediately associated with interior transformation, as the enthralled onlookers ask, "You look absolutely fabulous—how does it *feel*?"

As in *Sabrina*, however, the cinematic makeover is not only in terms of Hepburn's style, it is also yet another attempt to manage the debauched French influences believed to be corrupting young American women, for from the beginning, the film ridicules Stockton's philosophical pursuits. The bookstore where she works is named "Embryo Concepts," as if to suggest that the ideas found within not yet fully developed, while the Parisian café dwellers are pathetically one-dimensional characterizations—drunken, lecherous old men in berets as well as lewd women with tangled, Bardotesque hair and a penchant for being slapped by their lovers. The professor Emil Flostre and his philosophical cult, Empathecalism, are parodies of Jean Paul Sartre and Existentialism, respectively, while Stockton's declaration "I worship everything he stands for!" is emblematic of the veneration many young Americans voiced in regards to French authors who encouraged individual freedom and choice. Despite her supposedly dissolute Greenwich Village origins, Stockton is the quintessential American innocent abroad, and she naively believes that Flostre is interested in her mind, not, as he describes it, in her "burgundy velvet" mouth. When her morals are challenged, she is forced to recognize that the louche Frenchman is more interested in lascivious gratification than questioning the purpose of one's life, and she takes the sexually moral high ground. The subtext of *Funny Face* functions to affirm the Cold-War-era ethos of finding pleasure in material consumption and conforming to society's ideals, so as a good American girl in the 1950s should, Stockton chooses the pleasures of fashion over those of the flesh. The film's definitive transformation is the remaking of an astute iconoclast who declares fashion to be, at best, concerned with "synthetic beauty" into a weepy wanna-be bride, who, after one week of playing model in Paris, would now rather script fairy-tales about princesses and doves than pen a tract on Camus.

The increasingly mythic notion that Paris transformed a young woman reached its real life apotheosis when, not long after *Funny Face*, Jacqueline Bouvier Kennedy became First Lady. Kennedy, like Hepburn's filmic characters, had once returned from the City of Light a wiser and more womanly single girl with a penchant for Parisian couture (she even owned a French standard poodle named Gaullie), and I would suggest that one of the reasons Americans embraced her so readily was that she was visually similar to the adored Hollywood star.[23] Kennedy's travels abroad as part of Smith College's Junior Year in France, travels that she described as "the highpoint in my life, my happiest and most carefree year," were what began her enduring veneration for all things à *la Française*, and eventually, her undeniable chic cemented the idea that sophistication could be the province of American women via a continental education.[24] But she also further destabilized the preferred narrative as penned by Hemingway in *A Moveable Feast* that it was American men to whom the dearest memories of Paris belonged. When President Kennedy and First Lady visited the City of Light in 1961, reactions of enthralled Parisians who screamed "*Vive Jacqui, Vive Jacqui!*" caused her husband to later remark, "I am the man who accompanied Jacqueline Kennedy to Paris, and I have enjoyed it." Arguably, this deferential witticism was nothing more than an acknowledgment of his wife's popularity, but her theft of his limelight on the world political stage as well as her rumored preference for clothes purchased on the Champs Elysees rather than their American knockoffs only fueled partisan rumors that the president's wife was vainly frivolous and lacked the wifely deference of her Republican predecessor.[25]

Like the protagonist of the theatrical *Sabrina*, Mrs. Kennedy reified the supposition that an intelligent American woman who has been to Paris and spoke fluent French was dangerous and needed to be contained; this by now Machiavellian untruth was conveniently trotted out when Teresa Heinz Kerry used her proficient language skills to address voters in Spanish, Portuguese, Italian, *and* French.[26]

It is evident that the executive producers of UPN's *America's Next Top Model*, which "chronicles the transformation of everyday young women into potentially fierce supermodels" in only eight weeks, utilize more than a few conventions from *Sabrina* and *Funny Face*, not least among them is the latter's basic narrative that all successful models begin their careers in Gay Paree, as well as both films' central focus on a visual metamorphosis. But the two Parisian episodes of this reality television series provide an updated counterpoint to these managed 1950s productions, for they reveal not only the place of Paris in the current national imaginary, but also the dominance of the American nation in that same imaginary. The premiere season of this reductive "dramality" preceded what was arguably the most culturally divisive year in recent national history, and the producers meretriciously exploited the country's more acrimonious disputes, mainly that between the pious patriotism of the Red States and the liberal cosmopolitanism of the Blue States, with the aspiring supermodels functioning as cartoonish personifications of each faction's members.[27]

From the beginning, the girls are not only seen to epitomize definitive and thus competitive physical archetypes (the leggy Grace Kelly-like blonde, the exotic raven haired Hispanic, the Twiggy-ish pixie) but are also carefully set up in order to represent established and emergent social archetypes (the "small town girl" from Little Rock, Arkansas; the "All-American virgin" from Franklin, Ohio; the "the rock n' roll tomboy" from Joliet, Illinois) and are thus *a priori* oppositional in their mores. The intentionally cramped bedrooms, which replicate those that struggling, real-life models share, seems to heighten the competition's veracity, but they also help to heighten friction. For aside from the constant physical rivalry, which includes catty discussions of other models' hair-weaves and weight, the covert subtext of a "house soon divided" on the topic of religion becomes the subdominant conflict when "the three Christian girls decide to room together." As the episodes progress, clashes between the "militant atheist" Elyse and the proselytizing, fundamentalist Robin are aggrandized to keep viewers watching; and in this hyperbolical synthesis of reality and drama, Elyse's overt proclamations (such as, "I'm not going to pretend I don't believe in evolution just so I can be friends with Robin") and Robin's histrionic cries ("Oh Jesus, oh Jesus, I have to call on Jesus," as a scarlet colored snake is draped around her neck during a photoshoot) suggestively mirror the fervency of such national debates as that between Darwinism and Intelligent Design. I would also suggest that an additional opposition echoing the media's pet preoccupation with a nation torn asunder is the convenient "reality" that Elyse is white and Robin is black, although given the devious conventions of reality television, race is an issue always present but never directly addressed, so this card is never overtly played. Ultimately, the show's stagy dramatization of the antagonistic tension between rural girls of faith who are aghast at masturbation and homosexuality and the culturally liberal girls who feel completely at ease with nudity and tolerance reaches its seemingly natural crescendo in Gay Paree, for as it has in literature, cinema, and now, reality television, the libidinous French capitol provides a convenient site of difference in which an American's moral fortitude can be literally and figuratively contested.

From the start, the visual debt to *Funny Face* is obvious: the cartoon airplane and its five small windows with the smiling models' faces peeking out is a direct take-off on the 1957 film. In 2003, it is obviously played for laughs, but the successive shots of the Eiffel Tower and the idea that this is a young woman's ultimate fantasy are tropes that serve the dramatic aspect of the show quite well, as American viewers weaned on a visual diet of beret-wearing painters and baguette-waving chefs are thus cued to access their hackneyed sentiments regarding Gay Paree. As their taxi careens through the boulevards, the selected voice-overs express the magnitude of each girl's *naïveté* about going abroad and fittingly mimic those sentiments of their mid-century filmic counterparts. Kesse, a sweet Bible reader from the Sunbelt, states, "I used to say I was gonna move to Paris . . . I wanted to just get away from the whole environment of being in Arkansas, I just wanna be out on my own for while and experience, you know, the real world!" Robin, the pampered "pageant queen," is portrayed as a twenty-first century descendent of Twain's tourists when she is caught speaking a pedantic form of pig Latin to the taxi driver. After stating "I'm going to hold on to this" in English, she points once again to her pink teddy bear and slowly and loudly says to him, "Me kee-pee this-ay." And like the dogged "innocents" of the nineteenth century whose definition of the City of Light rests upon pictures they have seen in books, Robin is disappointed that reality does not live up to her Venetian cum Las Vegas expectation of seeing "people on boats with the violins."

Such delusions and reality converge and diverge consistently as the young women's experiences of Paris as masterminded by Tyra prove to be more challenging than pleasurable, and their trials on foreign soil are superficially evocative of those that their cinematic predecessors faced. Their first test is a photo shoot, but it does not quite resemble the *Funny Face* fantasy of running through the Tuileries with rainbow hued balloons. In the typical American imaginary, Paris is not Paris unless there is illicit sex and lacy lingerie, so the

photo shoot for the company Wonderbra is set up to imitate a lovers' tryst in
a hotel room and requires the young women to model with a muscular man
in skimpy briefs. This challenge and the photographer's advice to "be as bad
as you can be" are among the first of many that are deployed to delineate who
is willing to set aside Christian prohibitions and puritanical shame about
one's body in the name of fashion. Shannon, the blonde, toothy, "born-again
virgin," reveals that she never knew women could "touch themselves" and is
filmed scrunching up her face in disgust when the gay male makeup artist
talks about masturbation. Faith is also seen to be a formidable obstacle to
modeling in the shadow of the Eiffel Tower when neither Kesse nor Robin
can take the simulated physicality of the love affair as lightly as the photographer wishes they would. By this point in the series, Adrianne and Elyse have
been positioned as the personification of the cultural and political left, with
the former representing the Dionysian rock n' roller, and the latter the high-
brow "academic." As such, they are seen as American archetypes who would
predictably feel at home in Gay Paree, and it is no surprise when they both
follow the photographer's directions to the letter. Afterward, lusty Adrianne
is revealed bragging, "You're supposed to be on fire and I was," while intellectual Elyse says she treated it like art, "[It] was like posing with a statue."

As no fairy-tale transformation is complete without a gown, episode seven
begins at the House of Carven, "the oldest couture establishment in all of
Paris." To show off the clothes, Tyra has pulled all of the girls' hair back into
high buns, didactically informing them that in France, this style is called
"a chignon." She further instructs them that its simplicity is intentional, as it
is imperative that one's hairstyle not distract from the meticulous sartorial
craftsmanship. That a part of one's experience in France entails emulating the
sartorial *élan* that French women are reputed to naturally possess is evidenced
when the couturier tells them, "It's an attitude." To see if they can simulate
the requisite allure, their next test is to wear these couture gowns out for an
evening on the town, escorted by four young men from the upper echelons of
French society, who, at the night's close, will judge the girls on their ability to
"live up to the gowns." What Tyra is also having the Gallic men determine,
however, is each young woman's willingness to partake in another culture's
pleasures, whether that means being sated with a mere sliver of *bête noire* torte
or appreciate the nuances of the ballet. When the duly transformed
princesses, all wearing variations on "the famous black little dress from Paris,"
are shown to their stretch limo carriage, the enthusiastic Adrianne positively
squirms with delight. "I feel so good in this!" she exclaims, "I feel like some-
body else!" Certainly her metamorphosis is dramatic, considering that by day
the Midwestern cow-tipper has been wearing dirty jeans, black leather jacket,
and John Lennon style glasses. After she slicks her hair back and slithers into
a backless and nearly frontless dress, however, it is evident to viewers familiar

with contemporary sartorial codes that Adrianne has what it takes to be "America's Next Top Model," and the scene foreshadows the final episode, wherein Tyra tells Adrianne that she has "transformed like Cinderella."

The gourmet restaurant is another clichéd filmic locus where each potential model's desire to, as the filmic Sabrina says, be "in the world and of the world," or as Tyra updates it, "work the world," is further contested. Here, the camera shows plate after plate of artfully arranged, nouvelle style French cuisine: a dollop of red caviar, a slice of *pate de foie gras*, and that shellfish which never fails to challenge an American's palate, escargot. As could be expected, the dining tables are a microcosmic example of the easily parodied gustatory divide between the coastal wine snobs and the down home barbecues preferred by the great geographical swath that separates them, with Adrianne and Elyse sampling all that is offered and Robin and Shannon declaring that French food "isn't all it's cracked up to be." Likewise, the evening's entertainment at the Opera House seems calculated to determine who is, as one of the French men puts it, "interested in other people's interests": a thinly veiled criticism of the Bush doctrine's arrogant disregard for France's political concerns regarding the Iraqi invasion, as additionally the repeated shots of Robin reading her Bible in the back of the limousine serve to place her soundly on the side of those who would prefer to rename French toast. After the stroke of midnight, Adrianne is the girl rewarded with a luxurious suite at Le Meridian and chooses Elyse to remain with her. Relishing the sumptuous pleasures provided to them—bunches of roses, bottles of champagne, and a candlelit bubble bath, the girls smoke, drink, and declare their love for *la bonne vie*. Immediately, the camera cuts back to the crowded, walk-up hotel, where Robin and Shannon are shown reading their Bibles. The libertines' decadence is further reinforced when Adrianne entices Elyse to sleep topless with her, and the decisive challenge that awaits all of the girls when they awake is foreshadowed by each faction's choice of sleepwear: while the heathens lie half-naked, the "holiest holy-rollers" are bundled up in pyjamas and sweats.

The next day's photo shoot at the chic Buddha Bar seems to have been devised to lay bare all of the girls' pretenses to Parisian sophistication, as they are told they will be posing nude. To place emphasis on the latest collection of Serella diamonds, the art director has decided to forego clothing and settle for "greasy, smoky, make-up" and "very moody . . . lighting." This is a test that could theoretically happen in any city of the world; a nightclub in Paris, however, magnifies the Christian girls' increasing sense of alienation from the terra-firma of their moral beliefs, and despite the assurance that strategic placement of hair and hands will cover more private body parts, both Shannon and Robin are shown palpably nonplussed. The makeup artist offers the self-conscious girls thong underwear and flesh toned bands to wrap around their chests, but when pressed, Robin declares that the illusion of nudity is as immoral as being nude, and she delineates the slippery slope toward total abandonment of one's Christian principles that the atmosphere of Paris is believed to encourage when she is filmed vociferously asking, "Last week it was a bra and panties, this week it's two ribbons and a thong. What's it gonna be next week?"

When the four remaining girls return to New York, they are asked to "show [the judges] what they've learned in Paris." In keeping with the convention that a woman can reveal the degree of her continental education through dress, the aspiring models are given ten minutes to transform: They must choose a couture gown, shoes, and accessories to provide evidence of their sartorial sophistication. The results are, in some ways, as revealing to a fashionably knowledgeable audience as the nudity challenge is to a broader range of viewers. Elyse, whose bright red coat and semifluency in the French language made her seem a natural on Parisian cobblestones, nails the assignment. As Tyra tells her, "You're the one girl who took Paris by storm," and as she elegantly strides into the room in floral evening dress cut down to her navel and a sprig of silk flowers rakishly pinned in her hair, it is clear she is "still in the running." The next transformation fails, however, as Shannon proves that what is sexy in California is "too obvious" in the realm of couture. When she enters with her hair hanging like a surfer girl, Tyra reprimands her for not paying attention to what could be learned in Paris and expresses displeasure that Shannon has forgotten the transformational power of the chignon. Upon Adrianne's entrance, it is clear that the tomboy has remembered the secrets of French femininity. Although she lacks the natural grace of Hepburn, her reveal is similarly dramatic; her hair is pulled back into a lustrous bun, and her black lace mesh gown is understated in its elegance.

Robin's isolationist attitude in Paris, her pious Bible quoting, her desire to "shop" rather than "see" the city, and the footage of her wearing large white athletic sneakers around the boulevards have already demarcated her as the typical late twentieth-century American tourist, a woman who sees Paris not as a place to be transformed, but as a place to purchase. Her refusal to be made over by its atmosphere is visually represented by her inability to replicate a couture look back in New York City, and it is likewise analogous to her refusal to come to terms with her sense of privilege and patently false purity. When Banks informs Robin, the girl who proclaimed, "My religion teaches me that my body is a temple," that she was caught shaking her chest at the male makeup artist, she soundly chastises the hypocrisy: "What is this person that preaches all that [and yet does something different]?" This exchange, coupled with the understanding that Robin has declared herself "the representative of the American people," is emblematic of the Bush administration's claims to devout faith and a divinely ordained mission to "civilize" the rest of the world. Robin has nothing to learn, not from France, not from anyone.

Although many of the tropes of a young woman's Parisian transformation remain mere variations on the standards scribed in the eighteenth century and visualized during the twentieth, the fact that the City of Light is seen only as the penultimate test in the world of modeling reveals not only the contemporary place of Paris in the American imaginary, but also the consummate positioning in that same imaginary of their final challenge: Manhattan. That New York has usurped Paris's long standing position as the unparalleled style center of the world is visually reinforced by the banners that are shown flying around the city during the last episode, as well as by the appellations given to the bedrooms in the girls' living space. The five sleeping quarters are named after the globe's reputed "fashion capitols": Milan, Paris, Tokyo, London, and Miami. They all, however, lie within the preeminent realm of the New York penthouse, a neatly arrogant geographical metaphor for the city's capital dominance over other fashion markets in the early twenty-first century.[28] Following Dana Heller's superb analysis of *Sex and the City* and *Friends*, in which both of the lead female protagonists forsake Parisian expatriation for a male love interest in New York, I would also suggest that *America's Next Top Model*, like most postnational narratives of Americans in the City of Light, "reject[s] Paris as a transformative source of knowledge," even as it utilizes the site and its (by now, trite) challenges to affirm our own sense of what it means to be American. As Robin's refusal to change clarifies, there is no self-realization, only ultimate repatriation to "a state fantasy" that reflects one's "deepest internal desires."[29] True, the young models return from Paris with a better understanding of how to accessorize a couture gown, but the transformation is purely superficial. In the end they have simply flirted with the French, tried on their couture, eaten their cuisine, and said *bon jour*; the City of Light is nothing more than another stop in their global shopping mall of fashion fantasies. Although we will always have Paris and its "revealing" narratives, in our present state of isolated arrogance, it seems taking Manhattan is now the only way to "work the world."

NOTES

1. Henry James, *Daisy Miller* (London: Penguin, 1986), p. 56.
2. See Stephen Longstreet, *We All Went to Paris: Americans in the City of Light, 1776–1971* (New York: The Macmillan Company, 1972); *The Black Expatriates: A Study of American Negroes in Exile*, ed. Ernst Dunbar (New York: EP Dutton & Co., 1968); Stanley Karnow, *Paris in the Fifties* (New York: Times Books [Random House Inc.], 1997); Donald Pizer, *American Expatriate Writing and the Paris Moment: Modernism and Place* (Baton Rouge: Louisiana State University Press, 1996); and Georges Wickes, *Americans in Paris* (New York: Doubleday & Company, 1969).
3. Art Buchwald, "Paris! City of Nightlife," *Holiday* (April 1953), p. 103.

4. Dana Heller's forthcoming article "Sex and the Series: Paris, New York, and Post-National Romance" is an excellent analysis of how the city of Paris functions in the American national imaginary post 9/11. See *American Studies* 46, no. 1 (Summer 2005), pp. 5–29.

5. Musicals about singing GIs abroad, such as *So This is Paris* (1955), and even more serious dramas about ex-soldiers in France, such as *Kings Go Forth* (1958), met with lukewarm receptions at best.

6. Paul E. Deutschman. "American Girl in Paris." *Holiday* (October 1954), p. 107.

7. Foster Rhea Dulles, *Americans Abroad: Two Centuries of European Travel* (Ann Arbor: The University of Michigan Press, 1964), pp. 174–176.

8. Paul E. Deutschman. "American Girl in Paris." *Holiday* (November 1954), p. 59.

9. Dana Heller, *The Feminization of Quest Romance: Radical Departures* (Austin, TX: University of Texas Press, 1991), p. 26.

10. Frederic Jameson, "Reification and Utopia in Mass Culture," in *Signatures of the Visible* (New York and London: Routledge, 1992), p. 25.

11. Much of my understanding of fifties sexual mores comes from Elaine Tyler May and her ideas about domestic containment in *Homeward Bound: American Families in the Cold War Era* (New York: Basic Books, 1988).

12. The director knew *mise-en-scene* could insinuate what censorship disallowed. See *Conversations with Wilder*, by Cameron Crowe (New York: Alfred E. Knopf, 1989), pp. 218–220.

13. See my article, " 'Like Their First Pair of High Heels . . .' Continental Accessories and Audrey Hepburn's Cinematic Coming of Age" in *Abito E Identita: Recherché di Storia Letteraria E Culturale*, edited by Cristina Giorcelli (Italy: Ila Palma, Spring 2004), for a discussion of how the poodle functioned as a marker of sophistication. In regards to Wilder's pause, Rachel Moseley has rightly noted that it is geared toward "a feminine audience, one which is competent in reading sartorial codes." "Dress, Class and Audrey Hepburn: The Significance of the Cinderella Story" in *Fashioning Film Stars: Dress, Culture and Identity*, edited by Rachel Moseley (London: British Film Institute, 2005), p. 113.

14. Samuel Albert Taylor, *Sabrina Fair, or A Woman of the World* (New York: Dramatists Play Service, 1953), pp. 23, 45.

15. Anon, "Who's Seen Cinderella?" *Seventeen* (August 1954), p. 104.

16. Taylor, *Sabrina Fair*, p. 67.

17. Blanche Knopf purchased the rights to the English translation because she thought it was a "modern day sex manual, [like] Kinsey" and that the popularity of Existentialism among American college students would make for good sales. Alfred Knopf reiterated: "I think it is capable of making a very wide effect indeed and that young ladies in places like Smith who can afford the price . . . will be nursing it." See Deidre Blair's introduction to the 1989 Vintage edition of Simone de Beauvoir's *The Second Sex* (New York: Knopf, 1952), p. xiv.

18. For more on the Givenchy gown, see Stella Bruzzi, *Undressing Cinema: Clothing and Identity in the Movies* (London: Routledge, 1997) and Gaylyn

Studlar's "Chi-Chi Cinderella: Audrey Hepburn as Couture Countermodel," *Hollywood Goes Shopping*, edited by David Dresser and Garth S. Jowett (Minneapolis: University of Minnesota Press, 2000), pp. 179–204.

19. Margaret Halsey, *This Demi-Paradise: A Westchester Diary* (New York: Simon and Schuster, 1960), p. 55.

20. Neil Scovell, "Sacks Fifth Avenue," *Fashions of the Times, A Supplement to The New York Times* (Fall 2001), p. 114.

21. Molly Haskell attributed Hepburn's popularity to her ability to be both girl and woman simultaneously. See *From Reverence to Rape: The Treatment of Women in the Movies* (Chicago: The University of Chicago Press, 1973), pp. 267–268.

22. *Seventeen* (January 1956), p. 96.

23. In *America's Queen: the Life of Jacqueline Kennedy Onassis* author Sarah Bradford writes, "The Givenchy look, spare a-line dresses as worn by Audrey Hepburn—Givenchy's muse at the time—was the one that most appealed to [Jackie]. It suited her lean figure, while her own doe-eyed-dark fawn-like looks resembled those of the star of *Sabrina*, *Roman Holiday* and *Funny Face*" (New York: Viking Press, 2000), p. 146. A similar comparison is made by Geoffrey Perret in *Jack: A Life Like No Other* (New York: Random House, 2001), p. 237.

24. Robert D. McFadden, "Death of a First Lady; Jacqueline Kennedy Onassis Dies of Cancer at 64," *New York Times* (May 20, 1994), A1.

25. See Perret, 313, and also Robert Dallek, *An Unfinished Life, John F. Kennedy, 1917–1963* (Boston: Little, Brown and Company, 2003), p. 400.

26. Heinz-Kerry began her speech at the Democratic convention with the welcome "Y a todos los Hispanos, los Latinos; a tous les Americains, Francais et Canadiens; a tutti Italiani; a toda a familia Portugesa e Brazileria . . ."

27. The term "dramality" was conceived by *Survivor* producer Mark Burnett to define a show in which drama meets reality. http://www.wordspy.com/words/dramality.asp (Accessed on November 20, 2005).

28. As a recent article regarding *America's Next Top Model* stated, "Although fashion gives the illusion of being a global business, New York remains the hub for all the largest modeling and advertising agencies and also mass circulation magazines. And it is still the center of image creation, editorial clout and behind-the-scenes wheeling and dealing." *New York Times* (November 6, 2006), p. 91. For a more academic reading of "the geographies of fashion culture," see David Gilbert's superlative essay, "Urban Outfitting: The City and The Spaces of Fashion Culture" in *Fashion Cultures*, ed. Stella Bruzzi and Pamela Church Gibson (London & New York: Routledge, 2000), pp. 7–24.

29. Heller, "Sex and the Series," p. 28.

CHAPTER 6

MAKING OVER BODY AND SOUL: *IN HIS STEPS* AND THE ROOTS OF EVANGELICAL POPULAR CULTURE

CLAY MOTLEY

ONE SUNDAY EVENING IN 1896, the Reverend Charles M. Sheldon stood in front of his congregation at the Central Congregational Church of Topeka, Kansas, and read them part of a story he had recently written entitled "In His Steps: What Would Jesus Do?" Every fall since 1891, his second year at the Central Church, Sheldon had read his serialized stories to the congregation on Sunday nights to improve lagging attendance. Although his five previous stories were quite successful (their eventual publication working toward better church attendance), no one at the Central Church service that night could have known that they were witnessing the birth of one of the best-selling novels in American history. Within one year 16 different publishers would pirate the book,[1] selling over two million copies.[2] In a matter of years, *In His Steps* "saturated the reading public of the English-speaking world"[3]; it would eventually be translated into at least 25 languages[4] and is still purchased in the thousands annually in multiple editions. Often condensing the title to "WWJD," people across America wear it on such items as bracelets, t-shirts, license plates, and hats to advertise their evangelical Christian identity. From its birth in Topeka, Kansas, in 1896, "WWJD" has developed into the most prominent slogan for evangelical Christians in America today.

The persistent popularity of Sheldon's *In His Steps* reveals that it is a seminal text for understanding the roots of contemporary evangelical Christian culture, which is to say that *In His Steps* is important to our understanding of contemporary American culture. Although American society is more pluralistic than ever before, it is clear that evangelical Christianity has emerged as one of its most powerful forces. This is exemplified by the president of the United States frequently identifying himself as a "born again" Christian, by the millions of American men who annually fill football stadiums for Promise Keepers revivals, and by Franklin Graham, son of Billy Graham, carrying on his father's "crusades" on television and in sold-out arenas throughout America. In suburbs across America, evangelical "megachurches," such as the Willow Creek Community Church outside Chicago, can attract up to 15,000 worshippers a week to its "campus" of worship facilities.[5] A recent survey by the Barna Research group found that 40 percent of Americans consider themselves "evangelical Christians,"[6] which is a far larger percentage than any single religious denomination in America. Increasingly, evangelical Christianity is the face of modern American Christianity. By analyzing the social and historical context of Sheldon's *In His Steps*, we will see that his best-selling novel of the Social Gospel and today's media-savvy evangelical Christians respond quite similarly to profound social changes that evangelicals associate with a modernizing society." Their agenda is essentially an "antimodern" one of "making over" American society to fit with a mythic, idealized "past" that was more pious, coherent, and socially secure than the present.

Before proceeding, it is important to briefly define the somewhat nebulous term "evangelical." Although "evangelical" is a broad enough term to encompass both the cozy Christianity of a modern "megachurch" and the more austere fundamentalism of a rural sect, there are some important unifying characteristics across all evangelical beliefs. Evangelical Christianity in America can be traced back to the Great Awakening of the 1730s and 1740s, decades that were marked by a series of massive and emotionally charged religious "revivals" that helped expand such denominations as the Baptists, Methodists, and Presbyterians into the mid-Atlantic and Southern colonies. From its revivalistic roots, evangelicalism even today stresses a personal and willful conversion experience of being "born again" or "saved" into Christianity. Equally, most evangelicals stress a personal relationship with Jesus, and thus their services tend to stress emotional and dramatic experiences rather than liturgical formality. More so than in liturgical denominations, evangelicals typically believe in a literal interpretation of the Bible and in its inerrant authorship. Taking seriously the biblical charge to "evangelize" the world, evangelicals put a premium on making new converts by reaching out to the "unchurched."

It is the evangelical Christian emphasis on conversion and being "born again" that makes it significant to the deep-seated dynamic of the "makeover myth" in American culture. After all, to be "born again" through

Christ is presumed to be the ultimate "makeover" an individual can experience, radically transforming one's spiritual and personal identity. When George W. Bush calls himself a "born again" Christian, the implication is that he is a radically different person now than before his salvation experience because he has had a direct experience with Jesus. To be "born again" is to have a new "life in Christ" and thus a new identity. Of course, beginning with St. Paul's experience on the road to Damascus, Christianity has had a long history of dramatic conversions. However, it was not until evangelical Christianity began to take root with the Great Awakening that most Americans had a religious concept that was as transformative as being "born again." The early revivalist John Wesley revealed the radical nature of being "born again" when he wrote that conversion meant experiencing "God continually breathing, as it were, upon the human soul."[7] Thus, the unsaved are without the life-giving "breath" of God, but being "born again" is to be directly, constantly inspired by God. As an outward sign of a convert's inner transformation, evangelical Christianity stresses an outward "emotional experience of religion" as "the only proof of genuine faith and hence of salvation."[8] This could take the form of a tearful "testimony" of one's personal salvation experience, converts answering "the call" to salvation during a church service, or more dramatically, the dancing or convulsions associated with Pentecostalism.

The "makeover" of an evangelical Christian's identity is not limited to his or her inner life. On the contrary, evangelicalism calls for the radical transformation of the national identity as much as it calls for the transformation of personal character. The nineteenth-century Methodist minister William Arthur captured the social aims of evangelicalism when he wrote, "Nothing short of the general renewal of society ought to satisfy any soldiers of Christ."[9] This is where the evangelical "makeover" myth interestingly separates from its other versions in American culture. For example, in *The Great Gatsby* (1925), James Gatz leaves his home and his previous identity to invent a "platonic conception" of himself as "Jay Gatsby"; to use another example, at the end of *The Adventures of Huckleberry Finn* (1885), Huck and Jim famously "light out for the territories" when their lives become too "civilized." In these literary touchstones of American culture, we see the American makeover myth as highly personal and generally involving a break with society. Typically in secular culture, if an American does not like his or her current identity, he or she can move (literally or metaphorically) to where the "self" can be reinvented freely. Thus, more than ever before, Americans can drift without roots through careers, geographic regions, and even breast sizes and eye colors, as they continually shed old identities, unanchored to the unsatisfying past, or to larger social contexts.

In the evangelical Christian makeover myth, there is no retreat from society; in fact, the truly "born again" Christian has a duty to "renew" his/her national identity, to transform the nation's life as radically as one's own personal life. This evangelical social activism was prominently displayed at the end of the nineteenth century when such ministers as Charles Sheldon, Washington Gladden, and Walter Rauschenbusch promoted the "Social Gospel" to end "poverty, disease, filth, and immorality"[10] in America. Today, this evangelical social activism is likely to take the form of conservative politics, embodied by the Christian Coalition, Jerry Falwell's Moral Majority Coalition, or Pat Robertson's popular *700 Club* and Christian Broadcast Network. John Hagee, the popular San Antonio televangelist, concisely states the contemporary evangelical Christian's commitment to politics as a method of social change: "Learn God's position on abortion, homosexuality, and your obligation as a Christian to be involved in the political process."[11] Stephen Prothero observes that "evangelicals and fundamentalists have in recent decades become the most vocal critics of American Christianity's captivity to culture."[12] This does not mean that evangelicals are withdrawing from secular society, but rather that they are trying to transform American culture into their own evangelical image.

Due to the evangelical call to make converts and transform society, it is not surprising that evangelical Christians throughout American history have readily used the available media to transmit their message. David Morgan asserts that nineteenth-century evangelicals believed that "oral culture simply was not equal to the evangelical imperative of converting a world that was overwhelmingly non-Christian and a nation with a burgeoning population of Roman Catholic immigrants."[13] Thus, the advancement of inexpensive printing and transportation in the nineteenth century precipitated the publication of hundreds of evangelical novels and magazine titles, most prominent among them was the serially published *Uncle Tom's Cabin* (1852) by Harriet Beecher Stowe, which made a sentimental and evangelical Christian case against slavery. Upon their arrival in America in 1881, the Salvation Army waged a "campaign seeking to adapt popular media for religious purposes,"[14] as they acted out their evangelical Social Gospel in melodramatic plays that were easily transformed after the turn of the century into nickelodeon shows and early Hollywood films, such as *Fires of Faith* (1919) and *Salvation Nell* (1921). Although some twentieth-century evangelical leaders worried that new media of radio and television would lead to lower church attendance and degraded morality, most evangelicals quickly realized the power of new media forms to broadcast their message to larger audiences in more captivating forms than ever before. Early televangelists such as Oral Roberts and Jimmy Swaggart have given way to today's Benny Henn and Franklin Graham, but the basic premise—using the media to convert souls and change the moral order of America—has remained constant since the evangelical novels of the nineteenth century. The infamous "Heritage USA" community and theme park designed by televangelists Jim and Tammy Bakker in the 1980s was not designed to be a haven away from secular America, but rather a harbinger of what an evangelical America should look like.

Although the Social Gospel of the Progressive Era and the politics of modern day televangelists are remarkably different, they share the same fundamental evangelical qualities and both use the media for saving souls and "making over" the national identity. Thus, by closely analyzing Charles Sheldon's *In His Steps*, one of the most popular expressions of evangelical Christianity for well over one hundred years, we can gain insight into the roots and character of our modern evangelical culture. Specifically, we can better understand how the national "makeover myth" of evangelical Christianity is in many ways an "antimodernist" impulse, meaning it romanticizes qualities and experiences of the past as the key to transforming the present. The current televangelist minister John Hagee taps into this "antimodern" dynamic of the evangelical makeover myth when he proclaims, "Vote your Christian beliefs. We must take our nation back to the God of our fathers, the God of Abraham, Isaac and Jacob."[15] Hagee wants to take America "back" to a time when Christianity was pure and unthreatened by modern life. Of course, this religious "golden age" in America never existed, but this is why the evangelical makeover myth is so alluring: it promises to restore America to a better, more unified, secure, and righteous past that our modern society has lost touch with.

Charles Sheldon's *In His Steps* is also an evangelical makeover myth prompted by antimodern impulses. Sheldon's novel is mainly motivated by class fears and gender anxieties brought about by modern social changes, and in his novel he proposes a tangible plan to have America transformed into an evangelical Christian country by each of his millions of readers—in his own time and ours—simply asking "What Would Jesus Do?"

In His Steps reveals a multifaceted Social Gospel that treats the connections between gender, class, and religious belief in nuanced ways. To Sheldon, religious significance depended upon a person's class: for the relatively affluent middle class who made up the bulk of his congregation and readership, he argued that religion should be a masculinizing influence, forcing them out of their comfortable homes and padded church pews into the harsh world to suffer like Jesus in the fight for the lower class's souls. For the lower class, Sheldon's brand of religion was to be a domesticating and implicitly feminizing agent, pacifying their "dangerous," "violent" tendencies by inculcating middle-class domestic values. Thus, Sheldon's Social Gospel "makes over" the affluent and the poor differently, transforming both their spiritual lives and social circumstances for the better. Of course, their personal transformations will lead to the "making over" of the nation, taking it away from its modern troubles and leading it "back" to a safer and more recognizable culture.

THE SOCIAL CONTEXT OF *IN HIS STEPS*

One of the driving forces of Sheldon's *In His Steps* and the larger Social Gospel movement was the notion that turn-of-the-century American society had become "overcivilized" through its loss of the manly vigor of previous generations. Jackson Lears notes the prevailing sense that "the industrious had been corrupted by the fruits of their own success; wealth brought flaccidity and self-indulgence."[16] This corrupting success made "intense experience—whether physical or emotional—[. . .] a lost possibility. There was no longer the opportunity for bodily testing provided by rural life, no longer the swift alternation of despair and exhilaration which characterized the old-style Protestant conversion."[17] It was widely believed that what displaced the emotional, spiritual, and physical peaks and valleys associated with premodern life was a stable aridity that lulled modern society into a deep complacency. The middle class acutely felt this sensed burden of being trapped by their success in a world devoid of authentic emotions and actions.

These broad-based feelings of modern unease, termed "antimodernism" by Jackson Lears, was interpreted as "feminization" by many men who experienced it. This was because the same developments that helped create an affluent middle class, such as the rise of a national corporate culture and increased rates of urbanization, conflicted with existing definitions of manhood. E. Anthony Rotundo argues, "In the nineteenth century, middle-class men had believed that a true man was a self-reliant being who would never bow to unjust authority or mere position. The new structures of work and opportunity in the marketplace did not support such a concept of manhood."[18] Michael Kimmel adds that as America switched from an economy predicated on independent shop owners and rural labor to an urban, corporate economy, American men found themselves living an "oppressively crowded, depersonalized" way of life that was "economically dependent" and "subject to the regime of the time clock."[19] The very things that defined manhood to many American men increasingly seemed incompatible with middle-class life at the turn-of-the-century, making men feel that they had traded in their manliness for the trappings of modernity.

Because the Protestant church was one of the primary moralizing forces in America, it too became largely perceived as a feminized institution that suppressed manhood. Gail Bederman points out that "the American Protestant churches had been two-thirds female ever since the 1660s," but "despite this sexual imbalance, seventeenth- and eighteenth-century Protestants saw religion as gender-neutral."[20] It was not until the "cultural reorientation connected to the growth of a consumer-oriented, corporate order"[21] in the mid-to-late nineteenth century that the Protestant church became viewed as antithetical to manliness. The notion of the "feminized" church cast contemporary Protestantism as an emotional, ineffectual organization that concerned itself with "family morals" and "the social function of church going"[22] rather than with worldly problems. Thomas Wentworth Higginson captures early on the popular male derision toward a feminized Protestant church in his 1858 article "Saints, and their Bodies." He describes "an ill-starred young saint" wasting "his Saturday afternoons in preaching sermons in the garret to his deluded little sisters and their dolls."[23] While the other boys are no doubt outside, the future minister secludes himself in the house with the women, content with ineffectual "play" with girls and their toys. Higginson's caricature of a waifish minister surrounded by women and garreted from the "real world" sums up many late nineteenth-century, middle-class men's attitude that no "true" man would be involved with the church.

Arising from these feelings of a stifling "overcivilization" and feminization came a masculine revolt dubbed by E. Anthony Rotundo as "passionate manhood."[24] This manly "makeover" that arose in the late nineteenth century "took the negative labels affixed to [the male] character," such as "[p]rimitive, savage, barbarian," and "made them into virtues."[25] During this period of Teddy Roosevelt's "strenuous life," the popular images of the warrior, athlete, and backwoodsman in turn-of-the-century media implicitly contained the notion of a "retreat to a bygone era" that would return "historical notions of masculine virtue."[26] If "overcivilization" was tantamount to the feminization of society, then recapturing a premodern manhood was deemed by many to be the solution. This attempt to identify a manhood untouched by civilizing influences can be found, as Gail Bederman argues, in the turn-of-the-century fascination with the concept of "the natural man"—a man "unfettered by civilization, exempt from manly self-restraint."[27] Bederman notes that "ever since the Enlightenment, Westerners have invoked nature to explain whatever they found missing in their own cultures."[28] Thus, the passionate, unambiguously masculine "natural man" was antithetical to every notion of Victorian masculine restraint. However, many late nineteenth-century, middle-class men hoped this primal spirit still existed deep in their persons, waiting to be reclaimed.

American religious leaders in the late nineteenth century found themselves caught between the popular notion that religion was thoroughly feminized and irrelevant, and the emerging counterconcept of the passionate, primal man. Out of these circumstances emerged the Social Gospel that sought to present religion as something applicable to the larger world and, importantly, a location for profound manliness. Starting in 1882 with the beginning of Washington Gladden's 36-year tenure at the First Congregational Church of Columbus, Ohio, the Social Gospel gained one of its most recognized proponents as Gladden worked from his pulpit and popular writings to imbue Protestantism with the goal of personal redemption through social action. Gladden pointedly called upon the middle class to improve the lives of the lower class, thus "grant[ing] material aid to the impoverished and purposeful work for the affluent."[29]

The call to improve the conditions of the lower class appealed to many middle-class Protestants because the large number of poor, displaced people seemed problematic for a growing number of affluent Americans. The growing working-class culture partially seemed very unfamiliar to a dismayed middle class because many members of the working class did not share its Protestant faith and assumptions. With the infusion of southern and eastern European immigrants, Catholicism and Judaism became the religion of many of the urban poor by the turn of the century. In fact, by 1900 the combined numbers of Catholics (12 million) and Jews (1 million) almost equaled the combined number of Methodists, Baptists, Lutherans, and Presbyterians (14 million),[30] marking an unprecedented threat to Protestant cultural dominance. The urban, non-Protestant, working-class culture increasingly took on a pernicious appearance to many in the middle class as they focused on the urban boss system predicated on ethnic loyalty and corrupt politics, the saloon as center for social life, unfamiliar domestic arrangements, popular entertainments, and religious expressions.

Even more alarming to the Protestant middle class than the lower class's non-Protestant religious beliefs was the emergence of class-based hostility toward the middle class and its religion. Many working-class unionizers, socialists, communists, and anarchists viewed Protestant religion as "a sort of capitalistic soothing syrup"[31] and actively worked to persuade fellow laborers to this view. Even when Protestantism was not depicted in such conspiratorial terms, there was a pervasive and well-founded feeling in the lower class that affluent churches, "with [their] fine upholstery, stained-glass windows and expensive choirs," were places "where ill-clad worshipers were unwelcome and where the Nazarene himself would have been snubbed."[32] As the tenuous economy worsened through the 1890s, lower-class unrest, such as "riots, gang wars, and turbulent street brawls," was increasingly characterized "in terms of revolutionary violence"[33] toward the middle class. Strikes, labor violence, and protests from the working class, along with political agitation from anarchists, socialists, and communists, cast the lower-class laborer as a threat to the middle-class laborer, "not as a voter but as a destroyer of property. The absence of a home, the environment of the tenement slums," it was feared, "could drive men to vengeance against the propertied classes."[34] Thus, the call of the Social Gospel to improve the conditions of the lower class appealed to many middle-class Protestants as not only a righteous act but also as an act of cultural and political preservation.

IN HIS STEPS AND THE MANLINESS OF
THE MIDDLE CLASS

Near the beginning of *In His Steps* is a scene that encapsulates the problems and potential that Charles Sheldon sees in the relationship between the middle and lower classes. The Reverend Henry Maxwell of the First Church of Raymond is asked by one of his parishioners, a factory manager, to say a few words to his workers. Sheldon writes of Maxwell, "Like hundreds of other ministers, he had never spoken to any gatherings except those made up of people of his own class, in the sense that they were familiar in their dress and education and habits."[35] Before speaking to the crowd of workingmen, Maxwell felt "uneasy" and "was honestly in a condition of genuine fright over the prospect [. . .] of facing those men," and so he "shrank from the ordeal."[36] Despite his dread of the "grimy faced audience," Maxwell suffers through the uncomfortable task and delivers a fine speech about Christianity to the men. Afterward Sheldon writes, "never in all [Maxwell's] life had he known the delight he then felt in having the hand-shake from a man of physical labor. The day marked an important one in his Christian experience [. . .] It was the beginning of a fellowship between him and the working world. It was the first plank laid down to help bridge the chasm between the church and labor in Raymond."[37]

To Sheldon, America's central problem, as he illustrates in the above scene and throughout *In His Steps*, is the "chasm" between the world of the poor that laborers and that of the affluent middle class—those who are strangers to Christ and those who have religion and education but are strangers to honest hardship and sacrifice. People of the lower class, when employed, labor manually with "grimy" faces and distrustful attitudes toward the middle class who run the factories in which they work, and who control the social and religious institutions from which they are excluded. Conversely, Maxwell represents the middle class whose education and prosperity insulates it from authentic hardships to the point where panic ensues at the thought of interacting with actual laborers. Maxwell begins to bridge this gulf by bravely facing his fears of interclass interaction and trying to improve the lower class's lives through genuine Christian concern, as middle-class characters will do throughout the novel. To Sheldon, Maxwell's and the middle class's leaving their comfortable routines and coming forward to suffer hardships for the better-ment of the lower class is their Christ-like calling. Therefore, just as Maxwell and the laborers shake hands at the end of his speech, Sheldon implies that so too will the working class's mistrust of the middle class be replaced with trust, their coarse and self-detrimental habits adjusted, and eventually their lot improved as the middle class continues to reach out to them. Ultimately, Sheldon argues, such actions will result in a more manly, virile, and godly middle class and a more domesticated, moral, and religious working class, blending interclass differences.

Although Sheldon's Social Gospel is predicated on the middle class practicing Christ-like self-sacrifice for the betterment of the lower class, through much of *In His Steps* he depicts a lazy, effete middle class that is too bloated from its financial success to take meaningful social action. Echoing Alan Trachtenburg's assertion that "In its very success, middle-class culture had come to seem stifling, enervating, effeminate, devoid of opportunities for any heroism,"[38] no middle-class character will give up any personal convenience or luxury to assist the thousands of people living in poverty and sin in their midst—at least not until they take up Maxwell's challenge to do exactly as Jesus did. Maxwell's congregation, "composed of the leading people, representatives of wealth, society and intelligence,"[39] is content to utter pieties but never back them up with authentic actions, as when Maxwell hopes that it would not rain on Sunday because, if it does rain, "People will not come out to church."[40] As the comfortable congregants are not willing to suffer bad weather for their religion, they would also avoid the sight of sin, not out of piety, but rather for fear of upsetting their delicate sensibilities: Sheldon writes that the slum area known as "The Rectangle" was full of the "worst and most wretched elements" in town, "shut in by rows of saloons, gambling hells and cheap, dirty boarding and lodging houses," but "The First Church of Raymond had never touched the Rectangle problem. It was too dirty, too coarse, too sinful, too awful for close contact."[41] Sheldon portrays the middle class and its brand of religion as too frail to withstand any challenges.

Sheldon clearly links the middle class's self-indulgence and unwillingness to bear suffering as a sign of effeminacy. Drawing upon late nineteenth-century feelings of "overcivilization" and cultural feminization, Sheldon presents us with affluent characters such as Rollin Page who has "no purpose in life" save spending "time in club life, in amusements, in travel, in luxury," that is, in activities that affords him no time to "make the world better." When Rollin Page asks the pious Rachel Winslow to marry him, she alludes to his lack of manliness by asking him, "What is there in such a life [as yours] to attract a woman?"[42] Sheldon argues that the worldly success of modern men such as Charles R. Sterling, who became rich not through "an honest stroke of pure labor"[43] but by "grain speculation and railroad ventures"[44] has caused them to lose the manly virility necessary to endure hardship. For example, when Sterling loses his fortune through speculation, making him "practically a beggar," he is so dejected that even before a single piece of furniture can be sold from his house, he has given up, seeing "no escape from suicide."[45] Thus, unable to bear the thought of privation, let alone actually suffer a moment of it as millions do each day, Sterling kills himself, leaving behind a bedridden wife and two daughters. Sterling and the other middle-class men of *In His Steps* are portrayed as the "secret victims"[46] of their own affluence, hemmed in by their material comfort from the hard work and scrappiness that Sheldon believes makes "real" men. The president of Raymond College tells Reverend Maxell, "you and I [. . .] have lived in a little world of literature and scholarly seclusion, doing work we have enjoyed and shrinking from [. . .] disagreeable duties,"[47] this causes him to proclaim "professional men," like themselves, "cowards."[48] Through its seclusion in a false "little world" created by its class status, the middle class Sheldon portrays is separated and suffocating, away from the type of work and sacrifice for others that is the source of "true" manhood.

Maxwell and his male parishioners can "make over" their manhood through the Christian struggle of the Social Gospel. This is evident from the scene where the Bishop of Chicago states, "Our Christianity loves its ease and comfort too well to take up anything so rough and heavy as a cross."[49] The bishop's implication is that the "ease" and "comfort" that accompanies the middle class's affluence makes poor Christians of them, being too weak for the manly, "rough," and "heavy" duty of suffering like Christ. Thus, once the comfortable Christians of Raymond take Reverend Maxwell's challenge to act as Christ would in their daily lives, their suffering is described in masculine terms. President Marsh of Raymond College states, "If we bear this cross let us do it bravely, like men."[50] We see this again when Rollin Page, the former socialite who was anything but manly, accepts Maxwell's urging to live his life as Christ would. When describing his Christian suffering to Rachel Winslow, who formerly found nothing manly about Page, Sheldon writes, "Rachel again noted the strong, manly tone of his speech. With it all she knew there was a deep, underlying seriousness which felt the burden of the cross even while carrying it with joy." Rachel thinks to herself, "I am beginning to know what it means to be loved by a noble man."[51] Whereas the well-to-do college president and social gadfly were formerly examples of the "overcivilized" class; once they decide to take up the "burden" of suffering like Christ, Sheldon explicitly shows their suffering has developed their manliness to the point where it is a defining feature of their characters.

Although the question "What would Jesus do?" is predicated on the notion of manly suffering, it is crucial to note that this suffering is solely linked to social action that improves the material and spiritual conditions of the lower class. As Paul S. Boyer argues, "By organizing for a great urban moral purification drive [. . .] the middle class could not only become a powerful weapon for eradicating vice; it would also achieve a greater degree of internal order and cohesion, and overcome the social isolation and emotional aridity that seemed always to plague it."[52] Thus, the middle-class characters of *In His Steps* who willfully suffer for the lower class rescue themselves from feelings of "overcivilization" and feminization. There are multiple forms of suffering Sheldon links to Christ-like sacrifice, but the most significant type is direct physical injury. Twice characters are physically assaulted as they promote temperance in the slums. Rollin Page, now a "noble man," is pelted with "a shower of mud and stones"[53] by an angry, drunken mob outside of a bar, and the bishop of Chicago (described as bearing "on his body the marks of the Lord Jesus") is assaulted while trying to stop a man from drinking, causing him to learn "something of what it means to walk in His steps."[54] Besides physical injury, characters in the novel also undergo financial suffering, such as the newspaper owner Edward Norman, who decides to run the daily newspaper only as Christ would but finds "a great many men would lose vast sums of money under the present system of business if this rule of Jesus was honestly applied."[55] In each way the middle class suffers while living as Christ would, they directly do so in the context of attempting to improve the lot of the lower class.

What is perhaps most interesting about Sheldon's portrayal of middle-class suffering is his implication that by working to improve the material and spiritual circumstances of the lower class, the middle class actually takes on the "invigorating" characteristics of the lower class. Paul S. Boyer writes that "the characters of *In His Steps* are obsessed by thoughts of an immigrant working class of whose existence they are keenly aware, but from whom they feel totally cut off."[56] Wayne Elzey adds, "for Sheldon's characters, true Christian fellowship and discipleship emerge only in living among the poor and by adopting something of their dress, food, speech, and 'natural' lifestyle."[57] When the Bishop manfully bears "the marks" of Jesus after an assault; when the newspaper owner stoically has his fortune threatened by running his paper like Christ; and when President Marsh gives up academic seclusion for a political contest, Sheldon removes an aspect of middle-class life from each of these characters and adds what he feels is an aspect of a more "genuine" lower-class life. Sheldon is locating "authenticity" in the lower class, which matches Gail Bederman's argument that in the late nineteenth century the middle class was fascinated by the image of the premodern "natural man" who embodied "primitive masculinity,"[58] and pure "vitality."[59] By engaging in Christ-like suffering, Sheldon is arguing that the middle class can purify itself by shedding its "overcivilized" baggage and attaining the more "authentic" and manly attributes of the lower class.

Sheldon makes this point explicitly in a number of places. At the beginning of the story, he describes the pulpit presence of Reverend Maxwell as "scholarly," "refined," and free "from all vulgar, noisy or disagreeable mannerism,"[60] a description befitting the "best-dressed, most comfortable looking people of Raymond."[61] Everything about the church is polished, unassuming, polite, and sanitized. No strong emotions, either positive or negative, are possible in this benign atmosphere. This is the quintessence of "overcivilization." This early description can fruitfully be contrasted to one later in the novel, where Sheldon portrays a rousing temperance meeting held by the church: "it glowed with the Spirit's presence; it was alive with strong and lasting resolve to begin a war on the whiskey power in Raymond that would break its reign forever."[62] Once the church members have begun their reform work amongst the lower class, their ineffectual and insipid temperament is gone. The congregants at the start of the story would never have spoken in the above terms of "strong" and "lasting resolve" for "war" that would "break" the opposition. Clearly, Sheldon is showing that by taking up Christ's call to reform the lower class, the middle class will be imbued with a manly intensity and strength of will that was felt lacking in the middle class but was possessed by a more "natural" lower class.

THE DOMESTICATION OF THE LOWER CLASS

While Sheldon positions the lower class as a source of manly vitality and emotional intensity from which the middle class can draw in order to make over their own feelings of "overcivilization" and effeminacy, the lower class men of *In His Steps* are anything but "noble savages." In fact, the lower class is characterized as a hypermasculine, brute, and threatening force to the middle class. The very things that make them exotic and attractive to the middle class also make them overmasculinized and dangerous: Sheldon portrays the lower class as prone to violence, easily agitated, drunken, sexually charged, crude, and unhealthy. Made up of "wretched creatures who [have] lost faith in God and man, anarchists and infidels, free-thinkers and no-thinkers [. . .] all the city's worst, most hopeless, most dangerous, depraved elements,"[63] the lower class of *In His Steps* is the antithesis of Sheldon's middle class. However, Sheldon argues that the lower class's antisocial and dangerous behavior can be soothed through introducing middle-class, domestic practices, such as temperance, cleanliness, nutritious cooking, passivity, and religious faith. Thus, while the affluent Social Gospelers are invigorating themselves through their Christ-like suffering for the lower class, their efforts are ultimately for the domestication of the lower class into a group that more closely resembles middle-class values.

Although Sheldon's characterizations of the lower class encompass a wide range of attributes that he considered as opposite to that of middle-class Victorian values, one of his favorites is the attribute of brute violence and uncontrolled aggression. Describing the Rectangle slum area of Raymond, Sheldon uses words such as "brutal, coarse, impure,"[64] "dangerous," "troublesome,"[65] and he labels it "a festering sore."[66] Paul S. Boyer notes, "The shorthand symbol for [the lower class's] violent potential is alcohol,"[67] and Sheldon alludes to the ever-present threat of lower-class violence by stating, "The air of the whole city" is "impregnated with the odor of beer"[68] and the Rectangle is "shut in by rows of saloons."[69] The connection between lower-class violence and alcohol becomes clear when a riot breaks out in the Rectangle during a prohibition election. Sheldon writes, "The Rectangle was drunk and enraged," and "a howl [. . .] was beginning to rise from the wild beast in the mob."[70] The drunken mob is not only violent, it is also a "wild beast," reflecting Sheldon's belief in its atavistic, primal quality. Not only do the rioting slum dwellers lose their humanity in Sheldon's description, they also lose their individuality as well, becoming simply the Rectangle that is uprising, not the people in the Rectangle. The most crucial aspect of the drunken riot is that the violence is focused on the middle class. Reverend Maxwell, President Marsh, Rollin Page, and others are venturing into the Rectangle to campaign for temperance when they are assaulted by the rabid mob for their political and religious stance against alcohol. Sheldon makes it clear to his readers that the masculine, aggressive lower class is not simply different from the middle class, he would like to emphasize that its propensity toward violence makes it rather radically different, and that its violence can—at a moment's notice—be aimed at the middle class.

Sheldon suggests that the lower class's problems, including their drunken violence, can be traced back to their lack of domestic, middle-class values. The Protestant, Victorian set of values broadly adopted by many in the middle class held the family to be the sacred social unit, whereas "Social Gospelers" noted that it was "the deplorable living conditions of the urban poor that made family morality virtually impossible to maintain."[71] While "Church-going America" thought "religion might help produce family bonds and a set of manners,"[72] the lower class was considered either irreligious or at least non-Protestant. While Victorian values held that the home should be "a model of impeccable cleanliness and order," the environment of the urban poor was considered "a place of filth, disease, and disorder."[73] And although "piety and sobriety" were considered traits for "the poor to aspire to,"[74] as we see in *In His Steps*, the middle class felt that the lower class often fell short of this ideal. In the novel, Sheldon reflects these popular middle-class attitudes by repeatedly showing lower-class characters that are antithetical—and even hostile—toward middle-class domestic values. A prime example comes from the character of "Carlsen," a communist with a thick accent, who declares during a church meeting for the poor, "I thank God, if there is a God—which I very much doubt—that I, for one, have never dared to marry and make a home. Home! Talk of hell!"[75] Carlson's communist views, immigrant status, atheism, and enmity toward the middle class's most sacred moral unit, the family, signals how far Sheldon positions the lower class from the middle class's domestic ideal.

The actions of Sheldon's Social Gospelers, then, are ones pointedly devised to instill in the urban poor of Raymond middle class, Protestant, domestic values—at least to a degree. Each "problem" associated with the lower class, such as drunkenness, violent aggression, and chaotic home-life, is quickly assigned a cure predicated on middle-class values. One of the clearest examples can be found in the actions of Edward Norman, the owner and editor of Raymond's newspaper. Once Norman begins to run the paper as "if Christ was the editor,"[76] the paper "no longer printed accounts of crime with detailed descriptions, or scandals in private life [. . .] advertisements of liquor and tobacco were dropped, together with certain others of a questionable character."[77] Lurid crime, private scandals, and an abundance of alcohol and tobacco would not be permitted in a proper middle-class, Protestant home, thus the lower classes should be shielded from these "questionable" influences if they are to build a solid home as well. In the eyes of middle-class people, crime, rumors, and strong drink could only inflame the passions of the lower class, which they felt had an abundance of passions to begin with. With the middle-class Norman making editorial decisions with Christ and "the working man especially"[78] in mind, the newspaper becomes a type of guide for the lower class on their journey to domestic respectability, encouraging, in the words of one of Norman's editorials, "lovers of right, purity, temperance, and the home."[79]

Although men such as Edward Norman, Henry Maxwell, and President Marsh are important encouragers of middle-class, domestic behavior amongst the lower classes in the novel, Sheldon clearly portrays women as primary players in the Social Gospelers reform mission. Unlike the men, however, middle-class women's Social Gospel work is not described as masculinizing but rather as an extension of their domestic capabilities. Paul S. Boyer observes that "Drawing upon the familiar Victorian conception of femininity as the refining influence which softens the coarseness of the male and holds his lower nature in check, Sheldon thrusts the Middle-Class Woman—that spiritualized abstraction—into the battle against *lower class* brutality and violence."[80] Many of the female characters foster domestic values in traditional ways, such as the wealthy Virginia Page using her money to "build wholesome lodging-houses"[81] for the poor, and Felicia Sterling who opens a school in the Rectangle to teach "plain cooking, neatness, quickness, and a love of good work."[82] Both of these women use their culturally designated role as domestic and moral promoters to make "the city, as a physical and social environment, conform to the demands of an ideal home environment."[83] If the female-centered, middle-class domestic structure can be brought to the urban environment, reformers hope that then the lower class's hypermasculinized, violent tendencies can be discouraged and channeled toward more "productive," middle-class pursuits. Unlike the men's, The middle-class women's actions are never described as "fighting" or "suffering" because they are engaging in actions already within the domestic sphere, just as middle-class society expects. Just as Sheldon wants men to use their "innate" ability to "fight" like men for Christ, he positions women as using their "natural" domestic abilities for the benefit of society. "Christ-like" domestication differs from other forms of it when it is focused on the lower class as a whole rather than kept solely inside the home.

In His Steps clearly reveals that a prime motivation of the Social Gospel was to cope with and defuse the cultural changes precipitated by the period's industrialization, immigration, and urbanization. Susan Curtis observes that "Social Gospelers were among those who experienced anxiety when the matrix of beliefs and values that had given life meaning in the nineteenth century began to make less and less sense."[84] It is Sheldon's desire for a national "makeover" in the face of unsettling modern forces that most closely associates him and his Social Gospel with today's evangelical Christians, particularly those that, like Sheldon, use the popular media to broadcast their beliefs in order to change America's religious and social identity. Today, when evangelicals proclaim the need to "go back" to an older, more moral and more religious America, they are expressing a contemporary version of Lears's "antimodernism," where personal and national reinvigoration rest in the past, before the affects of unsettling modern change. This contemporary evangelical antimodernism can be seen in initiatives to define marriage "traditionally" to exclude gay couples and in the public pressure in some states to remove evolutionary biology from the public school curriculum. As evangelicals work to make America in their image, confident that they are acting as Jesus would, we can see that evangelical Christianity represents a prominent—and politically powerful—aspect of America's makeover mythology.

NOTES

1. Timothy Miller, *Following in His Steps: A Biography of Charleston M. Sheldon* (Knoxville: University of Tennessee Press, 1994), p. 83.
2. Frank Luther Mott, *Golden Multitudes: The Story of Best Sellers in the United States* (New York: Macmillan, 1947), p. 197.
3. Miller, *Following in His Steps*, p. 71.
4. Ibid., p. 87.
5. Stephen Prothero, *American Jesus: How the Son of God Became a National Icon* (NewYork: Farrar, Straus and Giroux, 2003), p. 154.
6. David Brooks, *On Paradise Drive: How We Live Now (And Always Have) in the Future Tense* (New York: Simon and Schuster, 2004), p. 67.
7. Karen Armstrong, *A History of God: The 4,000-Year Quest of Judaism, Christianity, and Islam* (New York: Ballantine Books, 1993), p. 316.
8. Ibid.
9. Brooks, *On Paradise Drive*, p. 122.
10. Susan Curtis, *A Consuming Faith: The Social Gospel and Modern American Culture* (Baltimore: Johns Hopkins University Press, 1991), p. 2.

11. John Hagee, *JHMagazine* September/October (2004): 6. <http://www.jhm.org/mag-pdfs/sept-oct04mag.pdf> (Accessed on June 26, 2006).

12. Prothero, *American Jesus*, p. 12.

13. David Morgan, "Protestant Visual Practice and American Mass Culture," in *Practicing Religion in the Age of the Media: Explorations in Media, Religion, and Culture*, ed. Stewart M. Hoover and Lynn Schofield Clark (New York: Columbia University Press, 2002), p. 41.

14. Diane Winston, "All the World's A Stage: The Performed Religion of the Salvation Army, 1880–1920," in *Practicing Religion in the Age of the Media: Explorations in Media, Religion, and Culture*, ed. Stewart M. Hoover and Lynn Schofield Clark (New York: Columbia University Press, 2002), p. 115.

15. Hagee, *JHMagazine*, p. 6.

16. T.J. Jackson Lears, *No Place of Grace: Antimodernism and the Transformation of American Culture, 1880–1920* (1983; Chicago: University of Chicago Press, 1994), p. 30.

17. Ibid., p. 48.

18. E. Anthony Rotundo, *American Manhood: Transformations in Masculinity from the Revolution to the Modern Era* (New York: Basic Books, 1993), p. 250.

19. Michael Kimmel, *Manhood in America: A Cultural History* (1996; New York: Free Press, 1997), p. 83.

20. Gail Bederman, " 'The Women Have Had Charge of the Church Work Long Enough': The Men and Religion Forward Movement of 1911–1912 and the Masculinization of Middle-Class Protestantism," *American Quarterly* 41 (1989): 437.

21. Bederman, "Women," p. 436.

22. Ann Douglas, *The Feminization of American Culture* (1977; New York: Noonday, 1998), p. 7.

23. Thomas Wentworth Higginson, "Saints, And Their Bodies," *The Atlantic Monthly* 1 (March 1858): 584.

24. Rotundo, *American Manhood*, p. 5.

25. Ibid., p. 253.

26. Kimmel, *Manhood in America*, p. 89.

27. Gail Bederman, *Manliness and Civilization: A Cultural History of Gender and Race In The United States, 1880–1917* (1995; Chicago: University of Chicago Press, 1996), p. 72.

28. Ibid., p. 73.

29. Curtis, *A Consuming Faith*, p. 45.

30. *The New York Public Library American History Desk Reference*, ed. Marilyn Miller and Marian Faux (New York: Macmillan, 1997), p. 102.

31. Arthur M. Schlesinger, Sr., "A Critical Period in American Religion, 1875–1900," *Religion in American History: Interpretive Essays*, ed. John M. Mulder and John F. Wilson (Englewood Cliffs, NJ: Prentice-Hall, 1978), p. 307.

32. Ibid.

33. Paul S. Boyer, *Urban Masses and Moral Order in America: 1820–1920* (Cambridge: Harvard University Press, 1978), p. 89.

34. Jan Cohn, *The Palace or the Poorhouse: The American House as a Cultural Symbol* (East Lansing: Michigan State University Press, 1979), p. 159.

35. Charles Sheldon, *In His Steps: What Would Jesus Do?* (1896; Uhrichville, OH: Barbour, 2000), p. 39.

36. Ibid.

37. Ibid., p. 40.

38. Alan Trachtenberg, *The Incorporation of America: Culture and Society in the Gilded Age* (1982; New York: Hill and Wang, 2000), p. 87.

39. Sheldon, *In His Steps*, p. 4.

40. Ibid.

41. Ibid., p. 57.

42. Ibid., p. 52.

43. Ibid., p. 182.

44. Ibid., p. 162.

45. Ibid., p. 183.

46. Lears, *No Place of Grace*, p. xv.

47. Sheldon, *In His Steps*, p. 88.

48. Ibid., p. 89.

49. Ibid., p. 178.

50. Ibid., p. 90.

51. Ibid., p. 142.

52. Boyer, *Urban Masses*, p. 179.

53. Sheldon, *In His Steps*, p. 115.

54. Ibid., p. 208.

55. Ibid., p. 107.

56. Paul S. Boyer, "*In His Steps*: A Reappraisal," American Quarterly 23 (1971): 60–78.

57. Wayne Elzey, " 'What Would Jesus Do?': *In His Steps* and the Moral Codes of the Middle Class," *Soundings* 54 (1975): 482.

58. Bederman, *Manliness*, p. 71.

59. Ibid., p. 101.

60. Sheldon, *In His Steps*, p. 6.

61. Ibid., p. 4.

62. Ibid., p. 119.

63. Ibid., p. 221.

64. Ibid., p. 59.

65. Ibid., p. 65.

66. Ibid., p. 66.

67. Boyer, "Reappraisal," p. 68.

68. Sheldon, *In His Steps*, p. 208.

69. Ibid., p. 57.

70. Ibid., p. 115.

71. Curtis, *A Consuming Faith*, p. 72.

72. Martin E. Marty, *Righteous Empire: The Protestant Experience in America* (New York: The Dial Press, 1970), p. 173.

73. Marlene Stein Wortman, "Domesticating the Nineteenth-Century American City," *Prospects* 3 (1977): 531–572.

74. Barbara Leslie Epstein, *The Politics of Domesticity: Women, Evangelism, and Temperance in Nineteenth Century America* (Middletown, CT: Wesleyan University Press, 1981), p. 4.

75. Sheldon, *In His Steps*, p. 228.

76. Ibid., p. 22.

77. Ibid., p. 66.

78. Ibid., p. 31.

79. Ibid., p. 92.

80. Boyer, "Reappraisal," p. 70. Original Italics.

81. Sheldon, *In His Steps*, p. 125.

82. Ibid., p. 211.

83. Wortman, p. 532.

84. Curtis, *A Consuming Faith*, p. 6.

CHAPTER 7

METROSEXUALITY: SEE THE BRIGHT LIGHT OF COMMODIFICATION SHINE! WATCH YANQUI MASCULINITY MADE OVER! [1,2]

TOBY MILLER

[A] metrosexual is a man who wants to be looked at [. . .] a collector of fantasies about the male, sold to him by advertising

Mark Simpson[3]

They call themselves the Fab Five. They are: An interior designer, a fashion stylist, a chef, a beauty guru and someone we like to call the "concierge of cool"—who is responsible for all things hip, including music and pop culture. All five are talented, they're gay and they're determined to clue in the cluttered, clumsy straight men of the world. With help from family and friends, the Fab Five treat each new guy as a head-to-toe project. Soon, the straight man is educated on everything from hair products to Prada and Feng Shui to foreign films. At the end of every fashion-packed, fun-filled lifestyle makeover, a freshly scrubbed, newly enlightened guy emerges

<bravotv.com/Queer_Eye_for_the_Straight_Guy/About_Us/>

ONE MUST PONDER HARD that in an avowedly pragmatic and instrumentalist nation where the vast majority attests to the existence of a devil and individuated angels, 45 percent of people think aliens have visited Earth, 64 percent of adult Internet users (i.e., 82 million Yanquis) go online in search of spiritual information, three times more people believe in ghosts than was the case a quarter of a century ago, and 84 percent credit the posthumous survival of the soul, up 24 percent since 1972.[4] Yet a major part of the bill of goods offered to U.S. residents is *secular* transcendence, the sense that one can become something or someone other than the hand dealt by the bonds of birth: one alternately loving and severe world of superstition (a.k.a. religion) is matched by a second alternately loving and severe world of superstition (a.k.a. consumption).

This chapter argues that U.S. secular commodity transcendence is undergoing renewal through a major change in the political economy of masculinity, allied to the deregulation of television. Together they have created the conditions for a new address of men as commodity goods, sexual objects, sexual subjects, workers, and viewers, thanks to neoliberal policies that facilitate media businesses targeting specific cultures. Viewers are urged to govern themselves through orderly preparation, style, and pleasure—the transformation of potential drudgery into a special event, and the incorporation of difference into a treat rather than a threat.

METROSEXUALITY

In the 1990s, traditional divisions of First-World consumers—by age, race, gender, and class—were supplemented by cultural categories, with market researchers proclaiming the 1990s a decade of the "new man." Lifestyle and psychographic research sliced and diced consumers into "moralists," "trendies," "the indifferent," "working-class puritans," "sociable spenders," and "pleasure seekers." Men were subdivided between "pontificators," "self-admirers," "self-exploiters," "token triers," "chameleons," "avant-gardicians," "sleepwalkers," and "passive endurers."[5] Something was changing in the landscape of Yanqui masculinity. The variegated male body was up for grabs as both sexual icon and commodity consumer, in ways that borrowed from but also exceeded the longstanding commodification of the male form. The most obvious sign of this was the emergence of the "metrosexual," a term coined in the mid-1990s by queer critic Mark Simpson after encountering "the real future [. . . and finding that] it had moisturised."[6]

Historically, male desire for women has been overlegitimized, while female and male desire for men has been underlegitimized. The metrosexual represents a major shift in relations of power, with men subjected to new forms of governance and commodification. Simpson calls his discourse of metrosexuality "snarky sociology, which is no good to anyone." But it has since been taken up and deployed—as a *pre*scription as much as a *de*scription—because it promises "highly profitable demography," guaranteed to stimulate any "advertiser's wet dream."[7] The metrosexual has been joyfully embraced by

Western European, Australian, South Asian, Latin American, and U.S. marketers. It was declared word of the year for 2003 by the American Dialect Society, ahead of "weapons of [mass destruction]," "embedded [journalist]," and "pre-emptive self-defense."[8]

The metrosexual "might be officially gay, straight or bisexual, but this is utterly immaterial because he has clearly taken himself as his own love object and pleasure as his sexual preference."[9] He is said to endorse equal-opportunity vanity, through cosmetics, softness, women, hair-care products, wine bars, gyms, designer fashion, wealth, the culture industries, finance, cities, cosmetic surgery, and deodorants. Happy to be the object of queer erotics, and committed to exfoliation and Web surfing, the metrosexual is a newly feminized male who blurs the distinction between straight and gay visual styles[10] in a restless search "to spend, shop and deep-condition"—and he is supposed to be every fifth man in major U.S. cities.[11] Single straight men now embark on what the *New York Times* calls "man dates," nights out together with other men without the alibis of work and sport or the props of televisions and bar stools—although Yanquis shy away from ordering bottles of wine together. That would be going a bit too far, other than perhaps in a steak house!.[12] Summed up by *Jet* magazine as "aesthetically savvy," the metrosexual appeared 25,000 times on google.com in mid-2002; three years later, the number was 212,000; and by the end of 2005, close to a million. He even managed to transform characters on *South Park*, which devoted an episode to criticizing the phenomenon in its mildly amusing, banally offensive way. In case men are not sure they qualify, an online metrosexual quiz is available. The average grade of the 100,000 who took it in its first year was 36.5 percent. I scored 54 percent and qualified![13]

In 2003, Californian gubernatorial candidate Arnold Schwarzenegger told *Vanity Fair* he was "a major shoe queen." *The Metrosexual Guide to Style* suggests that such a remark would have been "unthinkable ten years ago," but it is now "deeply in touch with the Zeitgeist," because the "new man" needs to display "style, sophistication and self-awareness."[14] The "Cultural Studies" section of the *New York Times* discerns a fully fledged "democratization of desire,"[15] because men are increasingly key objects of pleasure for female and gay audiences. Male striptease shows, for example, reference not only changes in the gender of power and money, but also a public site where "[w]omen have come to see exposed male genitalia [. . .] to treat male bodies as objects only." During the 1998 men's soccer World Cup, the French Sexy Boys Band, who had been performing in Paris since 1993 to sell-outs, offered strip shows for "les filles sans foot" (girls without soccer/girls who could not care less). The U.S. Chippendales toured across Northern Europe through the spring and summer of 1999 to crowds of women—*The Full Monty* (Peter Cattaneo 1997) writ large, even though some female spectators found the reversal of subject positions far from easy.[16]

Underwear for men has recently expanded to incorporate "action bikinis" and "athletic strings," some complete with condom pockets in the waistband and "sling support" to emphasize the male genitals. Worldwide sales of men's grooming products reached US$7.3 billion in 2002, accounting for 15 percent of all beauty products sold. *American Demographics* states that "baby-boomer" men allocate US$26,420 a year on "youth-enhancing products and services," and women just under US$3,000 a year more.[17] In 2004, U.S. men spent US$65 billion on fashion and grooming. ACNielsen issued *What's Hot Around the Globe: Insights on Growth in Personal Care* that year. A study of 56 countries, it was predicated on the existence of metrosexuality, and it duly discovered that the sector's key area of growth was shower gels, deodorants, blades, and moisturizers—for men. Euromonitor predicts that the male skin-care market will increase by 50 percent between 2001 and 2006, and Datamonitor expects a 3.3 percent annual increase in skin-care sales to men up to 2008. Men's antiperspirants outsell women's in the United States today, for the first time. Body sprays targeted at boys aged ten and up form part of "age compression," increasing both the sexualization of men and its impact across age groups. Gillette's Tag was promoted via an auction on eBay for teenage boys to buy a date with Carmen Electra, a married celebrity in her 30s. Hair-color sales to young males increased by 25 percent in the five years from 1998. In 2003, men's hair-care sales grew by more than 12 percent in the United States, to US$727 million. Teen boys in the United States spend 5 percent of their income on such products.[18]

Mid-town Manhattan now offers specialist ear-, hand-, and foot-waxing, with men comprising 40 percent of the clientele. Such sites provide pedicures and facials, to the accompaniment of cable sports and Frank Sinatra, and manly euphemisms to describe the various procedures—coloring hair becomes "camouflage," and manicures are "hand detailing." Both Target and Saks Fifth Avenue opened men's cosmetics sections for the first time in the new century, sections that were aimed principally at straights, while Lancôme announced that it had discovered eight differences between men's and women's skins, necessitating new products. "The Micro Touch" was released in 2003 as the first "unwanted hair" application for men, organized around a metrosexual campaign. Meanwhile, apologists for George Bush's economic record pointed to officially undercounted new jobs in spas, nail salons, and massage parlors as signs of national economic health: truly a digitally led recovery from recession. And men are now the fastest-growing segment of the jewellery market: up to 10 percent of sales as part of executive masculinity. In 2004, Garrad, Georg Jensen, and Cartier all launched comprehensive selections of male jewels.[19]

The metrosexual's ecumenicism has encouraged white-oriented companies to target Latinos and blacks for the first time. In Britain, he even appeared in diaper commercials—not to reflect the division of child-care labor, but to appeal to women consumers. The United States now sees 80 percent of grooms actively involved in planning weddings, as never before, and they dedicate vast sums to their own appearance. Banana Republic, a chain dedicated to casual-wear clothing, suddenly found that its catalog contained items worn as business attire and proceeded to establish partnerships with Credit Suisse, Home Box Office, and First Boston, setting up mini-stores that dispensed free drinks and fashion advice. Even Microsoft, seemingly as impregnable to high style as a Roger Moore James Bond film, saw its campus populated by Prada as the century turned. Macho magazines in Britain, such as *Loaded*, were forced by audience targeting to abandon their appeal to antifeminist, lager-swilling brutes in favor of "the caring lad in cashmere."[20]

The area of plastic, cosmetic, or aesthetic surgery is a particularly notable part of this transformation. Reconstructive surgery was pioneered on male veterans of World War I, most of whom reported the desire for economic autonomy as a key motivation. With the exception of wartime casualties, from the 1940s through to the 1960s, most U.S. surgeons reported treating women, and a few gay men, and pathologized their patients. But the *New York Times* declared "Cosmetic Lib for Men" in 1977, and three years later, *Business Week* encouraged its readers to obtain "a new—and younger—face." This tendency developed to the point where the major U.S. medical journal *Clinics in Plastic Surgery* dedicated a special issue to men in 1991.[21]

The 1990s and the years since have seen the shop well and truly set up. Bob Dole parlayed a political career representing Kansas into lucrative endorsements for Visa and Viagra after a facelift made him telegenic, John Kerry was rumored to have a Botox habit, and U.S. military recruiters began to highlight free or cheap elective plastic surgery for uniformed personnel and their families (with the policy alibi that this permitted doctors to practice their art). American Academy of Cosmetic Surgery figures indicate that more than 6,500 men had face-lifts in 1996. In 1997, men accounted for a quarter of all such procedures, and the following year, straight couples were frequently scheduling surgery together (up 15 percent in a year). Between 1996 and 1998, male cosmetic surgery increased 34 percent, mostly because of liposuction, and 15 percent of plastic surgery in 2001 was performed on men.[22] These 2001 figures from the American Society of Plastic Surgeons specify the distribution across gender of the procedures they performed (table 7.1).

Turning to the American Academy of Facial Plastic and Reconstructive Surgery,[23] we see a 316 percent increase in hair transplants from 1999 to 2001. Fourteen percent of female patients versus 30 percent of male indicate that they wish to undergo surgery for reasons connected to the workplace, a clear sign that men perceive age discrimination on the job. Youthfulness is a key motivation for 50 percent of women and 40 percent of men, dating for 5 percent of women and 10 percent of men. The top five male surgical

Table 7.1   American Society of Plastic Surgeons—2001 Procedures

Procedure	Patients	Male (%)	Female (%)
Breast augmentation	219,883	N/A	100
Breast implant removal	43,589	N/A	100
Breast lift	55,176	N/A	100
Breast reduction	18,548	100	N/A
Buttock lift	1,339	3	97
Cheek implant	8,494	26	74
Chin augmentation	28,736	33	67
Ear surgery	33,107	53	47
Eyelid surgery	238,213	19	81
Facelift	124,531	10	90
Forehead lift	74,987	12	88
Hair transplantation	31,012	90	10
Lip augmentation	23,044	9	91
Liposuction	275,463	18	82
Lower body lift	4,720	N/A	100
Nose reshaping	370,968	37	63
Thigh lift	3,495	3	97
Tummy tuck	58,567	3	97
Upper arm lift	3,241	N/A	100
Total	1,617,113	20	80

procedures (breast, hair, nose, stomach, and eyelid work) were not selected by men two decades ago.[24]

In 2002, U.S. men had more than 800,000 cosmetic procedures.[25] Data from both the American Academy of Cosmetic Surgery and the American Society for Aesthetic Plastic Surgery present popularity rates that are striking; these rates are for botox and collagen procedures, chemical peels, and hair surgery to conceal signs of ageing, and liposuction to reduce body weight, with similar rates of uptake by men and women.[26] Consider the figures in table 7.2. In 2003, cosmetic procedures were up by 33 percent, and 2005 brought the launch of the first magazine dedicated to patients, *New Beauty*.[27]

The new man is being governed as well as commodified. What the *New York Times*[28] calls "the rising tide of male vanity" has real costs to conventional maleness. The middle-class U.S. labor market now sees wage discrimination by beauty amongst men as well, and major corporations frequently require executives to tailor their body shapes to company *ethoi*, or at least encourage workers to reduce weight in order to reduce health-care costs to the employer. In 1998, 93 percent of U.S. companies featured fitness programs, compared to 76 percent in 1992. A 2004 ExecuNet survey of senior corporate leeches aged between 40 and 50 saw 94 percent complaining of occupational discrimination by age. A third of all graying, male U.S. workers in 1999 colored

Table 7.2 Estimated Number of Patients Treated by U.S.-based American Academy of Cosmetic Surgery Members 2002*

Procedure	Men Undergoing Procedure		Women Undergoing Procedure		Total Patients	
	No.	%	No.	%	No.	%
Abdominoplasty	414	0.3	8,065	1.15	8,479	0.99
Blepharoplasty	5,909	3.68	21,594	3.09	27,503	3.20
Upper lids	5,129	3.19	19,894	2.85	25,023	2.91
Lower lids	3,442	2.14	13,322	1.91	16,764	1.95
Botox	34,410	21.41	205,017	29.32	239,427	27.84
Breast Augmentation	122	0.08	31,096	4.45	31,218	3.63
Breast Lift	—	—	4,843	0.69	4,843	0.56
Breast Reduction	152	0.09	3,472	0.50	3,624	0.42
Buttock Lift	6	0.00	225	0.03	231	0.03
Calf Implants	38	0.02	41	0.01	79	0.01
Collagen injections	10,203	6.35	50,229	7.18	60,432	7.03
Chemical Peels						
Glycolic	13,669	8.51	52,904	7.57	66,573	7.74
Phenol	268	0.17	749	0.11	1,017	0.12
TCA	5,903	3.67	25,687	3.67	31,590	3.67
Total Chemical Peels	19,840	12.35	79,340	11.35	99,180	11.53
Facelift	1,961	1.22	13,517	1.93	15,478	1.80
Fat Injections	3,813	2.37	22,325	3.19	26,138	3.04
Forehead Lift	1,139	0.71	6,743	0.96	7,882	0.92
Genioplasty	1,748	1.09	3,704	0.53	5,452	0.63
Gynecomastia	2,376	1.48	305	0.04	2,681	0.31
Hair Transplant/Restoration	28,715	17.87	3,436	0.49	32,151	3.74
Laser Resurfacing	2,936	1.83	12,457	1.78	15,393	1.79
Liposuction	14,089	8.77	55,901	8.00	69,990	8.14
Malar Augmentation	573	0.36	1,498	0.21	2,071	0.24
Microdermabrasion	14,296	8.90	96,573	13.81	110,869	12.89
Otoplasty	804	0.50	1,072	0.15	1,876	0.22
Pectoral Implants	183	0.11	9	0.00	192	0.02
Rhinoplasty	3,417	2.13	7,206	1.03	10,623	1.24
Sclerotherapy	3,009	1.87	36,859	5.27	39,868	4.64
Thigh Lift	40	0.02	432	0.06	472	0.05
Penile Enlargement	1,919	1.19	—	—	1,919	0.22
Total	160,683	100.00	699,175	100.00	859,858	100.00

* American Academy of Cosmetic Surgery, 2003.

their hair to counter the effect of ageing on their careers, avoiding what is now known as the "silver ceiling." Studies by the hair-dye company Clairol reveal that men with gray hair are perceived as less successful, intelligent, and athletic than those without. Meanwhile, abetted by a newly deregulated ability to address consumers directly through television commercials, Propecia, a drug countering male hair loss, secured a 79 percent increase in visits to doctors by patients in search of prescriptions.[29]

Whilst the burden of beauty remains firmly on women, a new trend is unmistakable: the surveillant gaze of sexual evaluation is being turned onto men as never before. It is simultaneously *in*ternalized, as a set of concerns, and *ex*ternalized, as a set of interventions. *Playgirl* magazine's male centerfolds have undergone comprehensive transformations over the past quarter century: the average model has lost twelve pounds of fat and gained twenty-five pounds of muscle. GI Joe dolls of the 1960s had biceps to a scale of 11.5 inches, an average dimension. In 1999, their biceps were at a scale of 26 inches, beyond any recorded bodybuilder. Similar changes have happened to other dolls, such as *Star Wars* figures. Not surprisingly, in 1997, 43 percent of U.S. men up to their late fifties disclosed dissatisfaction with their appearance, compared to 34 percent in 1985 and 15 percent in 1972. The new century brought reports of a million men diagnosed with body dimorphism and the invention of the "Adonis Complex" by psychiatrists to account for vast increases in male eating and exercise disorders. The psy-complexes refer to "muscle dissatisfaction" among male TV viewers, and 40 percent of U.S. eating disorders are now reported by men.[30]

Clearly we should not assume that progressive change is bundled with metrosexuality. Reifying all is no good substitute for reifying some, while the US$8 billion spent each year on cosmetics could put the children of the entire world through basic education across four generations. Schwarzenegger's shoes may just register an "upgrade" of service-sector capitalism. And the *Metrosexual Guide* ends with a description of "The Metrosexual Mind-Set: The Bottom Line," which is that "Your life is your own creation." The metrosexual is a neoliberal subject who must govern himself as a new aesthete, generated from shifting relations of power and finance. Such cultural citizens are "more responsible for creating their own individuality than ever before," in the words of Britain's Cosmetic Toiletry and Perfumery Association Director-General.[31]

TELEVISION

In related developments, since the 1990s, the "pink dollar" has become more and more significant, as the gay media circulated information to businesses about the spending-power of their putatively childless, middle-class readership—*Campaign* magazine's slogan in advertising circles was "Gay Money Big Market Gay Market Big Money"—the mainstream media took notice. The *New York Times* made no references to queerness in its business pages throughout the 1970s, and only occasional—and male-oriented— pieces appeared in the 1980s. But news coverage tripled from 1992 to 1993 and has remained significant, if inconsistent. Hyundai began appointing gay-friendly staff to dealerships, IBM targeted gay-run small businesses, Subaru advertisements on buses and billboards had gay-advocacy bumper stickers and registration plates were coded to appeal to queers, Polygram's classical-music division introduced a gay promotional budget, Miller beer supported Gay Games '94, Bud Light was national sponsor to the 1999 San Francisco Folsom Street Fair, "the world's largest leather event," and Coors devised domestic-partner benefits through the work of Dick Cheney's daughter Mary, supposedly counteracting its antigay image of the past. Advertising expenditure in lesbian publications doubled from 1997 to 2001. On television, we have seen Ikea's famous U.S. TV commercial showing two men furnishing their apartment together, Toyota's male car-buying couple, two men driving around in a Volkswagen searching for home furnishings, and a gay-themed Levi Strauss dockers campaign, while 2003 Super-Bowl commercials carried hidden gay themes that advertisers refused to encode openly (known as "encrypted ads," these campaigns are designed to make queers feel special for being "in the know," whilst not offending simpleton straights). The spring 1997 U.S. network TV season saw 22 queer characters across the prime-time network schedule, and there were 30 in 2000—clear signs of niche targeting. Nineteen ninety-nine brought the first gay initial public offering, while gay and lesbian Web sites drew significant private investment. By 2005, Gay.com and PlanetOut.com had established themselves as the biggest queer affinity portals. They operated via a double appeal. On the one hand, they provided informational services desired by readers. On the other, they provided surveillance services desired by marketers. This combination attracted over eight million registered visitors and such major advertisers as United Airlines, Citibank, Procter & Gamble, Chase, Miller Brewing, CBS, and Johnson & Johnson. In 2004, Viacom announced that MTV was developing a queer cable network. Investors were animated by the US$400 billion consumer power, not cultural politics.[32]

Which is where we meet *Queer Eye for the Straight Guy* (*QESG*), a successful program that began in the northern summer of 2003 on the Bravo network. Regarded by many as a crucial metrosexual moment,[33] it teaches "the finer points of being a 'metrosexual'" (bravotv.com/Queer_Eye_for_the_Straight_Guy/Episodes/207/). What are its origins, beyond unfurling commodity interest in the queer dollar? *QESG* is part of the wider reality-television phenomenon, a strange hybrid of cost-cutting devices, game shows taken into the community, *cinéma-vérité* conceits, scripts that are written in post-production, and *ethoi* of Social Darwinism, surveillance, and gossip—bizarre blends of "tabloid journalism, documentary television, and popular entertainment."[34]

The genre derives from transformations in the political economy of television, specifically those that came about as a result of deregulation. When veteran newsman Edward R. Murrow addressed the Radio-Television News Directors Association in 1958 (recreated in the 2005 docu-drama *Goodnight and Good Luck*), he used the description/metaphor that television needed to "illuminate" and "inspire," or otherwise it would be "merely wires and light in a box." In a famous speech to the National Association of Broadcasters three years later, John F. Kennedy's chair of the Federal Communication Commission (FCC), Newton Minow, called U.S. TV a "vast wasteland."[35] He was urging broadcasters to embark on enlightened cold-war leadership, to prove that the United States was not the mindless consumer world that the Soviets claimed. The networks should live up to their legislative responsibilities to act in the public interest by informing and entertaining, and go beyond what he later recognized as "white suburbia's Dick-and-Jane world."[36] They responded by doubling the time devoted to news each evening and quickly became the dominant source of current affairs.[37] But 20 years later, Ronald Reagan's FCC head, Mark Fowler, celebrated the reduction of the "box" to "transistors and tubes." He argued in an interview with *Reason* magazine that "television is just another appliance—it's a toaster with pictures" and hence in no need of regulation, beyond ensuring its safety as an electrical appliance.[38]

Minow's and Fowler's expressions gave their vocalists instant and undimmed celebrity (Murrow already had it as the most heralded audiovisual journalist in U.S. history). Minow was named "top newsmaker" of 1961 in an Associated Press survey, and he was on TV and radio more than any other Kennedy official. The phrase "vast wasteland" has even, irony of ironies, provided raw material for the wasteland's parthenogenesis, as the answer to questions posed on numerous game shows, from *Jeopardy!* to *Who Wants to Be a Millionaire?*. The "toaster with pictures" is less celebrated, but it has been efficacious as a slogan for deregulation across successive administrations, and it remains in *Reason*'s pantheon of famous libertarian quotations, alongside those of Reagan and others of his ilk. Where Minow stands for public culture's restraining (and ultimately conserving) function for capitalism, Fowler represents capitalism's brooding arrogance, its neoliberal lust to redefine use value via exchange value. Minow decries Fowler's vision, arguing that television "is not an ordinary business" because of its "public responsibilities."[39] Fowler's phrase has won the day, at least to this point. Minow's lives on as a recalcitrant moral irritant, rather than a central policy technology.

Fowler has had many fellow-travelers. Both the free-cable, free-video social movements of the 1960s and 1970s and the neoclassical, deregulatory intellectual movements of the 1970s and 1980s saw a people's technology allegedly emerging from the wasteland of broadcast television. Porta-pak equipment, localism, and unrestrained markets would supposedly provide an alternative to the numbing nationwide commercialism of the networks.

The social-movement vision saw this occurring overnight. The technocratic vision imagined it in the "long run." One began with folksy culturalism, the other with technophilic futurism. Each claimed it in the name of diversity, and they even merged in the depoliticized "Californian ideology" of community media, much of which quickly embraced market forms. Neither formation started with economic reality. Together, they established the preconditions for unsettling a cozy, patriarchal, and quite competent television system that had combined, as TV should, what was good for you and what made you feel good, all on just one set of stations, that is, a comprehensive service. This was promised by the enabling legislation that birthed and still governs the FCC, supposedly guaranteeing citizens that broadcasters serve "the public interest, convenience and necessity," part of a tradition that began when in the 1920s CBS set up a radio network founded on news rather than its rival NBC's predilection for entertainment.[40]

In place of the universalism of the old networks, where sport, weather, news, lifestyle, and drama programming had a comfortable and appropriate *frottage*, highly centralized but profoundly targeted consumer networks emerged in the 1990s that fetishized lifestyle and consumption *tout court* over a blend of purchase and politics, of fun and foreign policy. Reality television, fixed upon by cultural critics who either mourn it as representative of a decline in journalistic standards or celebrate it as the sign of a newly femi-nised public sphere, should frankly be understood as a cost-cutting measure and an instance of niche marketing. Enter *Queer Eye*.

QESG won an award from the Gay & Lesbian Alliance Against Defamation and the Emmy for Outstanding Reality Program in 2004; it has also been heralded as a mainstream breakthrough text for queers.[41] But it embodies the advent of reality TV: originating on cable, an under-unionised sector of the industry, with small numbers of workers required for short periods. This contingent, flexible labor is textualized in the service-industry *ethos* of the genre, this creates "a parallel universe" for viewers.[42] *QESG* looks for male losers in the suburban reaches of the tristate area (New York, New Jersey, and Connecticut) who are awaiting a transformation from ordinary men into hipsters. Cosmopolitan queers descend on these hapless bridge-and-tunnel people, increase in whose marketability as husbands, fathers, and (more silently) employees they are charged with. The program's success can be understood in four ways. First, it represents the culmination of a surge of U.S. television that presents a sanitary, white, middle-class queer urban world in which queerness is fun, and gays and lesbians are to be laughed with, not laughed at. Their difference is a new commodity of pleasure—safely different from, but compatible with, heteronormativity. Second, it is a sign that queer-ness is, indeed, a lifestyle of practices that can be adopted, discarded, and redisposed promiscuously—in this case, disarticulated from its referent into metrosexuality. Third, it signifies the professionalization of queerness as a form of management consultancy for conventional masculinity, brought in to improve efficiency and effectiveness, like time-and-motion expertise, total-quality management, or just-in-time techniques. And finally, it indicates the spread of self-fashioning as a requirement of personal and professional achievement through the U.S. middle-class labor force.

Commodities are central to the secular transcendence that is *QESG*. They elicit desire by wooing consumers, glancing at them sexually, and smelling and looking nice in ways that are borrowed from romantic love; but they reverse that relationship: people learn about correct forms of romantic love from commodities. Wolfgang Haug's term "commodity aesthetics" captures this division between what commodities *promise*, by way of seduction, and what they are *actually about*, as signs of production.[43] For the public, this is "the *promesse du bonheur* that advanced capitalism always holds before them, but never quite delivers."[44] In media terms, the price paid for subscribing to cable or satellite (exchange-value) takes over from the program being watched (use-value).

Jean Baudrillard maintains that all products purchased within capitalist societies involve the consumption of advertising, rather than objects themselves. Such is the contest for newness. The culture industries are central to the compulsion to buy, through the double-sided nature of advertising and "the good life" of luxury: they encourage competition between consumers at the same time as they standardize processes to manufacture unity in the face of diversity. For all the pleasurable affluence suggested by material goods, the idea of transcendence has been articulated to objects. Commodities dominate the human and natural landscape. The corollary is the simultaneous triumph and emptiness of the sign as a source and measure of value. Baudrillard discerns four "successive phases of the image." It begins as a reflection of reality that is transformed when a representation of the truth is displaced by false information. Then these two delineable phases of truth and lies become indistinct. The sign comes to refer to itself, with no residual need of correspondence with the real. It simulates itself,[45] as "human needs, relationships and fears, the deepest recesses of the human psyche become mere means for the expansion of the commodity universe."[46] Commodities hide not only the work of their own creation, but their post-purchase existence as well. Designated with human characteristics (beauty, taste, serenity, and so on), they compensate for the absence of these qualities in everyday capitalism via a "permanent opium war."[47] In Alexander Kluge's words, "the entrepreneurs have to designate the spectators themselves as entrepreneurs. The spectator must sit in the movie house or in front of the TV-set like a commodity owner: like a miser grasping every detail and collecting surplus on everything."[48] *QESG* viewers are led gently toward a makeover that will meld suburban heteronormativity with urban hipness, as the fly-over states welcome a virtual gay parachute corps. The program's Web site offers the following: "FIND IT, GET IT, LOVE IT, USE IT. You've seen us work wonders for straight guys in need of some serious help. Get the same results at home with the same great products, services and suppliers that put the fairy dust in our Fab Five magic wands" at "QUEER EYE'S DESIGN FOR LIFE PRODUCT GUIDE" (www.bravotv.com/Queer_Eye_for_the_Straight_Guy/Shopping_Guide/).

CONCLUSION

In addition to this intrication with commodity fetishism, the trends I have outlined also produce a backlash. Attempts by queer marketers to emphasize the affluence of upper-class, white, male consumers have led to arguments by such groups as the American Family Association that there is no need for public subvention of AIDS research and prevention, or antidiscrimination protections for queers.[49] Cultural critic Richard Goldstein suggests that various testosterone tendencies in popular culture, such as masculinist hip-hop and talk radio, were preconditions for the rapturous turn to the right since September 11, 2001.[50] *American Enterprise* magazine headlined its post–September 11 cover "Real Men, They're Back," and it has been argued quite compellingly that hypermasculinity became not just patriotic but "a G[rand]O[ld]P[arty] virtue." Years later, JWT (previously J. Walter Thompson) announced the 2005 invention of the "ubersexual," who smoked cigars and was tough at the same time as he was sophisticated; this was marked by some, such as Rush Limbaugh, as the defeat of feminism and the triumph of traditional masculinity. For Simpson, though, it confirmed the onward march of the commodity—after all, even NASCAR marketers were now promoting it metrosexually. Meanwhile, *Foreign Policy* magazine nominated the European Union as "the world's first metrosexual superpower" because it "struts past the bumbling United States on the catwalk of global diplomacy," and public-opinion data indicate that this aura of sophistication leads to majorities around the world seeking greater European than Yanqui influence in foreign policy.[51]

Some of the hype surrounding metrosexuality may be overdrawn, but the numbers indicate that objectification and subjectification are on the move. Thanks to commodification and governmentalization, the male subject has been brought out into the bright light of narcissism and purchase—a comparatively enlightened culture of consumption. These trends register an epochal reordering of desire. Like most forms of commodification and governmentalization, it will have numerous unintended consequences. It has coalesced with the new neoliberal world of TV to produce the phenomenon of *QESG*. A country of ghost-fearing, god-bothering Yanquis and alien visitors has embraced new forms of superstition: neoliberal queerness. Watch this space.

NOTES

1. "Yanqui" is the term used by progressive Latin Americans and Latino/as within the United States to refer to the United States adjectivally, given the absence of a suitable alternative—"American" describes over twenty different countries, and it is inaccurate and, to many, offensive to appropriate it for one nation.

2. Many thanks to Dana Heller for her helpful comments on an earlier version.

3. Quoted in Andrew Williams, "Mark Simpson," *Metro Café*, September 15, 2005.

4. Will Hutton, "Crunch Time for Uncle Sam," *Observer*, January 5, 2003; Michael Mann, *Incoherent Empire* (London: Verso, 2003), p. 103; Pew Internet & American Life Project, *Faith Online*, 2004; Gallup Polls, gallup.com, 2002–2003.

5. Quoted in C. Fox, "Decade of the 'New Man' is Here," *Australian Financial Review*, January 21, 1989, p. 46 and see Sean Nixon, *Hard Looks: Masculinities, Spectatorship and Contemporary Consumption* (New York: St. Martin's Press, 1996), pp. 96–99.

6. Toby Miller, *SportSex* (Philadelphia: Temple University Press, 2001); Mark Simpson, "Meet the Metrosexual," *Salon.com*, July 22, 2002; Simpson quoted in Williams, "Mark Simpson."

7. Mark Simpson, "MetroDaddy Speaks!," *Salon.com*, January 5, 2004 and "Metrosexual? That Rings a Bell . . . ," *Independent*, June 22, 2003.

8. Warren St. John, "Un nuevo modelo de hombre, bien masculino pero sensible, invade los capitales del primer mundo," trans. Claudia Martínez, *Clarín*, June 25, 2003; Javier Casqueiro, "La Ola 'Metrosexual' Irrumpe en la Televisión de Estados Unidos," *El País*, August 24, 2003, 26; Sean Nixon, *Advertising Cultures: Gender, Commerce, Creativity* (London: Sage, 2003), p. 6; Deepti, "Watch Your Man," *Tribune*, October 22, 2005; American Dialect Society, "2003 Words of the Year," January 13, 2004.

9. Simpson, "MetroDaddy Speaks!"

10. St. John, "Un nuevo modelo de hombre."

11. Garth Fenley, "Image-Conscious Metrosexuals are Changing the Way Men Shop," *Display & Design Ideas*, August 1, 2004.

12. Jennifer Lee, "The Man Date," *New York Times*, April 10, 2005.

13. Marti Yarborough, "The Metrosexual Male: What Sisters Really Think of Them," *Jet* February 23, 2004, 34; Simpson, "MetroDaddy Speaks!"; D.C. Bachelor, "The Original Metrosexual Quiz" 2004, Available at: <dcbachelor.com/quiz/metro.cgi?quiz=metro> (Accessed on May 4, 2005).

14. Michael Flocker, *The Metrosexual Guide to Style: A Handbook for the Modern Man* (Cambridge, MA: Da Capo Press, 2003), p. x.

15. Guy Trebay, "When Did Skivvies Get Rated NC-17?," *New York Times*, August 1, 2004.

16. S.B. Barham, "The Phallus and the Man: An Analysis of Male Striptease," *Australian Ways: Anthropological Studies of an Industrialised Society*, ed. Lenore Manderson (Sydney: Allen & Unwin, 1985), pp. 51–65; Rose Marie Burke,

"Chippendales Let it All Hang Out in Europe," *Wall Street Journal*, April 8, 1999, A16; Richard Dyer, *Only Entertainment* (New York: Routledge, 1992), p. 104; Fiona Harari, "The New Face of Beauty," *Australian*, June 15, 1993, p. 15; Emily Jenkins, *Tongue First: Adventures in Physical Culture* (New York: Henry Holt, 1998) p. 92; Clarissa Smith, "Shiny Chests and Heaving G-Strings: A Night Out with the Chippendales," *Sexualities* 5, no. 1 (2002): 67–89.

17. Michael Weiss, "Chasing Youth," *American Demographics*, October 2002.

18. Trebay, "When Did Skivvies"; "ACNielsen: "Metrosexuals" Drive Growth in Personal Care Products," *Retail-Merchandiser*, June 23, 2004; Greg Lindsay, "Did Marketing Kill the Great American Alpha Male?," *Advertising Age*, June 13, 2005, p. 1; Rochelle Burbury, "Men Spending More on Grooming," *Australian Financial Review*, June 23, 2003; Datamonitor. *Changing Personal Care Behaviors and Occasions*, DMCM1020, 2004; Sally Beatty, "Cheap Fumes: Boys Have Their Reasons to Use Body Sprays," *Wall Street Journal*, October 29, 2004, A1, A10; Jack Neff, "Gillette Offers Teenage Boys Date with Carmen Electra," *AdAge*, May 3, 2005; Euromonitor, *Men's Hair Care: Virile Growth*, June 18, 2004; Virginia Postrel, *The Substance of Style: How the Rise of Aesthetic Value is Remaking Commerce, Culture, and Consciousness* (New York: HarperCollins, 2003), p. 29.

19. Joel Stein, "Only His Hairdresser Knows for Sure," *Time*, July 19, 1999, p. 78; Varda Burstyn, *The Rites of Men: Manhood, Politics, and the Culture of Sport* (Toronto: University of Toronto Press, 1999) 217; Stephen S. Hall, "The Bully in the Mirror," *New York Times Magazine*, August 22, 1999, pp. 30–35, 58–65; B. Lemon, "Male Beauty," *Advocate*, July 22, 1997, pp. 30–32; Weiss, "Chasing Youth"; "Salons are Catering to Men Who Want More," *Los Angeles Times*, January 4, 2006, C3; Fenley, "Image-Conscious Metrosexuals"; "Personal Care Products Aspire to Pamper Men," *BrandPackaging*, May 2004; Virginia Postrel, "A Prettier Jobs Picture?," *New York Times*, February 22, 2004; Emily Vencat Flynn, "Diamonds are for Men," *Newsweek*, October 31, 2005, p. 36.

20. "Ideavillage's as Seen on TV Line is an Alternative for Men and Women," *Retail-Merchandiser*, June 1, 2004; David Benady, "Playing Fairer with Sex," *Marketing Week*, August 5, 2004, p. 26; Jeremy Caplan, "Metrosexual Matrimony: When Modern Men Prepare to Wed, Many Wax, Tan and Help Plan. Here Come the 'Groomzillas'," *Time*, October 3, 2005, p. 67; Richard Florida, *The Rise of the Creative Class: And How it's Transforming Work, Leisure, Community and Everyday Life* (New York: Basic Books, 2002); James Robinson, "The Loutish Lad is Dead. Enter the Caring Lad in Cashmere," *Observer*, April 24, 2005.

21. Scott Burton, Richard G. Netemeyer, and Donald R. Lichtenstein, "Gender Differences for Appearance-Related Attitudes and Behaviors: Implications for Consumer Welfare," *Journal of Public Policy & Marketing* 13, no.1 (1995): 60–75; Kathy Davis, *Dubious Equalities and Embodied Differences: Cultural Studies on Cosmetic Surgery* (Lanham: Rowman & Littlefield, 2003), p. 123.

22. Christine Rosen, "The Democratization of Beauty," *New Atlantis* no. 5 (2004): 19–35; "Force Enlargement," *Economist*, July 31, 2004, 30; "Marketplace," National Public Radio, June 3, 1999; Sheerly Avni, "The Unkindest Cut," *Salon.com*, December 18, 2002.

23. American Academy of Facial Plastic and Reconstructive Surgery, *2001 Membership Survey: Trends in Plastic Surgery*, 2002.

24. Martin Miller, "Instant Brawn," *Los Angeles Times*, October 21, 2002, p. 1.

25. American Society for Aesthetic Plastic Surgery, *Cosmetic Surgery National Data Bank 2002 Statistics*, 2002.

26. American Academy of Cosmetic Surgery, *Estimated Total Number of Patients Treated by All U.S.-Based American Academy of Cosmetic Surgery Members 2002*, 2003 and the American Society for Aesthetic Plastic Surgery, 2002.

27. Suzanne Goldenberg, "Nip and Tuck Gets its Own Magazine," *Guardian*, January 17, 2005.

28. Ellen Tien, "The More Hairless Ape," *New York Times*, June 20, 1999, p. 3.

29. S.D. Hamermesh and J.E. Biddle, "Beauty and the Labor Market," *American Economic Review* 84, no. 5 (1994): 1174–1194; M. Wells, "Slimmer Dooner Revs up McCann," *Advertising Age*, October 10, 1994, 50; Milt Freudenheim, "Employers Focus on Weight as a Workplace Health Issue," *New York Times*, September 6, 1999, A15; Rosen, 2004; Weiss, "Chasing Youth"; Kamal Ahmed, "Britons Swallow Cure-All Drugs," *Observer*, January 26, 2003.

30. Daniel Agliata and Stacey Tantleff-Dunn, "The Impact of Media Exposure on Males' Body Image," *Journal of Social and Clinical Psychology* 23, no. 1 (2004): 7–22; Harrison G. Pope, Jr., Katharine A. Phillips, and Roberto Olivardia, *The Adonis Complex: The Secret Crisis of Male Body Obsession* (New York: Free Press, 2000).

31. Ziauddin Sardar and Merryl Wyn Davies, *Why Do People Hate America?* (Cambridge: Icon Books, 2002), p. 82; Flocker, *The Metrosexual*, pp. xi, xiii, xiv, 169; Angela McRobbie, "From Holloway to Hollywood: Happiness at Work in the New Cultural Economy," in *Cultural Economy: Cultural Analysis and Commercial Life*, ed. Paul du Gay and Michael Pryke (London: Sage, 2002), p. 100; Chris Flower, "Foreword," *The Self-Esteem Society*, Helen McCarthy (London: Demos, 2004), p. 5; Helen McCarthy, *The Self-Esteem Society* (London: Demos, 2004).

32. Ronald Alsop, "But Brewers Employ In-Your-Mug Approach," *Wall Street Journal*, June 29, 1999, B1 and "Cracking the Gay Market Code," *Wall Street Journal*, June 29, 1999, B1, B4; S. Rawlings, "Luring the Big Boys," *B and T*, February 12, 1993, 18–19; Stuart Elliott, "Levi Strauss Begins a Far-Reaching Marketing Campaign to Reach Gay Men and Lesbians," *New York Times*, October 19, 1998, C11; Tommi Avicolli Mecca, "Gay Shame," *AlterNet.org*, June 7, 2002; Michael Wilke, "Super Bowl Delivers Gay Ad Themes, Companies Remain Mum," *Commercial Closet*, February 18, 2003, www.commercialcloset.org (Accessed on May 4, 2005); Katherine Sender, *Business, not Politics: The Making of the Gay Market* (New York: Columbia University Press, 2005), pp. 126–128, 111; Angela T. Ragusa, "Social Change and the Corporate Construction of Gay Markets in the *New York Times*'

Advertising Business News," *Media, Culture & Society* 27, no. 5 (2005): 655, 658; J.J. O'Connor "Coming Out Party: The Closet Opens, Finally," *New York Times*, April 30, 1997, C18; David Bank, "On the Web, Gay Sites Start to Click," *Wall Street Journal*, September 28, 1999, B1; John Edward Campbell, "Outing PlanetOut: Surveillance, Gay Marketing and Internet Affinity Portals," *New Media & Society* 7, no. 5 (2005): 663–683; Bill Carter and Stuart Elliott, "MTV to Start First Network Aimed at Gays," *New York Times*, May 26, 2004, C1, C6.

33. Chris Nutter, "Circling the Square," *Gay & Lesbian Review Worldwide* 11, no. 6 (2004): 19–22.

34. Laurie Ouellette and Susan Murray, "Introduction," *Reality TV: Remaking Television Culture*, ed. Susan Murray and Laurie Ouellette (New York: New York University Press, 2004), pp. 8–9; Annette Hill, *Reality TV: Audiences and Popular Factual Television* (London: Routledge, 2005), p. 15.

35. Edward R. Murrow, Speech to the Radio-Television News Directors Association, Chicago, October 15, 1958; Newton Minow, "The Broadcasters are Public Trustees," *Radio & Television: Readings in the Mass Media*, ed. Allen Kirschener and Linda Kirschener (New York: Odyssey Press, 1971), pp. 207–217.

36. Newton N. Minow, "Television, More Vast than Ever, Turns Toxic," *USA Today*, May 9, 2001, 15A.

37. Michael Schudson and Susan E. Tifft, "American Journalism in Historical Perspective," *The Press*, ed. Geneva Overholser and Kathleen Hall Jamieson (Oxford: Oxford University Press, 2005), p. 32.

38. Not surprisingly, Alfred Hitchcock said it earlier and better: "Television is like the American toaster, you push the button and the same thing pops up every time," quoted in Janet Wasko, "Introduction," *A Companion to Television*, ed. Janet Wasko (Malden: Blackwell, 2005), p. 10.

39. Newton N. Minow and Fred H. Cate, "Revisiting the Vast Wasteland," *Federal Communications Law Journal,* no. 55 (2003): 408, 415.

40. Megan Mullen, "The Fall and Rise of Cable Narrowcasting," *Convergence*, 8, no. 1 (2002): 62–83; Richard Barbrook and Andy Cameron, "The Californian Ideology," *Science as Culture* 6 (1996): 44–72; Albert Scardino, "Sun Sets on U.S. Broadcast Golden Age," *Guardian*, March 9, 2005.

41. Beth Berila and Devika Dibya Choudhuri, "Metrosexuality the Middle Class Way: Exploring Race, Class, and Gender in *Queer Eye for the Straight Guy*," *Genders,* no. 42 (2005).

42. Justin Lewis, Sanna Inthorn, and Karin Wahl-Jorgensen, *Citizens or Consumers? What the Media Tell Us About Political Participation* (Maidenhead: Open University Press, 2005), p. 17.

43. W.F. Haug, *Critique of Commodity Aesthetics: Appearance, Sexuality and Advertising in Capitalist Society*, trans. Robert Bock (Cambridge: Polity Press, 1986), pp. 17, 19, 35.

44. Seyla Benhabib, *The Claims of Culture: Equality and Diversity in the Global Era* (Princeton: Princeton University Press, 2002), p. 3.

45. Jean Baudrillard, *Selected Writings*, ed. Mark Poster (Stanford: Stanford University Press, 1988), pp. 10–11, 29, 170.

46. Robert W. McChesney and John Bellamy Foster, "The Commercial Tidal Wave," *Monthly Review* 54, no. 10 (2003): 1.

47. Guy Debord, *The Society of the Spectacle*, trans. Donald Nicolson-Smith (New York: Zone, 1995), pp. 26–27, 29–30.

48. Alexander Kluge, "On Film and the Public Sphere," trans. Thomas Y. Levin and Miriam B. Hansen, *New German Critique* no. 24 and 25 (1981–1982), 210–211.

49. Helen Jefferson Lenskyj, "Gay Games or Gay Olympics? Corporate Sponsorship Issues," in *Global Sport Sponsorship*, ed. John Amis and T. Bettina Cornwell (Berg: Oxford, 2005), p. 287; Ragusa, "Social Change and the Corporate Construction," p. 656.

50. Richard Goldstein, "Neo-Macho Man: Pop Culture and Post–9/11 Politics," *The Nation*, March 24, 2003, 16–19.

51. Wendy Donahue, "Begone, Girlie Man. Hello, Confident Ubersexual," *Chicago Tribune*, October 30, 2005; Joe Kovacs, "Rush Limbaugh Wonders: Am I an 'Ubersexual'?," *WorldNetDaily*, October 11, 2005; Williams, "Mark Simpson"; Jennine Lee, "NASCAR Goes Metrosexual," *Time*, February 7, 2005, 18; Parag Khanna, "The Metrosexual Superpower," *Foreign Policy*, July/August 2004; Globescan/ Program on International Policy Attitudes, "In 20 of 23 Countries Polled Citizens Want Europe to be More Influential than U.S.," 2005.

PART II

MAKEOVER TELEVISION FORMATS, 1950–TODAY

THE CINDERELLA MAKEOVER: *GLAMOUR GIRL*, TELEVISION MISERY SHOWS, AND 1950S FEMININITY

MARSHA F. CASSIDY

IN JULY 1953, LONG BEFORE THE WORD "makeover" officially entered the American lexicon, the misery show *Glamour Girl* debuted on the NBC television network. Praised at the time for turning "ducklings into swans" and polishing up "diamonds in the rough,"[1] *Glamour Girl* was the country's first nationally broadcast daytime program that celebrated the beautification of women in a dramatic before-and-after format. The case study of this historically significant but rarely discussed program throws light on the gendered place of women in postwar America. *Glamour Girl*'s Cinderella storylines openly fostered the nation's emergent standards for American femininity— standards that required both a woman's realignment with traditional family roles and an artful and more opulent redesign of her physical appearance.[2] Yet because *Glamour Girl* followed the discursive arc of a "misery show," contestants' on-air explanations about why they desired a makeover also disclosed the social terms of their unhappiness. Taken together, these confessions implicitly served to underscore the gendered constraints of 1950s America and added a measure of rebellion to the makeover act.

Every weekday at 10:30 a.m. Eastern Time, four contestants on *Glamour Girl* described in interviews with host Harry Babbitt (and, later, Jack McCoy) their intimate reasons for wishing to be transformed; winners were selected by applause from the live audience. After receiving a key that unlocked the "gateway to glamour," the victor enjoyed 24 hours of beautification and pampering, returning to the studio the next day to display her new look to the world. Using Hollywood, the "glamour capital" of the world, as a backdrop, the program was recorded in NBC's Burbank Studio Number Three on 35 mm film for later network distribution from New York.[3] Winners on *Glamour Girl* were visibly reconstituted by means of consumer products and professional beauty advice—strikingly transformed by fashionable new clothes, a stylish hairdo, expertly applied cosmetics, and a complete line of beauty accessories—a process that trumpeted a new set of norms that had come to dictate feminine attractiveness and sexuality in postwar America.

Yet the program also explicitly attached a psychodynamic value to a woman's beautification. Historian Kathy Peiss, who has traced the public remaking of a woman's outward appearance across the twentieth century, explains that in modernity, beauty culturists promoted "the mutual transformation of external appearance and inner well-being."[4] Evoking these perceived connections between the inner and outer self, a winner's revitalization on *Glamour Girl* was presented as reflecting a much deeper transformation. In the words of an NBC sales brochure promoting the program, "[T]he girl is changed not only in appearance but also in her outlook on life. We see her poised, secure and smiling. This creation of a new personality has great human interest appeal."[5]

The television makeover on *Glamour Girl* thus represented a cultural crossroad where the demands of commercial television, financially dependent upon sponsorships from the world of cosmetics and fashion, intersected with long-standing traditions of feminine beautification and its therapeutic value, newly restored after the war. By promoting "glitz and glitter" to the masses— what Thomas Hines called "populuxe"[6]—television opened up a fresh category of consumer products to advertise—everything from hair coloring and chic hats to Fifi hosiery and Trapeze sports shoes. During the 1950s, television and the beauty industries were allied in the mutual promotion of a woman's never-ending pursuit of curative glamour.

GLAMOUR ON TV

The Oxford Dictionary of New Words reports that the noun "makeover" was first used in the late 1960s in professional hairstylist and beautician publications and began to appear as "stock vocabulary" in women's magazines only during the 1980s, when making a woman over came to mean transforming a woman's appearance through the help of experts.[7] Yet Peiss traces the practice of making women over much farther back in time. She reports that during the 1910s and 1920s, "before-and-after imagery" became a "pliable advertising concept" for the cosmetics industry.[8] In August 1921, at a beauty show in Atlantic City, cosmetic experts selected middle-aged or elderly women from the crowd and publicly transformed their complexions using creams and rouges; in 1928, an advertisement for zip, a facial depilatory, contrasted photographs of a lady's profile before and after the application.[9] Peiss further notes that in 1936, *Mademoiselle* featured a "Made Over Girl," nurse Barbara Phillips, who experienced a transformation of "herself and her life chances" through beauty aids.[10]

As visual spectacle and performance, the makeover was ideally suited to early television. While radio could—and did—supply beauty tips to women,[11] television provided the dramatic visual display of results. Moreover, television arrived in American homes at the very time the country was embracing a new spirit. In a postwar climate of revitalization and hope, the fantasy of glamorization and the therapeutic value attached to it gained heightened currency. Christian Dior famously captured this trend in the fashion world when he introduced his "New Look" for the American woman, a look that represented, in Karal Ann Marling's view, "a form of living sculpture . . . a kind of body engineering" that exuded the decade's "palpable optimism."[12] If the basic shape of fashion could change the "soldier woman" of the 1940s into a flower, as Dior hoped it would,[13] then so could the human condition change, or "at the very least, the life of the lady in the son-of-Dior suit."[14]

The cosmetics industry fully exploited the fashion renaissance. During the war, the government had asked women to curtail their purchases of cosmetics, and manufacturing companies discouraged glamour on the job. Once the war ended, sales of beauty products skyrocketed. Consumers were now offered a limitless array of choices, and the two Goliaths of the cosmetics world, Hazel Bishop and Revlon, invested richly in television sponsorships.[15] Peiss calls the postwar years "a rococo period" for the beauty industry, when the war's end served as a "catalyst for [a] psychological interpretation of cosmetics," promoting the fantasy of feminine beauty as an antidote to the unsettling transitions women faced in the shift from war to peace.[16] According to Peiss, beautification during the 1950s "became even more aligned with therapeutic claims" than it was in the 1930s, as women contended with social transformations and a return to domesticity.[17]

Yet in both fashion and makeup, these new aesthetic standards for the female form demanded artful coordination and design[18] under the strict guidance of glamour experts. To meet this demand, early local television across the country featured a number of programs devoted to beauty and fashion advice. In San Francisco, KPIX aired *Your Beauty Clinic* as one of its first women's shows,[19] while WGN-TV in Chicago premiered *Individually Yours* in 1949, sponsored by the Blair Corset Company, whose commercials boldly pictured the latest girdles and bras in closeup.[20] Former model and fashion columnist Inga Rundvold conducted regular beauty school segments on WNBW in Washington, DC,[21] and, just months before *Glamour Girl* debuted, a "Pygmalion"-style show, which made "a beauty of a rather dowdy looking girl," was already airing daily on WKRC in Cincinnati.[22]

By the time NBC decided to develop a national Cinderella show of its own in 1953, the premise of transformative glamour permeated television to such an extent that NBC worried *Glamour Girl* could face unlawful infringement suits. In April of that year, NBC lawyers fretted over the proposed show's similarities to Mutual's West Coast hit, *Queen for a Day*, and advised *Glamour Girl*'s production company to purchase at least $200,000 worth of liability insurance.[23] After *Glamour Girl* premiered, NBC was hectored by letters that claimed prior rights to the concept, including controversial inquiries and legal notices by representatives of *The Lucky Lady Show*, *Glamour Jury*, and *Lady Be Beautiful*.[24]

Notwithstanding these challenges, NBC launched the country's first national daytime program that predicated its beauty treatment on a woman's confession of hardship or misery, balancing elements from the beauty clinic and the misery show in a new combination.

GLAMOUR AND MISERY

Glamour Girl was but one misery show among many during the 1950s that centered its game upon contestants who had suffered hard luck or mistreatment in their lives.[25] More benignly labeled "human interest" programs by the industry, these extraordinarily popular shows featured "everyday" participants chosen from the home or studio audience who were brought on stage to trade the public recitation of their life stories for the chance to win prizes.[26]

With an emphasis on personal confession, the misery shows of the 1950s complied with a television mode that Mimi White calls "therapeutic discourse." For White, who traces this form across multiple television genres of the 1980s and 1990s, confession mediated through television is "repeatedly linked with consumer culture and social subjectivity."[27] *Glamour Girl* exhibited the same discursive pattern. Women on *Glamour Girl* first confessed the reasons for their displacement in the social world and were then transformed by consumer products in a renewal that promised to change their lives.[28]

Utilizing television's visual potential, *Glamour Girl* magnified the poignancy of a woman's confession by focusing attention on the flaws of her body. In the lexicon of *Glamour Girl*, the mark of social misfortune, inadequacy, dissatisfaction, or abuse was the "unattractive" body, presented for close inspection by the television camera.

Just as the story of each day's contestants stigmatized them as misfits within the gender structures of American life, their plain, bedraggled, or unconventional bodies confirmed their marginal position within the social world and supplied a reason for it. Jane Bennett, the ultimate winner on October 1, 1953, was an unmarried woman from Nashville, Tennessee, who told McCoy that she had been unable to "trap" a husband because "glamour [is] floatin' one way and me floatin' the other." McCoy immediately recognized Bennett's precarious position within 1950s culture: "[You] represent lots of single girls in America who are a miss and want to be a missus."[29]

On the following day, Elizabeth Launer of Hawthorne, California, won out over her competitors when she confessed, "I'm big. I want to prove you can be big *and* glamorous." Elizabeth divulged that she had tried and failed to "reduce" and hoped to please her disapproving husband by demonstrating that big can be beautiful. Here, Elizabeth's substandard figure demarcated an erotic shortcoming that threatened to destabilize her marriage.[30]

The next day, Joyce Torres's story exposed a much more volatile and disturbing marriage, on the brink of collapse. Married for three years, she was now pregnant with her second child. She haltingly told McCoy that her husband thought she was not very glamorous and had threatened to leave a number of times because she did not take care of herself. McCoy probed further. "Now, let me understand this properly," he continued, "Mr. Torres has criticized openly your appearance? . . . Have you talked this over with anyone?" Joyce conceded that she had discussed the problem with a social worker, whose therapeutic advice turned out to be in accord with the ethos of *Glamour Girl*: the social worker advised Joyce to improve her appearance. After gently assuring Torres that her husband loved her and that she was a good wife and mother, McCoy asked enthusiastically, "Do you think glamour could help cohese [sic] this Torres home? Put it right back together the way you'd like it?" When she agreed, he added, "I hope it will do the trick . . . It won't hurt any . . . [Men need] a little help every so often." Despite McCoy's reassurances, Torres was reintroduced to the audience before the final vote as the contestant who wanted to be glamorized as a "last resort to keep her husband from leaving home."[31]

As attentive interlocutors to each woman's confession, the studio audience, almost exclusively composed of women, listened, evaluated, and then meted out judgment, electing Miss. Jane Bennett and the full-figured Elizabeth Launer by clear margins, while sustaining such wholehearted clapping for Joyce Torres that the applause meter pegged past 100 on her victory day. Women in the studio knew full well the jeopardy each winner faced under postwar gender rules, and their applause recognized and affirmed a contestant's social malady, coded as homeliness.

Of course, for every winner there were three losers, and in just one week, audiences heard a total of 20 distressing tales. Like the players on *Strike It Rich* and *Queen for a Day*, woeful contestants on *Glamour Girl* sobbed out their stories day after day: a hardworking farm wife in her late 40s who never had a honeymoon; a polio victim who wanted to thank her husband for his life-saving support; a foster mother to 21 children who longed to attend her youngest daughter's wedding; a young woman whose face was disfigured in a fire; a wife who worked to put her husband through college while nursing a three-year-old daughter with leukemia; and a woman named Mabel McKinzie, who was widowed at age 17 and worked all her life to raise her children alone. Collectively, these stories reiterated a melancholic discontent, a simple longing for a life less prosaic. McKinzie summed up the bleakness experienced by so many of these women when she said simply, "The years have been long and the work hard."[32]

The accumulated narratives of these dispirited women, representing all possible gradations of misery from deep tragedy to the drabness of everyday routines, conveyed the lurking potential for dissatisfaction and even despair in women's lives. Historian Elaine Tyler May found that "women in Levittown [the prototypical postwar suburb] often complained about feeling trapped and isolated . . . For them suburban life was not a life of fun and leisure but of exhausting work and isolation."[33] Verifying the cheerlessness and monotonous toil that often circumscribed women's lives during the 1950s, the television camera on *Glamour Girl* scrutinized in closeup how distress crept into a woman's appearance—visible in her face, her voice, the cut of her hair, her sloping posture, or the drabness of her figure.

For a brief moment, television rescued her. After confessing the reasons for her displacement in the social world, the damaged woman won renewal in a glamour treatment the very next day. Corsetry and crinolines close to the body, and hats, furs, charm bracelets, gloves, ball gowns, and chiffon artfully arranged on the surface, all served to define the glitz, glitter, and glamour of a new self. (One woman was even awarded a poodle as a fashion accessory.) Five days a week, *Glamour Girl* championed the principle of psychodynamic refiguration outlined by Peiss and Marling and turned one lucky contestant into what Jack McCoy called "an exciting, thrilling, brand-spankin' new personality."[34]

THE HOLLYWOOD CONNECTION

This personal restoration was underscored on *Glamour Girl* through the fantasies of Hollywood. Not only did the show's opening sequence remind viewers that the program was filmed in the world's "glamour capital," but each transformation was also managed by Mary Webb Davis, introduced as a "consultant to the stars" and the "finest glamour expert in America."[35] (In fact, Davis ran a modeling school and agency for aspiring starlets.[36]) Moreover, the narrative terms of *Glamour Girl* were borrowed from a familiar antecedent in Hollywood film, what Maria LaPlace calls "the spectacle of metamorphosis—the thrill of 'before and after,' " when a protagonist's outward transformation becomes "part of her cure," as it was for Bette Davis in *Now, Voyager*[37]—or for Calamity Jane and Sabrina.[38] Whereas another 1950s program, the primetime celebrity show *This is Your Life*, claimed to expose the authentic self within the glamorous star, as Mary Desjardins has explained,[39] *Glamour Girl* sought to express the ordinary woman's authentic but hidden beauty in Hollywood terms. As Jack McCoy lucidly phrased it on air, beneath the surface of every woman lay a genuinely stunning creature. "I think almost every lady is basically very glamorous," said McCoy, "[it just takes] outside touching around" to bring out the glamour from within.[40]

As Denise Mann suggests, postwar television "re-presented" the unattainable sumptuousness associated in earlier decades only with Hollywood stars. She calls this the "spectacularization" of the everyday, by which Hollywood's entry into the television industry evoked nostalgia for "an opulent world that existed outside the home."[41] In Mann's view, postwar beauty ideals conflated "the star's wardrobe with that of the average suburban housewife," in a two-way leveling effect that superficially homogenized class difference.[42] Accordingly, shows such as *Glamour Girl* hinged on the fantasy that every woman could be as royal and glamorous as a Hollywood star. In his appeal for letters from prospective home contestants, host Jack McCoy offered every viewer the hope for stunning self-fulfillment in the TV studio. "I know every one of you, no matter who you are, wants to be right here and see yourself transformed into a beautiful, beautiful glamorous lady," he proclaimed on air.[43] A month into the show, *Glamour Girl*'s executive producer in New York, Adrian Samish, expressed the same vision when he instructed the Los Angeles team to begin flying in contestants from around the country, to "give [the] audience the assurance that they too can appear no matter where they live."[44] *Glamour Girl* reassured every woman trapped by housework drudgery and isolated at the hearth that she too could become a princess.

Glamour Girl accomplished this leveling effect by offering the ordinary contestant temporary celebrity and the chance to experience the thrill of Hollywood nightlife. *Glamour Girl*'s original host, Harry Babbitt, was a night club singer and a former featured vocalist with Kay Kyser and his band,[45] and he radiated a B-level version of stardom. Adding to the Hollywood fantasy, *Glamour Girl* pampered each winner as if she were a star herself, treating her not only to the ministrations of Mary Webb Davis, but also to "an evening of fun and excitement on the Sunset strip."[46]

When *Glamour Girl* premiered on July 6, 1953, NBC appeared to have discovered a winning formula, one that linked the Hollywood-style makeover of body and soul to redemption from misery. Early reviews of *Glamour Girl* were filled with praise. On July 31, Samish at NBC headquarters bragged about the show's "great reviews" across the country and called upon the network to publish print ads that stressed the press acclaim.[47] Plaudits came in from various corners: Ted Green at *Radio Daily-Television Daily* called the program a "sensational new hit" that "will be on the network for a long, long time"; TV columnist Sid Shalit praised NBC vice president Charles Barry for creating "a sure-fire winner" that might, he joked, eventually provide Barry with enough votes from grateful housewives to propel him into the U.S. presidency.[48] Harriet Van Horne of the *New York World-Telegram* attributed the show's popularity to her conviction that "perfection of face and form is the dream of every woman still young enough to have a dream, that is, under 80."[49] And Hal Humphrey, the Radio-TV Editor for the *Mirror* in Los Angeles, gushed that the new daytime show "makes the author of 'Cinderella' look like a bum."[50]

Seeking to capitalize on the favorable publicity, the NBC's sales department prepared a 20-page brochure targeting potential advertisers whose business was glamour: "[H]ere is the program especially produced for you . . . loaded with the proven elements of TV success"—feminine appeal, human interest, personal identification, and day-to-day suspense and continuity. Using remarkable before-and-after photographs of contestant Delores Napolitano, the brochure highlighted the drama created each day at the moment when the refurbished woman appeared before the cameras for the first time, accompanied by fanfare, music, and applause. "The effect is exciting and moving," the promotion read.[51]

Glamour Girl may have been off to a strong start, but when *New York Times* critic Val Adams finally got around to reviewing the show on August 21, 1953,[52] the program soon fell victim to a public battle over vulgarity on television. At odds were conflicting taste values articulated by the era's elite critics, who upheld a doctrine of uplift for television and censured ever more forcefully the cheap appeals they attributed to women's shows. Social critics worried that the substandard programming that they believed had sullied radio would negate television's potential to enlighten the masses. In the opinion of these critics, it was deplorable that the radio genres especially favored by women viewers—notably the misery show and soap opera—were transferring their tawdriness and mediocrity straight to television.[53]

MORBID MISERY OR INSPIRATION?

In keeping with this elite attitude, Adams's two-column review lambasted *Glamour Girl* in no uncertain terms.[54] Under a headline that labeled the show a "new twist in exploiting human misery," Adams denounced NBC's morning schedule as having "deteriorated to an unbearably low level." There is no excuse, he said, for a show "that exploits human misery and intentionally victimizes the innocent people who appear on the show." Adams expressed outrage that before NBC agreed to make a woman glamorous, she was "encouraged to tell pitiful and tragic things about her personal life," and he wondered sardonically how glamour could improve the plight of a contestant whose husband suffered an incurable disease. "It is impossible to understand," Adams fumed, "why NBC would choose to present such a cheap, vulgar program." While conceding that a "glamour show for the ladies could really be fun," he censured NBC for choosing "to play it offensively for tears instead of laughs." He concluded, "The whole shoddy business is a sin against the viewing public."[55]

Adams's stinging review in the *Times* could not have appeared at a worse time for *Glamour Girl*. It immediately caught the eye of the legendary RCA founder David Sarnoff, who was serving as interim president of NBC that August,[56] and it triggered an uproar at the network. Sarnoff composed an unambiguous memo to John K. Herbert, his next-in-command, demanding a response and precipitating a flurry of in-house correspondence debating the show's propriety.[57]

These documents reveal how NBC executives tried to salvage a potentially profitable show by fine-tuning the idea of "misery."[58] At the same time, these documents also make clear that the era's power players (almost all of them men) failed to comprehend that this very expression of misery supplied a deep-seated reason for the show's unflagging popularity with women.

Responding to the Sarnoff memo, New York producer Adrian Samish did his best to defend *Glamour Girl*. "It is unfortunate that daytime television shows which appeal to housewives seem to require a measure of unhappiness in them to succeed," he wrote his supervisor Charles Barry.[59] Samish then tried to spell out the subtle difference between a "good heart act" that demonstrated "moral strength" and the mere outpouring of "*acute* unhappiness,"[60] which he considered to be in "just plain bad taste." "What I am trying to get our Hollywood producers of Glamour Girl to realize," he continued in his memo to Barry, "is that there is a great difference between a guest who has an inspirational story coming out of hardship and a guest who simply gives a recital of her trials and tribulations."[61]

In Samish's estimation, the "perfect heart act" was a story from a previous show of a young nurse who had fallen in love with a paralysis patient in an iron lung. Her wish was to be glamorous for her lover, who had only seen her in a nurse's uniform. In a letter to Jack McCoy, who was then serving as the show's producer, Samish granted that the story "had sickness attached to it," but he praised its "great romantic twist," including "a theme of courage overcoming [a] great handicap," maybe even leading to marriage. He told McCoy that it would have been entirely appropriate to have "brought the guy to the show, iron lung and all, to see her transformation." He concluded, "No one could have criticized us for presenting this act and, if they did, I would have told them to go to hell."[62] For Samish, a TV executive held accountable for both decency and dollars, an inspirational story made misery defensible.

His boss, Charles Barry, took a decidedly more pragmatic approach in his response to General Sarnoff on August 27. "We must give the audience a chance to vote as to the show's appeal," Barry reasoned, "and if we get the audience, that's what counts in this particular instance."[63] Barry, Samish, and even Sarnoff himself could not ignore the fact that misery shows were "leading the pack" in daytime TV ratings, as Samish had made clear in an earlier memo.[64]

Less than six weeks later, the audience got its chance to vote. Two promotional announcements for a prize giveaway on *Glamour Girl* in the first few days of October 1953 drew over 10,000 letters, a number so impressive that Barry circulated the good news to his NBC superiors.[65] Within two weeks, the show's Trendex rating had increased by 1.3, and the American Research Bureau (ARB) rating was likewise showing a "good increase," even against its toughest competitor, *Arthur Godfrey Time* on CBS.[66] In Los Angeles, *Glamour Girl*'s 3.2 ARB rating led all other NBC programs in the daytime lineup for the days from September 12 to 14, second only to another CBS favorite, *Art Linkletter's House Party*.[67]

Even more astonishing were the mail-in results for two consecutive promotions inaugurated during the weeks of October 5 and October 12. In the first week, *Glamour Girl* announced that its beauty experts would study letters and photographs from home viewers and offer suggestions for individual improvement over the air. When the program received 30,000 letters, the offer had to be withdrawn because "the glamour experts were up to their coiffures in letters and photographs," according to an NBC press release.[68] The following week, *Glamour Girl* announced it would select a single winner and reward her with "a trip to Hollywood, an appearance on the show, and a full glamour treatment." The new contest drew 42,000 letters in one week; NBC calculated that between October 5 and October 16, approximately one in ten viewers of *Glamour Girl* had entered the contest.[69]

These promising numbers temporarily quelled NBC's anxieties about airing what Samish had called *Glamour Girl*'s "museum of horrors."[70] In the long run, however, nothing could protect *Glamour Girl* from mounting public disapproval of misery shows in general.[71] The effort to rid daytime television of shows such as *Glamour Girl* was powerfully ingrained in 1950s notions of vulgarity, morality, and "bad taste." And it was this prevailing assessment of the misery genre and its predominantly female viewers that led beleaguered NBC executives and critics such as Adams to misread the genre's underlying attraction. While Adams condemned *Glamour Girl*'s "vulgar" appeal and Samish trumpeted inspirational suffering as an antidote to crassness, both men failed to grasp the misery show's bittersweet attraction for women viewers. As feminist scholars would articulate many years later, *Glamour Girl* and its sobbing counterparts authorized "girl talk" on television, what Mary Ellen Brown has called "feminine discourse." She explains that feminine discourse is "a way of talking and acting among feminine subjects . . . in which they acknowledge their position of subordination within patriarchal society" but are empowered by the comfort of validation and by the recognition that others understand their culturally determined restrictions.[72]

Like other misery shows, *Glamour Girl* granted contestants a kind of public forum that was never available before to women. The misery format on TV authorized visible confessions that served to expose the perils of 1950s gender relations. Like women of the 1920s, contestants on *Glamour Girl* "staked a claim to public attention, [and] demanded that others look," to quote Kathy Peiss.[73] Day after day, an assemblage of women, injured, wronged, or ensnared by patriarchy, explained their troubles to a sympathetic television community, openly seeking recognition and redress.[74] As a remedy for body and soul, a Hollywood-style makeover served as a temporary but defiant gesture.

PSYCHOLOGY PLUS GIRDLE

At *Glamour Girl*'s center was glamour expert Mary Webb Davis, whose team of beauty consultants transfigured each winner. A stylish woman herself, Davis conveyed a mood of supportive daring when she appeared on stage with the day's future glamour girl, and kindly holding the woman's hand she would promise to use her expertise to bring out the "innate possibilities for a tremendous picture tomorrow."[75] To the full-figured Elizabeth Launer, Davis declared boldly, "There's no law that says all women should be slim . . . There can be *big* glamorous women, too. Glamazons . . . the Junoesque type."[76] To the pathetic expectant mother Joyce Torres, fearful of divorce, Davis pledged passionately that the next day the world would see "one of the most glamorous mothers-to-be of all time . . . I promise this." Davis predicted that after the makeover, Mr. Torres "might feel like leaving, but for another reason . . . Every man [Joyce] meets will be so interested in her, he will get jealous."[77] The defiant tone of prescriptions such as these accented the makeover on *Glamour Girl* as an act of insubordination. Davis's plans of redemptive adornment liberated both the inner and the outer self, a precept she called "psychology plus girdle."[78]

Under Davis's direction, the *Glamour Girl* makeover served to rehabilitate a woman by momentarily shifting her power within the social world. Winners donned the mantel of Hollywood celebrity and temporarily enjoyed all its privileges and prestige. To become a glamour girl for 24 hours was a performance that conspicuously overturned her mundane and subordinate position at home. TV critic Hal Humphrey observed this reversal in winner Sophie Ritson, who lived in a housing project with her husband of 15 years, Wilbur, and their two children. Humphrey, as he sat next to Wilbur after Sophie's transformation, reported that Wilbur, completely thrown by the change, had said, "I guess I'll have to get a better job." When Wilbur "forged through" the crowd of photographers surrounding Sophie to give her a kiss, she cried, "Don't smear me! Kiss me on the cheek." Later, when Davis announced she might even train Sophie as a professional model, Wilbur was forced to "ogle" his wife from the sidelines and snap his own photograph of her from a distance.[79] Columnist Sid Shalit noted a similar response in another winner's husband, who felt that "the balance of marital power had been shifted too suddenly" and asked for a glamour treatment for himself "to even things up."[80]

Certainly *Glamour Girl*'s remedies were anything but revolutionary. New hairdos, opulent clothes that promised "sophisticated perfection,"[81] and the luxury of 1950s beauty products, accessories, and perfumes ultimately worked to constrain women within the decade's new material culture and to draw the reformed winner back into traditional patriarchy after her day in the sun. In the program's narrative fall and rise, winning contestants regained an erotic appeal that ensured their success in husband-hunting or husband-keeping. Yet it was the process of glamorization, not merely the Cinderella outcome, that affirmed for audiences the defects in Prince Charming's system.

Viewed inside-out, *Glamour Girl* chronicled the pitfalls and discontents of 1950s femininity, offering only fleeting pleasure in the celebration of Davis's defiant remedies. Just as Thomas Elsaesser and others have interpreted 1950s Hollywood family melodramas as "critical social documents" whose falsely happy endings expose the powerlessness of women,[82] *Glamour Girl* exposed the faultlines buried deep beneath the decade's dominant thinking about gender. Studio visitors and viewers alike were asked to look intimately at the bodies of distraught women and to listen every day to their stories of struggle and disappointment. Ten years later, second-wave feminists would call these same recitations "consciousness-raising."

In retrospect, even the sharp criticism directed against *Glamour Girl* served to affirm the misery show's capacity to spotlight the plight of women in postwar America. By giving voice to the "abject," *Glamour Girl* and the other misery shows of the 1950s prefigured the "narrative irritation, complication, catch" that Gloria Jean Masciarotte observed in early *Oprah*.[83] The revulsion with which the misery show was greeted by the era's television critics and social moralists suggests that these programs rendered the repressed visible, thus charting the "contradictions of the social field."[84]

Near the end of 1953, this very revulsion against the exploitation of misery gained a momentum that *Glamour Girl* could not withstand.[85] NBC in particular continued to debate suitable standards of taste and decency for its daytime offerings. When columnist John Crosby criticized the show again in the *New York Herald Tribune* on October 9, 1953, Sarnoff remained mum, but Barry reproached Samish again by asking, "[S]houldn't we be the 'Happy Glamourizers'[?]"[86] Within this uncertain corporate climate, efforts to sanitize the program through happier glamorization or inspirational lessons were too little, too late. *Glamour Girl* aired its final episode on January 8, 1954, just as the network's chief of programming, Sylvester "Pat" Weaver, well known for advocating the high-brow production strategy he called "Operation Frontal Lobes," was planning the launch of an ambitious new show for women called *Home*, in the same timeslot.[87]

Among the daytime misery shows that captivated audiences during the 1950s, *Glamour Girl* stands out for so faithfully articulating the terms of the era's misery/makeover equation. For women accustomed to "girl talk," the formula of *Glamour Girl* served to communicate the shared hazards of women caught up in a newly revived patriarchy and to record every day a discontent that glamour could hold in abeyance only for another decade.

ABBREVIATION

NBCR The National Broadcasting Company, Inc. Records, 1921–1969, Wisconsin Historical Society, Madison, WI.

NOTES

1. Sid Shalit, "Diamonds in Rough Polished Up," clipping in NBCR, Box 368, Folder 60.
2. Karal Ann Marling, *As Seen on TV: The Visual Culture of Everyday Life in the 1950s* (Cambridge: Harvard University Press, 1994), p. 15.
3. Adrian Samish to Frederic Wile, memorandum, June 4, 1953, NBCR, Box 368, Folder 60; Ernest Theiss to "List Below," memorandum, June 11, 1953, NBCR, Box 368, Folder 60.
4. Kathy Peiss, *Hope in a Jar: The Making of America's Beauty Culture* (New York: Metropolitan Books, Henry Holt and Co., 1998), p. 144.
5. "Glamour Girl" pamphlet, attached to John Porter to "All Salesmen," memorandum, July 27, 1953, NBCR, Box 397, Folder 40.
6. Quoted in Marling, pp. 14–15.
7. *The Oxford Dictionary of New Words* (New York: Oxford University Press, 1991), p. 189.
8. Peiss, *Hope in a Jar*, p. 144.
9. Ibid., pp. 127 and 145.
10. Ibid., p. 144.

11. Michele Hilmes, *Radio Voices: American Broadcasting, 1922–1952* (Minneapolis: University of Minnesota Press, 1997), pp. 52, 148–149.

12. Marling, pp. 10, 15.

13. Quoted in Marling, p. 9.

14. Marling, p. 15.

15. Peiss, *Hope in a Jar*, p. 244–246.

16. Ibid., pp. 245, 248.

17. Ibid., p. 248.

18. Marling, p. 15.

19. Steven C. Runyon, "San Francisco's First Television Station: KPIX," in *Television in America: Local Station History from Across the Nation*, ed. Michael D. Murray and Donald G. Godfrey, 364–365 (Ames: Iowa State University Press, 1997).

20. "Individually Yours," *Variety Review Book*, March 9, 1949.

21. David Weinstein, "Women's Shows and the Selling of Television to Washington, DC," *Washington History* 11, no. 1 (Spring/Summer 1999): 17–19.

22. Royal to CCB, memorandum, May 18, 1953, NBCR, Box 368, Folder 60.

23. Richard Harper Graham to James E. Denning, memorandum, April 24, 1953, NBCR, Box 368, Folder 60.

24. See Richard Harper Graham to Scott Shott, Legal, memorandum, June 11, 1953; Phillips Carlin to Charles Barry, October 6, 1953; and John Rayel to Wayne Haydun, August 31, 1953, NBCR, Box 368, Folder 60.

25. *Strike It Rich* (1951–1958), *Stand Up and Be Counted* (1956–1957), *On Your Account* (1953–1956), *Turn to a Friend* (1953), *Welcome Travelers* (1955–1956), and *Queen for a Day* were considered other prominent examples.

26. See Marsha Cassidy, *What Women Watched: Daytime Television in the 1950s* (Austin, TX: University of Texas Press, 2005), chapter 5.

27. Mimi White, *Tele-Advising: Therapeutic Discourse in American Television* (Chapel Hill, NC: University of North Carolina Press, 1992), see pp. 8, 10, 67, 181.

28. For a fuller discussion of *Queen for a Day*, one of America's most notorious and long-running misery shows, see Cassidy, *What Women Watched*, pp. 40–43 and 185–194, and Amber Watts in this volume.

29. Los Angeles, California. Radio and Television Archives, University of California at Los Angeles. *Glamour Girl*, NBC, October 1, 1953, Videotape VA6095T. The three episodes of *Glamour Girl* recorded on this videotape were filmed on three consecutive days during October 1953, when Jack McCoy first replaced Harry Babbitt as the program's host.

30. *Glamour Girl*, NBC, October 2, 1953, UCLA, Videotape VA 6095T.

31. Ibid., NBC, October 3, 1953.

32. Ibid.

33. Elaine Tyler May, *Homeward Bound: American Families in the Cold War Era* (New York: Basic Books, 1988), pp. 173–174.

34. *Glamour Girl*, October 1, 1953, UCLA.

35. Ibid.

36. Hal Humphrey, "It's a Great Gimmick," *Mirror*, clipping in NBCR, Box 368, Folder 60.

37. Maria LaPlace, "Producing and Consuming the Woman's Film: Discursive Struggle in *Now, Voyager*," in *Home Is Where the Heart Is: Studies in Melodrama and the Woman's Film*, ed. Christine Gledhill (London: British Film Institute, 1994), p. 144 .

38. See Alisia G. Chase in this volume.

39. Mary Desjardins, "Maureen O'Hara's 'Confidential' Life: Recycling Stars Through Gossip and Moral Biography," in *Small Screens, Big Ideas: Television in the 1950s*, ed. Janet Thumim (London: I.B. Tauris, 2002), pp. 12–13 .

40. *Glamour Girl*, October 2, 1953, UCLA.

41. Denise Mann, "The Spectacularization of Everyday Life: Recycling Hollywood Stars and Fans in Early Television Variety Shows," in *Private Screenings: Television and the Female Consumer*, ed. Lynn Spigel and Denise Mann (Minneapolis: University of Minnesota Press, 1992), p. 47.

42. Mann, pp. 49–59.

43. *Glamour Girl*, October 1, 1953, UCLA.

44. Samish to Jack McCoy, telegram, August 26, 1953, NBCR, Box 368, Folder 60.

45. "Glamour Girl" pamphlet.

46. Ibid.

47. Adrian Samish to Sydney Eigers, memorandum, July 31, 1953, NBCR, Box 368, Folder 60.

48. Clippings of these reviews were found in NBCR, Box 368, Folder 60.

49. Undated clipping, NBCR, Box 368, Folder 60.

50. Ibid.

51. "Glamour Girl" pamphlet.

52. Val Adams, "NBC's Morning Show, 'Glamour Girl,' Called a New Twist in Exploiting Human Misery, *New York Times* August 21, 1953, clipping in NBCR, Box 368, Folder 60.

53. For a fuller discussion, see Cassidy, *What Women Watched*, pp. 15–16, 157–159.

54. Adams, " 'Glamour Girl,' . . . Called a New Twist in Exploiting Human Misery."

55. Ibid.

56. "Outlook: Sarnoff to Steer NBC for Remainder of Year," *Broadcasting/Telecasting* August 3, 1953: 71.

57. Sarnoff to John K. Herbert, memorandum August 21, 1953, NBCR, Box 368, Folder 60.

58. For an interesting look at how much "misery" was considered acceptable on *Queen for a Day*, see Amber Watts.

59. Samish to Chas. Barry, memorandum, August 24, 1953, NBCR, Box 368, Folder 60. See Cassidy, *What Women Watched*, chapter 5, for a full discussion of this correspondence.

60. Adrian Samish to Jack McCoy, August 21, 1953, NBCR, Box 368, Folder 60.

61. Samish to Barry, August 24, 1953.

62. Adrian Samish to Jack McCoy, August 24, 1953, NBCR, Box 368, Folder 60.

63. Barry to General Sarnoff, memorandum, August 27, 1953, NBCR, Box 368, Folder 60.

64. Samish to Barry, August 24, 1953.

65. Frank Cooper to Charles C. Barry, October 6, 1953, NBCR, Box 368, Folder 60.

66. Ibid., October 19, 1953.

67. Frank Cooper to Adrian Samish, October 23, 1953, NBCR, Box 368, Folder 60.

68. " 'Glamour Girl' Draws 30,000 Letters in One Week," Television Sales Promotion, October 16, 1953, NBCR, Box 397, Folder 40.

69. "Second Week Mail Response," Television Sales Promotion, October 23, 1953, NBCR, Box 397, Folder 40.

70. Adrian Samish to Jack McCoy, September 2, 1953, Box 368, Folder 60.

71. See Jack Gould, "TV's Misery Shows," *Sunday New York Times*, February 7, 1954: 11.

72. Mary Ellen Brown, "Motley Moments: Soap Operas, Carnival, Gossip, and the Power of the Utterance" in *Television and Women's Culture: The Politics of the Popular*, ed. Mary Ellen Brown (London: Sage, 1990), p. 204.

73. Peiss, *Hope in a Jar*, p. 55.

74. Brown, "Motley Moments," p. 206.

75. *Glamour Girl*, October 1, 1953, UCLA.

76. Ibid., October 2, 1953.

77. Ibid., October 3, 1953.

78. Ibid., October 1, 1953.

79. Humphrey, "It's a Great Gimmick."

80. Shalit, "Diamonds in Rough Polished Up."

81. *Glamour Girl* October 2, 1953, UCLA.

82. Thomas Elsaesser, "Tales of Sound and Fury: Observations on the Family Melodrama," in *Imitations of Life: A Reader on Film and Television Melodrama*, ed. Marcia Landy (Detroit: Wayne State University Press, 1991), pp. 88–89 .

83. Gloria Jean Masciarotte, "C'mon, Girl: Oprah Winfrey and the Discourse of Feminine Talk," *Genders* 11 (1991): 83.

84. Masciarotte, "C'mon, Girl," p. 103.

85. See Cassidy, *What Women Watched*, chapter 5.

86. All that remains of this final correspondence is a one-page summary of the Herbert-Barry-Samish communication, marked "751," NBCR, Box 368, Folder 60.

87. See Cassidy, *What Women Watched*, chapter 6.

CHAPTER 9

QUEEN FOR A DAY: REMAKING CONSUMER CULTURE, ONE WOMAN AT A TIME

AMBER WATTS

QUEEN FOR A DAY, THE MOST POPULAR DAYTIME PROGRAM IN AMERICA in the late 1950s, billed itself as "the Cinderella show," where every day, a woman's wishes would come true. The Mexican Department of Labor, however, viewed it very differently. In August 1960, the department issued an official statement that *Queen for a Day* should be banned. The rather pointed criticism said that the show "accentuate[d] the exhibition of human sorrow for commercial ends," adding that the prizes themselves were excessive and inappropriate. What good is an expensive vacation when a family cannot afford shoes, they asked, or "an electric refrigerator in a one-room shack?"[1] The show stayed on the air for another four years in America, this censure notwithstanding, but the Mexican Labor Department's statement encapsulates a number of key ideas about *Queen for a Day*'s significance within postwar North American media. The show integrated pathos and product plugs into a seamless narrative, in which there was a direct correlation between the alleviation of misery and the acquisition of consumer goods, even if the goods were potentially useless for the recipient. While the *Queen for a Day* contestants' incessant tales of misfortune appear to challenge the post–World War II mythos of middle-class domestic bliss, the show simultaneously rearticulated the agenda it deflated, offering each contestant a glorious transformation via rampant consumerism, the "solution" to all problems. In this way, *Queen for a Day* positioned itself as the ultimate makeover, where the winner's physical *and* material selves could be reincorporated into middle-class society, a makeover that nonetheless served a larger commercial agenda.

Los Angeles housewife Clarice Singer was chosen to appear as a contestant on an episode of *Queen for a Day* (October 9, 1960), and, when prompted by host Jack Bailey, she told her story. Eight years earlier, her brother had been mistaken for someone else and shot five times in the back, leaving him paralyzed from the waist down. Because of the chronic pain, he was forced to always remain lying on his stomach. He lived with their mother who, now in her late seventies, had "sugar diabetes and high blood pressure, and could go at any minute." Singer wished for a special wheeled bed to help her brother get around and take care of their ailing mother.

After a fashion show, several commercials, and innumerable product plugs, the studio audience voted by applause-o-meter for their favorite candidate. Singer was crowned Queen after receiving more applause than others: a woman who wanted a washer/dryer in order to take in laundry and pay bills accumulated during her husband's unemployment, the housewife desiring educational toys for her brain-damaged son, and the mother of five asking for a hole in the ceiling to heat her children's bedrooms. Jack Bailey led the tearful woman to her throne, where he draped her in ermine, handed her four dozen roses supplied by Carl's of Hollywood, and showered her with prizes. She not only received a Baumgartner hydro-level cot, which Bailey told her was "designed to make life easier for paralyzed patients and provide the ultimate comfort in the process," but also all the clothes from the episode's fashion show, a day of pampering that included a tour of MGM studios, dinner, and a night on the town, a dinette set, a tape recorder, eight place settings of silver, her own twin canopy bed, a food processor, a washer/dryer, a gift certificate for the Spiegel catalogue, and, as a special surprise, a trip to Tennessee to visit her mother and brother—a prize package worth over $2,550.

Such was a typical episode of *Queen for a Day*, which premiered on the Mutual radio network in 1945, was simulcast by a local Los Angeles television station in the late 1940s, and was televised nationally from 1956 to 1964, first on NBC and later, after 1960, on ABC. Every weekday, producers chose four or five women from the 800 or so audience members in Hollywood's Moulin Rouge Theater to be contestants. Each would get a chance to tell her often tragic life story and describe one specific product that would ameliorate her situation. The audience would then determine the winner, that day's Queen, who was almost inevitably the woman with the saddest, or at least the most sympathy-inducing, story.[2] The winner received her desired item plus thousands of dollars worth of other sundry prizes, which the show was always pleased to enumerate for viewers at home. By 1961, the show had given away 2,282 washing machines, 918 vacuum cleaners, 1,334 refrigerators, and 137 hearing aids to its winners, the sum total of which averaged over $1,200,000 a year.[3] This unrivaled combination of pathos and rampant consumerism was a boon for NBC's daytime lineup. In 1957, it averaged a 12.3 rating, peaking at a 13.8 in its last 15 minutes, when not only would the Queen be crowned, but also her prizes described in detail—a boon for their advertisers, as well.[4]

Historians are not quite sure what to make of *Queen for a Day*. It has been called both one of the "best TV games of the fifties" and one of the "worst TV shows ever."[5] When *Queen for a Day* was on the air, the press seemed equally ambivalent about its status. When the show first debuted on NBC, Jack Gould reported that "the awfulness lasted thirty minutes," lamenting, "What hath Sarnoff wrought?"[6] Close to a decade later, Cleveland Armory claimed that "it is, literally, miserable."[7] Most of *Queen for a Day's* press coverage was not so blatantly disparaging, however—the general tone was rather somewhere between amusement and bewilderment. Many critics focused on the sheer emotionality of the program. *Variety* pointed out the number of "emotional tugs that are tossed aplenty to the setowning [sic] hausfraus."[8] *Time* described a candidate "obviously teetering on the brink of a good cry" as having "all the tearmarks of a winner," while Armory pithily stated that *Queen for a Day* was "a bawl."[9] The show was indeed a site for the female confession and emotional display that elicited derision from its critics. At the same time, however, they were equally focused on, and seemingly in awe of, the Queen's prizes. When press articles described an individual show, they inevitably concluded with a list of the winner's rewards.[10] Many enumerated the total amount of merchandise the show had given to all its winners up to that point. By the time *Queen for a Day* was cancelled, for example, the 5,000-plus winners had received nearly $23 million in gifts.[11] Even more bemused were critics who listed some of the more unusual requests winners had received, including a wooden leg for a performing duck and an army surplus Flying Fortress.[12] The prizes were just as important as, if not more important than, the sob stories to the critics. At its heart, as its press reveals, *Queen for a Day* was essentially about two things: pathos and products. The critical contempt for the pathos may say more about male critics' reactions to female emotional display than the show itself. When this contempt for emotionalism is coupled with the same critics' fascination with *Queen for a Day's* multitude of prizes, however, the combination hints at the show's larger implications.

The Mexican Labor Department's condemnation of *Queen for a Day* tied together the show's interweaving of pathos and product plugs in a very clear way, showing how the former was put to use in the service of the latter. The contestants' sob stories were necessary to underscore the importance of the products, and the two were tightly intertwined within the structure of the show. In part, this interdependence may explain early television critics' discomfort with the emotionality of *Queen for a Day*. Even if the contestants' pleas were genuine, the women's ultimate goal was to win merchandise, while the show's goal was to sell network advertising and the products it plugged. Emotional display, for both parties, became a means to a commercial end. However, the metamorphosis that the show promised its contestants and, by proxy, viewers, not only spoke to the fantasy of commodity consumption but also hinted at certain very real social conditions of the postwar era.

Queen for a Day premiered on Mutual radio just as World War II was coming to an end, and it is in many ways a product of its time. The show's portrait of women's material transformation fed into, and off, the myriad social and economic changes facing postwar America and its renewed focus on middle-class family life. Beginning in World War II, both marriage and birth rates climbed steadily for all social groups. More couples married, and at younger ages, than ever before, and each woman had, on average, 3.2 children, up from the 2.4 children born of women who came of age in the 1930s.[13] The number of new families, coupled with the mass migration to the suburbs, led to an increased focus on domesticity. In part, this resulted from the relative isolation of suburbia as compared to the urban communities many families left behind. Without the larger social structure of extended families and close neighborhoods as support, the home became the focus, and the nuclear family the core social unit for many suburbanites.

As historian Elaine Tyler May demonstrates, however, an equally large factor influencing the return to domesticity was the perceived need for security in an uncertain political era. The 1950s generation had distinct memories of the Depression and World War II, and the postwar era offered a new relative tranquility. Americans sought to keep it that way, both internationally and domestically, desiring above all "secure jobs, secure homes, and secure marriages in a secure country."[14] Thus, many postwar families applied the Cold War foreign policy of containment as protection against communism, with a slightly different inflection, to the domestic sphere. The Cold War certainly produced its own anxieties for Americans, but the cohesive nuclear family became its own protection against—as well as something to protect from—the uncertainties of the outside world. The domestic sphere was a haven and a respite, especially for the "Organization Men" who worked outside the home, and a major source of personal fulfillment for the American middle class in the postwar era.[15]

As the marriage and birth rates rose, so did the percentage of Americans in the middle class. In *The Mass Consumption Society*, behavioral economist George Katona discusses the increased affluence of the United States after World War II. During and after World War II, class mobility became much more possible for Americans. After the Depression, according to Katona, almost everyone from every class improved their economic position (if not their percentage of the total collective American income), but the most notable increases were within what he calls "the discretionary-income group," or the middle class. Between 1929 and 1961, the number of family units in America increased by 55 percent, the overall national income 60 percent, but the percentage of those with discretionary income—families with the power to purchase more than basic needs on a regular basis—increased 400 percent.[16] Most Americans had more money to spend than ever before, and the number who could spend freely had quintupled. The result, Katona said, was a new kind of affluence—a middle-class society, where most people had the ability to buy what they wanted rather than solely what they needed to survive.[17] Because of their numbers and their purchasing power, the middle class became the ideal representation for all American families.

This movement toward middle-class domesticity brought about a number of changes in the meaning of women's social roles. In wartime, it had been women's patriotic duty to work. After the war, however, Rosie the Riveter was expelled from the factory and returned to the home, to make room for (and cook and clean for) the returning GIs. At the time, a number of discourses came together, from popular media to pop psychology to women's magazines, to endorse women's "natural" role as mothers and homemakers.[18] A woman's most important job became taking care of her family and home. The employed wife was either condemned by or annihilated from public discourse, in favor of the ideal housewife and mother. Many women did continue to work after World War II, however, and indeed 1955 saw more employed women in America than ever before.[19] However, in 1950, while 27 percent of women in the general population worked, only 9 percent of suburban women sought employment outside the home.[20] Indeed, it was this latter group of women—living as middle-class housewives in safe suburban homes—that best exemplified the ideal social role for postwar women.

The majority of contestants on *Queen for a Day* did not fit into this social or economic ideal, however, and their stories certainly seem to indicate how unrealistic the image of postwar domestic tranquility was for many people. As Georganne Scheiner points out, most candidates were from the lower-middle or working classes, a large number of the women worked, and many were in severe financial distress. Their pleas for help showed that not everyone was, or could be, a middle-class suburban housewife. In addition, they demonstrated the dearth of options for women, particularly single mothers and widows, to change unacceptable domestic and economic situations.[21] The wishes of each potential Queen—wishes that in the episodes sampled included a prosthetic leg for the contestant's brother who was hit by a drunk driver, a crib for a par- alyzed child, two wheelchairs, a wedding dress for the contestant's daughter, and the aforementioned hole in the ceiling—demonstrated a need that, albeit material, was indicative of a larger issue. Each contestant, whether as the result of her own failing or of extenuating circumstances, had lost some degree of control over her proper social role as wife and mother of happy, healthy children. The contestant asking for the hole was unable to provide a warm house for her family; the woman who needed a wedding dress did not have the means to launch her daughter into the social sphere. Women with handicapped children often appeared on the show, as did political émigrés who had been forced to leave their children behind the Iron Curtain.[22] Although neither disability nor politics were within a woman's control, the contestants' inabilities to ameliorate their situations (by obtaining the equipment to help the child in one case, or physically obtaining the child in the other) signified a general powerlessness within their capacities to be the best mothers they could be.

Ironically, the winning Queen would often be the one least in control of her social sphere. Viva Birch, crowned Queen on October 17, 1960, wished for a wheelchair and special bike for her son with cerebral palsy. She had promised him these things, but her husband's sales job was in jeopardy, she needed knee surgery and had lost *her* job as a waitress, and they were thus unable to alleviate their son's problems. Mrs. Birch's inconsistencies with the ideal middle-class family structure were myriad. Not only was she unable to fully take care of her incapacitated son, but she herself was also incapacitated. She had worked outside of the home but could not do so anymore, even though her family was without a steady income. Mrs. Birch's description of her life presents a sharp contrast to the postwar ideal, although the two are not necessarily in opposition. Mrs. Birch clearly loved her son. Like all *Queen* contestants, she *wanted* to provide for her family but she could not. It was this desire to be the best mother possible, to recover some degree of her depleted social and economic role, that ostensibly appealed to the audience, who crowned Mrs. Birch Queen.[23] *Queen for a Day*'s contestants' stories certainly showcased myriad difficulties and constraints associated with postwar domesticity. Ultimately, however, the show reasserted the importance of women's inscribed social roles by articulating the need to reclaim them.

In the same vein as other 1950s "misery shows" such as *Strike It Rich* and *Glamour Girl*, *Queen for a Day* allowed American women to hear types of stories that were normally ignored by mainstream media, thus making usually invisible social contradictions visible. In addition, as Marsha Cassidy argues about *Glamour Girl* in this volume, *Queen for a Day* opened up the possibility for mediated "feminine discourse," where women spoke to other women about their troubles in a public forum.[24] However, *Queen for a Day*, both structurally and affectively, mitigated the potential for defiance that feminine discourse can offer by framing the stories within a light game show format and placing the audience in a position of judgment.

The use of the contestants' hard luck stories on *Queen for a Day* seems to serve a dual purpose. At one level, their pleas had the potential to induce a kind of *schadenfreudic* attraction for the viewer at home. Certainly not all 1950s housewives were happy with their role. The secure home, working men's leisure space, was for women the site of both work *and* leisure and, as Elaine Tyler May indicates, of much unspoken isolation and discontent. The postwar ideal of domestic containment could have literal implications for the housewife. Women were much more likely than men to report dissatisfaction with their marriages, and much less likely to rate their mental health as "excellent" on survey questions.[25] The reaction to being a housewife was occasionally more than mere resentment, for married women in the 1950s experienced a considerably higher rate of schizophrenic episodes than their male counterparts, often stemming from the housewife's isolation from familial and social connections.[26] *Queen for a Day* contestants, however, almost inevitably had it worse than the average suburban housewife, and surely there was a pleasure to be found in hearing their stories.

John Portmann has called *schadenfreude* "the emotional manifestation of beliefs about justice," an almost puritanical pleasure in seeing punishment meted out to those who deserve it, without having to mete it out oneself.[27] In a way, *Queen for a Day* was a show inherently about justice—in terms of both the injustice of the contestants' situations, and the eventual judgment given by the audience voting on the winner. The nature of the contestants' stories, so focused on breaches of social and economic contracts, often sounded like real-life punishments in and of themselves. Even worse, however, was that the women were in a position where they needed to go on national television and enumerate their problems for millions of viewers to try to repair the breach. For the contestants, it was a double punishment; for the audience, a double judgment. There was the encouragement to judge which contestant was most worthy of winning, of course, but the format also encouraged viewer judgment in a more general sense: namely, weighing the merits of contestants' lives against their own. Perhaps part of the spectatorship position, then, was similar to what Neal Gabler has described as the lure of talk shows: "the reassurance of our superiority over the guests and over the programs themselves."[28] Indeed, *Queen for a Day*'s format encouraged this view by putting the audience in a position of judgment. If a housewife was unhappy with her social role, watching *Queen for a Day* could serve as a reminder that there were worse positions to be in. At least she was not competing on the show, nor did she need to. By making judgments about contestants and enjoying the search for the worst possible sob story, she could feel distinct moral superiority over the participants. However, this trace of power was contingent on the viewer not falling into the same hardship as the contestants. The ultimate result was that experiencing *schadenfreudic* pleasures while watching *Queen for a Day* made one complicit with the meanings of her own social role—otherwise, there could be no superiority attached to judging those who failed to achieve it.

At the same time, and for similar reasons, *Queen for a Day* pleas could also act as a warning of what could potentially happen if a woman stepped outside her role. If, as May indicates, postwar families desired security above all else, *Queen for a Day* showed myriad situations in which circumstance could quickly erode a secure foundation. For many reasons and in many ways, contestants' lives failed to live up to the ideal. Their appeals showed not only the difficulties of trying to do so, but also the hardships suffered when one could not. Viewers looking for security, then, could compare their own lives to both the contestants' sob stories and the ideal; almost certainly, even for an unhappy housewife, the ideal would be more desirable. While *Queen for a Day* did indeed reveal inconsistencies among postwar social ideals, it simultaneously reaffirmed the importance of trying to live within them.

Even though the show depended on contestants' sad stories—and many *were* upsetting, if one took the time to think about them—the misery rarely got out of control. Despite what the 1950s television critics wrote about *Queen for a Day*, Jack Bailey did his best to keep women from crying, at least until they won (for how could one *not* cry at the multitude of prizes?). Marsha Cassidy has described his interview style as "a glib folksiness that rapidly alternated between humor and gravity."[29] Bailey would extract a contestant's pathetic story from her, carefully guiding each step of its narration, while simultaneously interjecting his own quips and one-liners to keep it light.[30] On one 1962 episode, for example, Bailey skillfully bantered a contestant away from tears. Lillian Ayres wanted a record player for her 15-year-old son, who had just had open-heart surgery. As she began to tell her story, her voice broke, and she was visibly close to crying. Bailey asked Ayres for her son's name (Ayres said, "Chester." Bailey cheerfully responded, "Old Chet"), his age, and what type of music he liked, and joked with her until she calmed down. As soon as she was smiling, as Bailey complained about "that new 'Twist' junk" the kids listened to, he interrupted himself to say, "You see how I moved in on you? You were going to start sniveling here, and I was going to have to take you out to the chicken house and talk to you about that." For the rest of the interview, Mrs. Ayres smiled.

In a 1957 *TV Guide* interview, Jack Bailey said about "the sob stuff," "I just don't let it happen if I can possibly help it."[31] In fact, despite the need for good stories, *Queen for a Day* producers shied away from women who would be *too* emotional, or whose stories were too sad. Contestants were always chosen from the day's studio audience. Upon entering the studio, each woman wrote what she would wish for on an index card. Producers read each card and shortened the list to the 25 most likely candidates; Bailey would then speak with each of the 25 and, on the basis of those interviews, choose the finalists. In the 1957 interview, Bailey stated that "a woman who looks as though she'll really break down doesn't get picked as one of the five daily contestants."[32] Howard Blake, a former producer, concurred, noting that many stories were too pathetic to make it to the air. He cited a number of "wish cards" that expressed desires too sad or too bizarre for television. One potential contestant wished for $100 for a divorce, because, as she put it, "Husband attempted rape on my 6-year-old daughter, then left with money and car. Must be divorced so I can testify against him in court."[33] Another wanted a new mattress because her husband had recently died in bed. Yet another said she wanted "a typewriter or a recording machine. Because my husband hit me over the head with a shoe and completely paralyzed me for seven-and-a-half months. It left me with my right side paralyzed and I am a writer."[34] Despite *Queen for a Day*'s reliance on stories of need, some were too dismal for daytime TV.

What this balance between Jack Bailey's patter and sad-but-not-*too*-sad stories created was a show borne of misery that could still be taken lightly— in part not only because there would be a happy ending, at least for the winner, but also because of its aversion to emotional excess. While the show's premise depended on tales of woe, it did not dwell on them, except superficially. Candidate interviews rarely lasted for more than two and a half minutes, at least one minute of which consisted of light banter between the woman and Bailey. Bailey always concluded interviews with either a joke or a compliment for the contestant—he told Lillian Ayres, "You're a swell mother," for example, before she left the stage—thus ending on a positive note. The audience's position as decision-makers likely mitigated the immediate impact of the candidates' stories even further. Because the show was a competition, the viewer weighed the relative merits of each candidate's narrative, and would ultimately root for whomever she felt to be the most deserving. Whether that contestant won or lost, the show's competitive nature refocused attention from the stories themselves to the candidates as game show contestants vying for prizes. *Queen for a Day* thus rewrote the *schadenfreudic* dynamic of misery-as-punishment as misery-for-merit through the game show format. The focus, then, would be more on the *idea* of misery-for-merit than on the particular implications of each contestants' misery. Certainly, the underlying themes of pathos and insecurity lingered behind *Queen for a Day*'s game show sensibility, but the final effect was not wholly one of sadness. The result was that a viewer could take pleasure in the sob stories without feeling any guilt about a *schadenfreudic* enjoyment of the contestants' misfortunes. The forced lightness of contestants' storytelling, along with the Queen's happy ending, created a narrative that elicited feelings of superiority without delving too deeply into any of the social problems contestants' situations hinted at. The stories could still be a site of judgment and a mild warning, without either dynamic creating any outright moral anxiety for the audience. Candidates' stories were necessary within *Queen for a Day*'s narrative as an excuse for prize-giving. However, holding back both emotion and the potential for social inquiry made it possible for both participants and audiences to believe in the power of the prizes.

Indeed, the greatest factor mitigating the pathos was the prizes. By the end of each episode, the effect of *Queen for a Day* was a feeling of consumerism gone mad. Product plugs abounded. Each episode's fashion show featured the elegant Jeanne Cagney's detailed narration as six or seven women modeled the latest styles, complete with jewelry, perfume, and the inevitable pair of Mojud stockings. Each losing contestant would receive at least two small appliances as a consolation prize. The spoils of the Queen herself, usually totaling well over $2,000, invariably included a washer/dryer or refrigerator, furniture, tableware, and a vacation, *plus* the items from the fashion show, *plus* whatever she had wished for. All of these items were described in as much detail as time allowed by a frenetic Jack Bailey and announcer Gene Baker; all were wonderful; and, as was made clear, all were available for the viewer to purchase for her own home, in order to feel like a queen, if not be one. The Queen's excitement at winning often seemed to increase in accordance with the quantity of prizes bestowed upon her, and it would be difficult not to associate her happiness with commodity consumption.

At one level, of course, *Queen for a Day*'s rapid-fire commercial sensibility served a straightforward economic purpose for its producers. Because of the show's popularity, advertisers for both home products and larger durable goods filled a months-long waiting list in order to pay to get a plug on the show. The result was that the more "gifts" given to the Queen and runners-up, the more money the show would make. One episode from the early 1950s included 52 product plugs in half an hour, not including the five commercial breaks. When *Queen for a Day* expanded to 45 minutes in 1956, only 15 minutes of the show were actually devoted to the contestants' confessionals and audience voting; the other 30 were consumed with plugs, further increasing the show's revenue while still maintaining its original format.[35] Producer Ray Morgan netted $5,000 a week himself from advertisers' money.[36] In short, the product plugs paid.

Implicit in each contestant's story was the idea that a specific product could solve her problems, which, according to Blake, was another opportunity for advertising. Although many potential candidates needed doctors or lawyers, producers could never find any medical or legal professionals who would work in exchange for a plug, so these women were never chosen. Rather, in order to be selected, contestants had to want something that could be received in exchange for free advertising.[37] Eliminating the possibility of nonpluggable wishes resulted in a narrative in which commodity consumption solved all problems. Each contestant claimed to need only one commercial product, the lack of which encapsulated, and the acquisition of which would surely fix, the major problems in her life. Her specific issue could thus instantly be taken care of with a phone call to "Carl Woodall, maker of artificial limbs," for example.[38] As a bonus, her acquisition of the multitude of other prizes would, in theory, secure her future happiness and ensure that her problems would not resurface. The products plugged on the show were thus intertwined with the contestants' hard luck stories into a seamless narrative, presenting a problem and offering a clear solution. If the contestants' pleas for help were a warning about the dangers of losing control, the solution became one of prevention through consumption. In the *Queen for a Day* narrative, commodities could solve all problems, no matter how severe, so the best way to avoid personal crisis was to buy more. Merchandise was thus equated with security as well as a return to the stable nuclear family. Recovery of self-control could be purchased.

The consumerist implications of *Queen for a Day* were not out of line with other contemporary discourses. George Katona named postwar America a "mass consumption society," in which, as never before, consumers themselves were a major factor in economic growth.[39] As Gary Cross and George Lipsitz have noted, the transition from a booming wartime economy to one equally successful in peacetime brought about certain changes in both federal economic practices and citizens' status as consumers. Business leaders at the time sought to invigorate the postwar economy primarily through increased federal spending, exports, and consumer debt. They believed a 30 to 50 percent growth in consumer spending was necessary in order to jumpstart the economy. Increased consumption allowed for the creation of new jobs, and would eventually offset consumers' initial postwar debts—largely mortgages—and stabilize the federal economy.[40] Personal spending thus became "a patriotic duty," as well as the discursive antithesis to communism.[41] And consumption did increase dramatically in the postwar era, particularly in terms of household goods. Consumer spending itself increased 60 percent between 1945 and 1950, but purchases of household goods went up 240 percent.[42] In this case, consumerism and domestic containment ideologies were in perfect synch. Richard Nixon and Nikita Khrushchev's 1959 "kitchen debate," where Nixon argued the supremacy of capitalism by showing the supremacy of the suburban kitchen, made this ideology explicit.[43] According to Nixon, Americans' ability to purchase products for the home inched the country ahead in the Cold War; consumerism was anticommunism. Buying household goods could embody national security while simultaneously providing consumers with secure home lives.

The commercial media was an important promoter of consumerism. Indeed, as Lipsitz indicates, the postwar broadcast media was a key site for advancing a consumerist agenda, particularly on the urban ethnic sitcoms popular on radio and television in the late 1940s and early 1950s. Shows such as

The Goldbergs, Life with Luigi, and *Mama,* which focused on working-class immigrant family life, helped Americans transition from a wary Depression-era mentality into the new consumer society. By invoking characters whose lives could be vastly improved through commodity culture, advertisers could highlight the joys of consumerism within the body of a show as well as during commercial breaks. Immigrant characters could be taught about their new economic conditions without the instruction patronizing the audience—even if viewers needed to learn the same lesson. Episodes of *Life with Luigi,* for example, included detailed instructions on how to open a bank account and receive a department store credit card.[44] Because the title character was a childlike immigrant, these lectures were not out of place in the narrative, but they clearly existed for the audience's benefit as well. Many episodes of working-class comedies focused on consumption as the means to achieve happiness and economic mobility. A conflict about the run-down furniture in the Goldbergs' home, for example, is resolved when mother Molly restores family unity by purchasing a new living room set through Macy's installment plan. Buying durable goods on credit therefore becomes the route to contentment. By showcasing characters learning the American way of life, these shows both instructed viewers and legitimated their new social and economic conditions.[45]

Queen for a Day functioned in a similar way, although its pedagogy was less explicit. The show never specifically instructed the audience about how to get store credit, but rather showed viewers the security a middle-class consumer lifestyle could offer, especially when compared to the alternatives. Watching working-class women plea for products to reclaim their social roles reinforced not only the importance of the roles but also the importance of merchandise in maintaining them. Contestants' product-based wishes were rooted in the less material fantasy of a problem-free life, and the winner's prizes promised her this stability in the future via entry into a middle-class consumer lifestyle. Viewers who were better off than *Queen for a Day* contestants, who were already middle-class consumers and did not *need* products in the same way, were similarly encouraged to enter into the fantasy of consumption the show presented. Even if one did not require an economic transformation, new products could still make dreams come true, or prevent nightmares from happening.

That *Queen for a Day* called itself "the Cinderella show" underscores the importance of fantasy within the show; for if Jack Bailey was your fairy godmother, you too would live happily ever after. However, unlike Cinderella's pre-ball makeover, the transformation on *Queen for a Day* was a material, rather than physical, one. Winners always got the clothes from the fashion show, and their "day of pampering" always began with a haircut, but what the show truly made over was their material existences through the products they received. As the Mexican Department of Labor statement implied, the

Queen's material transformation—in real life, at least—was probably not always perfect. Because producers kept the show "light," however, viewers would be much less likely to dwell on the fact that, as the Labor Department pointed out, a trip to Acapulco would not be a long-term solution to a severely troubled woman's problems. Mrs. Viola Netherland, a 1950 winner, complained to the *Chicago Daily Tribune* 10 weeks after her coronation, "I feel as though I've been put through a wringer." Netherland, a widow living in a converted chicken coop with her two teenage children, had won based on her request for a graduation dress for her daughter. After the broadcast, she was bombarded with phone calls and letters from *Queen for a Day* viewers across the country, even though she claimed she had not won that much. A welfare worker came to investigate, and her monthly Children's Aid payments were subsequently halved. Although Netherland said the prizes were welcome, she vehemently stated that she "would not go through a similar experience."[46] Clearly, this was not the "happily ever after" scenario that *Queen for a Day* promised. The annoyance of dealing with phone calls from strangers combined with her reduced income seems to argue the opposite, in fact—her life very well may have gotten worse.

Netherland's story may or may not be typical. It is difficult to tell, because *Queen for a Day*, unlike its contemporary, *Glamour Girl*, did not follow up with its winners. While *Queen for a Day* may have promised women the ultimate material transformation, this lack of follow-through made it a unique type of makeover. While traditional makeovers build to an eventual reveal—highlighting the process of moving from "before" to "after"—the "after" is only implied on *Queen for a Day*. Rather, it is the "before" that matters, the setting up of problems that material acquisition can fix; on the show's terms, the desirable "after" is sure to follow. How could someone's life *not* get significantly better with a new leg and a washer/dryer, especially if the lack of a leg prevents her from holding a job? Surely the absence of follow-ups on the show is related to the fact that the "after" might not be as wonderful as promised, but leaving each winner's story open-ended allowed for the possibility that it *could* be. *Queen for a Day* was thus ultimately more about the fantasy of transformation than the transformation itself, for the viewers and even for some queens.

For one 1950 winner, Catherine Schmidt from Chicago, the fantasy of her time as queen outweighed her material gains. Six months after her win, according to the *Chicago Daily Tribune*, her family responsibilities remained heavy, her sons were approaching draft age, and she was looking for a second part-time job to supplement her truck driver husband's income. However, she claimed that "the precious memories serve as a buffer. When things go wrong, I switch my mind back to the trip [to the show]."[47] Schmidt's win gave her the hot water heater she desperately needed, but more importantly, she received a permanent mental escape from day-to-day drudgery via the fantasy of her one day as royalty. Her "happily ever after" was a mental rather than material transformation, but it nevertheless improved her life in an apparently significant way. For the viewer at home, as well, it was possible to daydream a similar fantasy—not as a memory, like Schmidt's, but as a future investment. By encouraging viewers to dream about and wish for products that could solve their problems, the show highlighted the promise of material transformation through commodity consumption. On *Queen for a Day*, each Cinderella could do nothing *but* live happily ever after, and each viewer could learn to live like Cinderella on her own.

NOTES

1. "For the Record," *TV Guide (Southern California Edition)*, August 20, 1960.
2. A *TV Guide* interview with Jack Bailey described how the show's crew would wager each day on who would win. One episode's backstage favorite was the elderly schoolteacher who wanted books and records for her students. Ralph Widman, the still photographer, disagreed. He instead favored the mother of three with the ill husband who wanted groceries for a month, saying, "Woman can't stand to see kids go hungry." He was right; she, with the saddest story, won. "Jack Bailey: Mesmerizer of the Middle Aged," *TV Guide*, March 11, 1961.
3. "Jack Bailey: Mesmerizer of the Middle Aged," "The Stuff that Tears Are Made Of," *TV Guide*, June 22, 1957.
4. "TV's Hottest Battleground," *Sponsor*, May 14, 1957. Beginning in 1955, *Queen for a Day* ran for 45 minutes instead of half an hour, apparently to fit in the fashion show and more product plugs. The second highest-rated daytime program of this year, incidentally, was the CBS soap opera *Secret Storm*, with a 10.2.
5. See Maxene Fabe, *TV Game Shows* (New York: Doubleday, 1979) and Bart Andrews, *The Worst TV Shows Ever* (New York: E.P. Dutton, 1980).
6. Jack Gould, " 'Queen for a Day' Is Not for Crowning," *New York Times*, January 6, 1956.
7. Cleveland Armory, "Queen for a Day," *TV Guide*, March 7, 1964.
8. "Queen for a Day," *Variety*, January 11, 1956.
9. "Troubles & Bubbles," *Time*, April 15, 1957; Armory, "*Queen for a Day.*"
10. See, e.g., "Queen for a Day," *Variety*, January 11, 1956; "Troubles & Bubbles"; Larry Wolters, "Where to Dial Today," *Chicago Daily Tribune*, January 6, 1956; and Larry Wolters, "Joker Out as Queens Pick Queen," *Chicago Daily Tribune*, June 14, 1959.
11. Val Adams, " 'Queen for a Day' to End Reign of 20 Years Over Radio-TV," *New York Times*, August 26, 1964. Also see Larry Wolters, "Queens for Day Get 13 Million in Last Decade," *Chicago Daily Tribune*, May 21, 1955; "The Stuff that Tears Are Made Of," *TV Guide*.
12. "Troubles & Bubbles," Wolters, "Where to Dial Today."

13. Elaine Tyler May, *Homeward Bound: American Families in the Cold War Era* (New York: Basic Books, 1988), pp. 20, 137.

14. Ibid., p. 13.

15. Ibid., pp. 13–36.

16. George Katona, *The Mass Consumption Society* (New York: McGraw-Hill, 1964), pp. 13–14.

17. Ibid., pp. 5–6.

18. See, e.g., May; Lynn Spigel, *Make Room for TV* (Chicago: University of Chicago Press, 1992), Mary Beth Haralovich, "Sit-coms and Suburbs," in *Private Screenings: Television and the Female Consumer* (Minneapolis: University of Minnesota Press, 1992), and Susan Douglas, *Where the Girls Are* (New York: Random House, 1994).

19. "Employment of Women Reaches All-Time High in 1955," *Personnel Guidance Journal* 34, no. 6 (February 1956), p. 339.

20. Haralovich, "Sit-coms and Suburbs," p. 119.

21. Georganne Scheiner, "Would You Like to be Queen for a Day?: Finding a Working Class Voice in American Television of the 1950s," *Historical Journal of Film, Radio and Television* 23, no. 4 (2003): 380–381.

22. See "*Queen for a Day,*" *Variety*, January 11, 1956 and "Those 800 Babies," *TV Guide*, June 28, 1958.

23. Incidentally, one of the losers on this particular episode had lost control over her capability to run her household because she was *too good* of a mother. Mrs. Arlene Harding had three sons in the navy, who would bring at least a dozen friends home each weekend because the men enjoyed her cooking so much. She asked for bunk beds to put them up because she had run out of room in the house. Not surprisingly, she received the least applause.

24. See Cassidy in this volume.

25. May, *Homeward Bound*, pp. 193–203.

26. Jeffery Sconce, *Haunted Media* (Durham, NC: Duke University Press, 2000), p. 148.

27. John Portmann, *When Bad Things Happen to Other People* (New York: Routledge, 2000), p. 15.

28. Quoted in Joshua Gamson, *Freaks Talk Back* (Chicago: University of Chicago Press, 1998), p. 8.

29. Marsha F. Cassidy, "Visible Storytellers: Women Narrators on 1950s Daytime Television," *Style* 35, no. 2 (Summer 2001): 360.

30. Ibid., pp. 360–362.

31. "The Stuff That Tears Are Made Of," *TV Guide*.

32. Ibid.

33. Howard Blake, "An Apologia from the Man who Produced the Worst Program in TV History," in *American Broadcasting: A Source Book on the History of Radio and Television*, ed. Lawrence W. Lichty and Malachi C. Topping (New York: Hastings House, 1975), p. 418.

34. Ibid., pp. 418–419.

35. This was before the FCC regulation limiting the number of product plugs on a game show to no more than five "fee items" per half-hour.

36. Blake, "An Apologia," p. 416.
37. Ibid., p. 417.
38. Which occurred on the July 4, 1955 episode. To enhance the product plug, guest host Adolphe Menjou added, "You can be assured that if Mr. Woodall makes it, it's going to be right."
39. Katona, *The Mass Consumption Society*, p. 25.
40. George Lipsitz, "The Meaning of Memory" in *Time Passages: Collective Memory and American Popular Culture* (Minneapolis: University of Minnesota Press: 1990), pp. 44–47.
41. Gary Cross, *An All-Consuming Century: Why Commercialism Won in Modern America* (New York: Columbia University Press, 2000), pp. 138–139.
42. May, *Homeward Bound*, p. 165.
43. That the kitchen debate itself was a politically loaded product plug, engineered by then-PR consultant William Safire for a kitchen manufacturer client, only enhances the link between politics, business, and the patriotic meaning of consumption.
44. On the 1952 pilot and the 1953 episode "The Dress," Italian immigrant Luigi Basco receives five-minute lectures from bank and credit managers explaining, almost as if from a textbook, what banks do with money, and how the credit process works.
45. Lipsitz, "The Meaning of Memory," pp. 39–57.
46. Anton Remenih, "Queen for a Day Finds Crown Is Target for All," *Chicago Daily Tribune*, May 6, 1950.
47. Joan Beck, "Thrill Over Being Queen for a Day Lingers On," *Chicago Daily Tribune*, March 5, 1951.

BIBLIOGRAPHY

Adams, Val. " 'Queen for a Day' to End Reign of 20 Years Over Radio-TV," *New York Times*, August 26, 1964.
Andrews, Bart. *The Worst TV Shows Ever* (New York: E.P. Dutton, 1980).
Armory, Cleveland. "Queen for a Day," *TV Guide*, March 7, 1964.
Beck, Joan. "Thrill over Being Queen for a Day Lingers on," *Chicago Daily Tribune*, March 5, 1951.
Blake, Howard. "An Apologia from the Man who Produced the Worst Program in TV History," in *American Broadcasting: A Source Book on the History of Radio and Television*, ed. Lawrence W. Lichty and Malachi C. Topping (New York: Hastings House, 1975).
Cassidy, Marsha F. "Visible Storytellers: Women Narrators on 1950s Daytime Television," *Style* 35, no. 2 (Summer 2001).
Cross, Gary. *An All-Consuming Century: Why Commercialism Won in Modern America* (New York: Columbia University Press, 2000).
Douglas, Susan. *Where the Girls Are* (New York: Random House, 1994).
"Employment of Women Reaches All-Time High in 1955," *Personnel Guidance Journal*, 34, no. 6 (February 1956).

Fabe, Maxene. *TV Game Shows* (New York: Doubleday, 1979).

"For the Record," *TV Guide* (Southern California Edition), August 20, 1960.

Gamson, Joshua. *Freaks Talk Back* (Chicago: University of Chicago Press, 1998).

Gould, Jack. " 'Queen for a Day' Is Not for Crowning," *New York Times*, January 6, 1956.

Haralovich, Mary Beth. "Sit-Coms and Suburbs" in *Private Screenings: Television and the Female Consumer*, ed. Lynn Spigel and Denise Mann (Minneapolis: University of Minnesota Press, 1992).

"Jack Bailey: Mesmerizer of the Middle Aged," *TV Guide*, March 11, 1961.

Katona, George. *The Mass Consumption Society* (New York: McGraw-Hill, 1964).

Lipsitz, George. "The Meaning of Memory: Family, Class and Ethnicity in Early Network Television" in *Time Passages: Collective Memory and American Popular Culture* (Minneapolis: University of Minnesota Press: 1990).

May, Elaine Tyler. *Homeward Bound: American Families in the Cold War Era* (New York: Basic Books, 1988).

Portmann, John. *When Bad Things Happen to Other People* (New York: Routledge, 2000).

"Queen for a Day," *Variety*, January 11, 1956.

Remenih, Anton. "Queen for a Day Finds Crown Is Target for All," *Chicago Daily Tribune*, May 6, 1950.

Scheiner, Georganne. "Would You Like to be Queen for a Day?: Finding a Working Class Voice in American Television of the 1950s," *Historical Journal of Film, Radio and Television* 23, no. 4 (2003).

Sconce, Jeffery. *Haunted Media* (Durham, NC: Duke University Press, 2000).

Spigel, Lynn. *Make Room for TV* (Chicago: University of Chicago Press, 1992).

"The Stuff that Tears Are Made Of," *TV Guide*, June 22, 1957.

"Those 800 Babies," *TV Guide*, June 28, 1958.

"Troubles & Bubbles," *Time*, April 15, 1957.

"TV's Hottest Battleground," *Sponsor*, May 14, 1957.

Wolters, Larry. "Joker Out as Queens Pick Queen," *Chicago Daily Tribune*, June 14, 1959.

———. "Queens for Day Get 13 Million in Last Decade," *Chicago Daily Tribune*, May 21, 1955.

———. "Where to Dial Today," *Chicago Daily Tribune*, January 6, 1956.

CHAPTER 10

INTERIOR DESIGN: COMMODIFYING SELF AND PLACE IN *EXTREME MAKEOVER*, *EXTREME MAKEOVER: HOME EDITION*, AND *THE SWAN*

JUNE DEERY

I

THE TERRITORY

Contemporary television's latest version of the makeover translates the American Dream and other notions of self-improvement into profitable vehicles for the new media economy. Not only are makeover shows relatively inexpensive to produce, not only do they generate respectable ratings and offer TiVo-proof platforms for advertising goods and services, but they also promote an all-encompassing and infallible consumerist ethos. By commodifying both the process of making over and its mediation, this programming reinforces basic tenets of consumer capitalism and extends the market into previously unmined areas of experience. Reality makeovers simultaneously demonstrate the power of commodities and the power of the medium that promotes these commodities. In fact, the Reality phenomenon in general has shown television to be a cultural device with the potential to commodify every imaginable zone of experience and sell it at a profit.

On Reality makeovers, participants are sold to viewers, and viewers traded to advertisers in the usual fashion: that is, ratings establish what advertisers will be charged to access a certain number or type of viewer (usually CPM, or cost per thousand). But the shows also promote the capitalist credo that one can buy happiness, that through consumption you or your life experience can be fixed or improved. What is being depicted in the makeover show is not change for its own sake—though change alone could stimulate demand—but change for the better. So there is a deep psychological and even a residual moral component to this transaction. Consumers are urged to improve self and environment or be perceived as both materially and ethically lacking. Furthermore, in the new crop of makeover shows the very distinction between self and physical environment, between body and edifice, is becoming blurred. The extent to which this relaxation of boundaries makes the concept of *being* closer to that of *having* is something this chapter will explore.

The transformations wrought by Reality producers take place on camera and thus involve translating the unmediated into the mediated. As with other Reality shows, the inclusion of the real-because-unmediated, the virgin scopic territory, is what defines the genre and attracts viewers, but only because the territory is inevitably stripped of this virgin status once the cameras roll. So-called Reality programming asserts that there is a real to begin with, but then asks us to enjoy its being contained and transformed—an example perhaps of the desperate search for reality and its inevitable eradication that Baudrillard and others have pegged as characteristic of our era.[1] Even if a universal hyper-reality is still beyond the horizon, we do see a central tension being played out on Reality TV between the novelty of the unmediated and the voyeuristic enjoyment of its annihilation, a self-conscious process that undercuts the genre's pretensions to realism. But while all Reality formats claim to capture the previously unmediated, makeover shows in particular foreground the way in which the unmediated becomes not just mediated but mediatized, or something that more closely conforms to a media image. Hence the makeover show, because it centers on mediatizing or making media-worthy, becomes the quintessential Reality TV format.

There are two main points to focus on here. First, that makeover shows amplify the commercial imperative to purchase in order to improve, and second, that, even more markedly than in other Reality programming, the process of mediation becomes the makeover format's selling point. Of course, the theme of improving self and situation is not new, neither in American history nor even in television programming where it has featured for some time in talk shows and the likes of Oprah's Change Your Life TV. But what is increasingly evident in the new round of prime-time programming is the link to consumerism; what is hard to miss is the turning of self-identity into a commodity and a lucrative, media event. In addition, Reality makeovers illustrate the broader truth that the economy of the media turns attracting attention into something one can sell, thus creating not just a society of the spectacle but of the commercial spectacle.

As already mentioned, the makeover clearly invokes the self-consciously entitled and undoubtedly hegemonic "American dream," a shared societal aspiration that for generations has succeeded in managing economic demand while masking sociopolitical inequality. No exact equivalent exists elsewhere (there is, e.g., no commonly circulated British or French Dream!). Contemporary makeover shows reinforce the consumerist base to this and other notions of self-improvement in American culture, the extent to which acquisition of home and car rather than less tangible sociopolitical rights constitute the fulfillment of said dream. But what is also significant is a shift away from Emersonian self-reliance toward a dependence on outside—and paid for—agencies. Hence while older TV formats incorporated elements of D.I.Y., the new wave of lifestyle programming tends to subject passive "participants" to expert eyes. This meshes well with an era of privatization, with a scaling back of both public services and public life and with various forms of accommodation to surveillance.[2]

The newer programs maintain the individualist focus of the American Dream as this suits the political economy. They decontextualize, and in so doing, reinforce the supremacy of the individual by ignoring or downplaying actual sociopolitical arrangements and erasing any expectations of public support. What is offered instead is private agency that is made public only because it is *mediated*, and not because it is socially mandated and tax-based. In other words, the act of giving to those in need is public only to the extent that it is performed on camera. Moreover, this making public is its genesis; the transaction occurs because it will be broadcast and thereby generate "publicity," a commercially valuable outcome. This is what motivates private givers, rather than elected legislators, to offer support and to do so on an individual or personal basis.

By commodifying the self—or an image of the self—Reality makeovers perform an important function in demonstrating the extent and power of consumerism. Their focus is on how purchases affect identity and well-being, both of which are perceived as cultural assets capable of change, exchange, and interchangeability. This occurs in the context of a postindustrial falling away of traditional institutions such as religion, extended family, and community that previously helped define and fix one's position and sense of self. In other words, the economic practices that helped alienate the individual now promise to aid those burdened with the work of forming subjectively imagined definitions of self. For what makeover programming reflects is the extent to which the self is now regarded as a project and cultural construct, something that must be self-reflexively worked on and continually performed.

As part of the process of refurbishment and resultant commodification, individual subjects are to a greater or lesser extent objectified. This is to be expected. But what is interesting is how Reality shows conflate the improvement of person and of place to reinforce the notion that aspects of the self are forms and acquisitions not unlike those belonging to an architectural space. Watching both home and personal makeovers brings several analogies to mind: first, an initial cataloging and display of problems and inadequacies; second, dramatic intervention and transformation by experts; and finally, before-and-after revelations displaying the new product. Blueprints, marked up bodies, and project timelines, all schematize the same dramatic process, and so the body, like the house, is regarded as a place, as a project to be worked on by others. All of which makes being (e.g., unattractive) more equivalent to having (e.g., an unattractive room).

The bad news is that something needs fixing; the good news is that it can be fixed. This is the central faith of an advertising-driven consmerist economy which makeovers amplify by focusing on the gap between the imperfect and the ideal. Moreover, the idea of a makeover not only implies the correction of an original flaw but also allows for, and even encourages, an open-ended process: as with advertising, both perception of imperfection and hope of rectification are essential, with absolute fulfillment generally being deferred. Makeover programming reinforces the commercial imperative to improve and keep on improving, to consume and keep on consuming. It is the latest contribution to what might be termed Imperative TV, an increasingly large category of programming that nags, urges, or disciplines viewers, be it through talk shows, news magazines, or shopping channels. Imperative programs which do not have an overt commercial function are nevertheless totally in line with the commercial messages that support them—or rather they support—and constantly impress upon us the need to acquire something that we do not have. On Reality TV this lack may take the form of an adventure, a wedding, a better home/garden/body, or just more money.

In particular, Reality makeovers provide exemplary modes of consumption, thematizing how subjects can participate in the process of self-commodification and get with the program of capitalist expansion. Each episode instructs viewers how to regard consumption as a form of production and how, through consuming goods and services, they can make their lifestyle or selves over into a new product. In what follows, I will examine both home and personal makeover series to highlight the relationship between transformation and consumption. In the words of Henri Lefebvre, I wish to examine how "Displays of reality have become a display trade and a display of trade" and, thereby uncover some of the ideological underpinnings of a promotional culture.[3]

II

HOME IMPROVEMENT

The first type of programming focuses on the sine qua non of the American Dream, the acquisition of a home one can be proud of. It has its roots in a venerable TV genre, the home improvement show, a concept that began in America and elsewhere as instructional, how-to programming of Bob Vila's *This Old House* variety.[4] More recently, several home improvement shows have begun to appear on commercial channels and to serve more clearly defined commercial purposes. In America, *Trading Spaces*,[5] imported from Britain, was the first to break through in 2000 and soon its ratings began to rival the networks, the first cable programing to do so. By 2005, on TLC alone, there was *Moving Up*, *Town Haul*, *Clean Sweep*, *In A Fix*, and *While You Were Out*, in addition to wall-to-wall home improvement shows on HGTV.[6] Not to be outdone, even the iconic Bob Vila has gone commercial, making the most of his years on the PBS by becoming a frequent pitchman. Meanwhile, *This Old House* has become a lucrative franchise, spawning commercial TV shows, merchandise, and publications.[7]

What makes the Reality version of the home improvement show distinctive is not only the increasingly overt forms of commercialism but also an attention to person as well as place. The new element is the construction of a human story alongside that of a building, complete with a condensed dramatic arc to increase suspense, emotion, and therefore ratings. The emphasis is no longer on "how-to," unless it be how to buy the goods and services that are integrated into the program and listed in considerable detail on the accompanying Web site. Linking person to product works on a commercial level and reflects an historical trend in modern advertising toward an emphasis on associated persons and lifestyle rather than product description. Advertisers did not need semioticians to tell them that commodities can function as legible signs which express one's cultural identity. One result is a form of mass individualism—always a paradox at the heart of advertising and consumer culture—whereby one is expected to express one's individuality by acquiring mass-produced items. Many of these home makeovers reassure viewers that the choice is sufficiently wide and the parameters not too confining, though they often do so with the aid of customization and on-site carpentry that regular audience members can only dream of.

A good example of the Reality home makeover series is *Extreme Makeover: Home Edition*, which not only personalizes and dramatizes but even adds a moral tale, to the delight of large Sunday-night audiences.[8] Rather than making over an interior in a few days, here we have the radical redesigning or building of an entire house with an enormous team of workers laboring for long hours over the period of one week. Certainly in terms of before-and-after, this programming has upped the ante from home decor shows such as *Queer Eye for the Straight Guy*[9] or *Trading Spaces*. The investment is worthwhile because it achieves a larger and more dramatic import, teaching viewers that changing real estate and the commodites therein can radically improve a whole family's prospects and even chance of survival. Since it involves a permanent life change and not simply the attempt to improve one's chance of dating, the perceived power of commodities is greatly enhanced.

Subjects are selected because of both need and moral dessert: someone who is down on his/her luck yet who manages to look after others is a typical profile. In personal makeover shows, subjects are generally made over simply because they perceive themselves to be inadequate, whereas producers of *Extreme Makeover: Home Edition* foreground the idea of moral worth and reward for good deeds, a formula that more closely resembles the rags-to-riches narrative of much earlier commodity-oriented programming such as the 1950s *Queen For a Day*.[10]

Rewarding the deserving poor makes everyone feel—and, it must be said, look—good. This includes the sponsor or advertiser who is not just financing a show but is now framed as a charitable organization; thus *Home Edition*'s major sponsor, Sears, is thoroughly embedded in the programming, yet its spot announcements thank producers for being "included," as though Sears, Roebuck and Co. were either an invited guest or a helpful volunteer instead of a corporation which is paying to advertise its products. In addition, CEOs from mortage and insurance companies regularly appear on camera to grant the deserving subjects a release from financial burdens, just, it seems, out of the goodness of their hearts and not for the priceless PR this generates. Likewise, the behind-the-scenes show *How'd They Do That?* highlights how morally uplifting it all is for those who build the new space; their appearace on the show is portrayed less as a career break and more as a social project.[11] Even the network brand stands to benefit, for ABC is also ritualistically thanked on camera and it must indeed be gratifying for a media company to look heroic for producing profitable programming. In fact, the narrative gets downright religious at times. In one episode, when producers actually found deaf parents of a blind as well as autistic son, host Ty Pennington remarked with a straight face, "I'm just reflecting a light."[12] Reflecting it rather profitably it seems, since he not only appears on Sears ads, but now also has his own line of products.

Without being too cynical, one could argue that this kind of programming reflects the larger political economy in which public support is being replaced by privatized giving, a model that gratifies the (known) giver and obligates the (known) recipient. Subjects of *Extreme Makeover: Home Edition* have less input than those in shopping advice shows such as

Queer Eye for the Straight Guy. While the home transformation is taking place, family members are absent and, if contacted, are often teased by the host who pretends to approve changes he knows they would not like to see happen in their formerly private space. And he does have this kind of license. The agents of change have therefore become even more paternalistic, if not deified, and the products they or their sponsors offer are suffused with the warm glow of personal drama. Sears is not supplying a fridge, but a future life. People do not just transform things; things transform people. The lesson is clear.

The price, as always on Reality TV, is that subjects must lay bare and let go once they have offered themselves to be transformed as public spectacle, in this case often out of desperation. Little thought is given to long-term consequences or social context when these new edifices rise, consequences such as subsequent tax bills, shoddy workmanship, or the sudden appearance of a new mansion in a poor neighborhood. For producers, all that matters is what occurs on camera: there is no attempt to follow up or examine with a wider lens.

Those who create and fund the shows are content because the makeover format has proven to be an inexpensive way to outsmart DVRs by embedding advertising discourse on many levels. In the first place, the life affirming and (often literally) constructive context promotes an ethos of buying one's way to happiness and of being empowered by purchases. More specifically, these shows promote home improvement products, a notable growth sector in American and other western economies. While it would be difficult to prove a direct influence, the TV format and sales figures have certainly grown together and retailers such as Lowes and Home Depot are happy to sponsor these series.[13]

Actual advertising techniques vary, but they often follow the advertorial approach of merging program content and paid-for advertising. This can take the form of product placement and retailer plugs during the program, or specially geared designer ads during commercial breaks that refer back to the show. On *Home Edition*, team members invariably refer to products provided by Sears, and they are even shown shopping in the store. Meanwhile, every other embedded brand gets at least a closeup, or even what sounds like a scripted dialogue extolling its virtues. Opening up another form of integration, the Sears Web site also links to the show and, among other things, itemizes how many of its products were used in each episode. Hinting at the ever-present American Dream, Sears.com urges viewers to "start building your own dream now," presumably by shopping at its stores. Finally, to complete the commercial loop, elements of the show have migrated into regular advertising, as when the show's host fronts Sears' spot advertising.

THE BODY SHOP

Clearly, the home makeover has been an economic godsend, modeling privatized giving to passive recepients who benefit by being mediated for our pleasure. Both the medium, and the way it summons commodities, are shown to be life transforming. An analogous and also popular format is the personal makeover of the surgical variety. The flagships of this variety are *Home Edition*'s sister show, *Extreme Makeover*, and later *The Swan*.[14] Here the focus is less on the consumption of commodities than on consuming the self as commodity. Cameras are aimed at the objectivized, corporeal body and its presentation to the world. While psychological therapy is offered to participants, this kind of alteration is hard to detect on film and is therefore largely ignored. The only "inner" change that interests producers is the one that takes place when the knife goes under the flesh to produce a new surface. (Hence it should come as no surprise that *The Swan*'s therapist acquired her much-quoted doctorate from what is essentially a diploma mill.)[15]

As mentioned, one can immediately see broad analogies between home and personal makeover shows: the cataloguing of inadequacies, the handing over to a team of experts, the creation of suspense, and the final reveal of the new product. But clearly, surgical makeovers are more radical than clothes-and-make-up or home decorating shows, in that they physically and permanently reshape the body in a process that lasts not days but months. Rather than merely donning new apparel or inhabiting a different room, the shows aim to permanently transform the image one presents to oneself and to the world: a more complex proposition since, however much we accept the consumerist notion that our dress or décor express our personality, the relation between body and identity is clearly much more intimate. Although a proper exploration of this relationship is outside the scope of this chapter, one can say that, unlike the interior space of a room, the body is not only what we think of as very private, but also inevitably exterior and public, and something that goes out in the world. Consciously or not, those who undergo surgical makeovers are radically internalizing the idea of style and its media representations, a process reminiscent of Baudrillard's observation that today we not only find "the forced extraversion of all interiority"—which almost any Reality series pushes to the limit—but also the "forced introjection of all exteriority," in this case because subjects are literally in-corporating external social imagery.[16]

Once again the gap between the ordinary and the mediated is bridged by a team of experts, not surprising in a culture where the notion of a "life coach" is not risible, and authoritative self-help texts sell in the millions.

Elsewhere, but especially in America, the urge to improve the self is taken for granted as a cultural norm, a norm that generates enormous profits. Its latest turn in Reality programming conforms to the larger corporatization of private life and the professionalization of social relationships whereby one pays for everything from "personal trainers" to "life organizers" rather than look for familial or other forms of nonbillable advice. While not unique to this country, the desire to start again—and the belief that it is possible—is a core myth of American identity. Today it is simply being outsourced and, in this case, handsomely renumerated.

With surgical makeovers, we encounter a very technologically mediated event that promotes the centuries-old scientific proposition that one can, and should, alter natural processes for the greater glory of humankind. Fox's ironically titled *The Swan* works counter to Andersen's original "Ugly Duckling," a tale that admonished that nature will take its course and does not need our intervention. Whereas in surgical makeover programs, nature clearly lets us down, and therefore human devices such as money and technology have to be called upon to correct it. On a much larger scale, the same kind of intervention opened up the new American continent, where technology and force of will made over the landscape to better conform to European ideals.[17]

But even more immediately, the makeover is born of a commercial culture that communicates through advertising, a discourse that generates enormous numbers of images, especially idealized images, until these appear to be something everyone must aspire to have or to be. This is particularly striking with regard to the human body, for never before in history has there been such a daily intake of ideal body images, images rarely found in nature but rather constructed by surgery, Photoshop, or severe diets. These remarkably high standards of beauty—and, particularly in the female's case, the prioritization of this aspect of her self—are promulgated by all forms of media, largely for commercial purposes. Beauty attracts attention—the basic currency of the media—and the drive to achieve an ideal beauty also usefully shifts a lot of products. No wonder, then, that postmodern commentators remark on the current drive toward an aestheticization of the self.[18]

Personal makeovers reify the image, the ideal image, which is itself made into a commodity by being constantly mediated. Indeed, what particularly struck Fredric Jameson about Debord's depiction of the society of the spectacle was his observation that "the ultimate form of commodity reification in contemporary consumer society is precisely the image itself."[19] The surgical makeover goes further in that the media image finds flesh and physically imprints itself on the subject. One can see it as an extreme version of the advertiser's exhortation of viewers to translate media images into real products by purchasing them in stores.

As is usually the case with Reality TV, personal makeovers offer only a truncated and depoliticized back-story with no serious investigation of forces at play outside the hermetic, and hegemonic, world of the program. An abrupt intervention cuts subjects off from larger forces that might have formed their identity up to this point, so they possess little more context than the figures of advertising, to which they are related. The focus on a decontextualized individual inspires broad identification and empathy, factors that generally improve ratings. Ignoring larger sociopolitical forces also adds to the magic of the solution and reinforces the commercial ideology of individually buying one's way to happiness without questioning the social arrangements under which one lives. This, again, is perfectly in tune with the American Dream.

As with other Reality formats, personal makeovers have had a real commercial payoff. Just as shopping primers such as *Queer Eye* have helped expand the market in, for example, "male products," so have shows such as *Extreme Makeover* helped normalize and sell plastic surgery to a wide audience. Those who may not have considered it before come under increasing pressure to look like those on screen, further colonizing the unmediated and spurring consumption. Episodes actually take the form of infomercials, with personal testimony and before-and-after narratives. Ordinary participants are chosen not only because they appear to need improving (unlike celebrity demigods) but also because most viewers (who are also "ordinary") will identify with these clay-footed or "out of shape" bodies and perhaps with their course of action as well. Again, the extent to which this programming has contributed to a national boom in cosmetic surgery is hard to determine, but certainly those surgeons featured on the show attest to long waiting lists for their services since appearing on TV: that is, their appearance on the show constitutes an advertisement of self and services. This is reinforced by spot advertising for cosmetic services during the programming and by the show's Web site which promotes similar businesses.[20]

With body makeovers, surgical sculpting positions the individual's body as an area to be worked on by others. This most intimate of spaces is publicly exposed, analyzed, and then handed over to experts who work to improve its appearance, just as others beautify bedrooms and backyards. Surgeons literally inscribe the cultural ideal on the patient's body by applying a marker to the flesh in pre-op. Some such as *Extreme Makeover* also display a rotating, schematic image of the body and mark off specs on a digital blueprint, rather like a modern-day "Million Dollar Man"—or perhaps "Several Thousand Dollar Woman" would be more accurate. In any case, both the technology and the price tag are meant to impress. The early spatialization and objectification of the individual's body reinforce the idea that the person has become part of the object world and, with adequate investment, will emerge as more valuable, as someone who will undergo a promotion both in the sense of display and increased status. All this contributes to an historic shift away from defining and improving the self in terms of the inner, the ethical, or the spiritual. As Jean Kilbourne ruefully remarks, "These days, self-improvement seems to have more to do with calories than with character, with abdomens than with absolutes, with nail polish than with ethics."[21]

One suspects that, at least for some participants, this objectification of the body may actually be a relief. On entering the doctor's surgery, their problems are in some ways legitimized because medicialized, and it is likely to be of some comfort to embrace the notion that their problematic body is an area that others can manage and fix. For viewers, the experience is therefore one of watching not resistance but capitulation: capitulation to the rule of the expert and to the power of the camera.

THE REVEAL

Although the term goes back to Allen Funt's 1960s *Candid Camera*, "the reveal" has quickly gained currency as a trademarked segment of Reality makeover shows.[22] The personal reveal is equivalent to the moment in home improvement shows when homeowners view what has been done to their room, and involves the same mix of unfamiliairty and ownership, of distance and possession. To reveal means both to uncover and to display; on surgical makeovers, the new body is uncovered (which could be done privately) and simultaneously displayed to a dual audience of subject and TV viewers. The term may even retain some of the religious associations attached to the notion of revelation. Noting the economic and psychological investment we now place in the body, Baudrillard observes how it "has today become an *object of salvation*. It has literally taken over that moral and ideological function from the soul"[23] (author's emphasis). As cultural construct and obsession, the body is open to fetishism and even spiritual endowment. Hence, before being granted a revelation, makeover subjects are asked to sacrifice (e.g., privacy and familial contact), go into the deep sleep of a surgical operation, and then are resurrected anew.

The Swan maximizes the drama of the subject's first encounter with her new self by removing all mirrors prior to the reveal. Producers put their superintendence into militaristic terms by referring to "mirror police" who they employ to remove all reflecting surfaces in the subject's new living quarters. One of the many ironies here is that the selling point of the show is viewing access, but subjects are not allowed to view themselves. In fact, their not being able to see themselves is a major reason why audiences are persuaded to watch. The viewed have further restrictions. They may not see family members except through mediated and one-way systems, such as video tapes, and they are not permitted to be seen by these loved ones until producers grant permission at the show's conclusion. As always on Reality TV, since scopic access is the vital currency, the subjects' viewing of both themselves and others is carefully controlled in order to produce an entertaining and profitable spectacle. The restriction that this imposes underlines how, by handing over their body to be worked on, they have lost some ownership of this now marketable commodity.

After seeing no reflection for three or four months, *Swan* contestants are instructed to stand before a draped mirror and indicate when they are ready to view themselves, thus producing a modest sense of agency as well as dramatic suspense. When the curtain is lifted, viewers scrutinize the new image at the same moment as the former patient, who now looks in the mirror and sees herself as a product, as an Other. Almost always the first gesture is to cover the face with both hands and collapse the body, thus ironically blocking the image they are so captivated by. There is also generally some touching of the contours of the body in an attempt, it seems, to reconcile the image with their new physical reality and perhaps verify its authenticity. After a minute's examination, subjects usually manage to articulate some reaction such as "Is this me? I can't believe this is me!" or "I don't look anything like that girl!"

Subjects then dutifully turn to thank the experts who have gathered to admire their handiwork like so many Pygmalions cooing over this week's Galatea. Those who underwent the surgery are essentially being congratulated for attempting to conform to the image the media helped convince them they lacked. The subsequent re-imaging of the self is, in Foucauldian terms, a quite literal internalization of surveillance and the Other's gaze.[24] It is the culmination of a process that is about control, both physical and representational, as much as it is about aesthetics. Anthony Giddens, who comments on the primacy of the reflexive project of the self in contemporary culture, notes that "the body is less and less an extrinsic 'given' [. . .] but becomes itself reflexively mobilized. What might appear as a wholesale movement towards the narcissistic cultivation of bodily appearance is in fact an expression of a concern lying much deeper actively to 'construct' and control the body."[25]

MEDIATIZATION

In any Reality makeover, services are provided only if the camera has full access: the program, after all, is not about changing, but about exhibiting change. A brilliant reconstruction must be earned by undergoing a humiliating deconstruction in which flaws are publicly exposed in graphic detail simply to gratify others' voyeuristic and theatrical desires. It seems we are now at a point when closeups of people's sagging stomachs or crooked noses are an acceptable form of commercial entertainment. This is not exploitation of the freak, something that for centuries we have paid to view, but rather of the ordinary and pathetic. The invasion of the ordinary, the foregrounding of intimate imperfection, suggests that commercial forces are somewhat desperately pushing us further and further into any area that was previously off-limits. And it is the push, the transgression, that is the selling point.

Sometimes counterdiscourses are vocalized in ways that suggest some tension in establishing motives and effects. For example, participants will frequently proclaim that they are "doing it [the makeover] for themselves" or that inner beauty is what really counts—an astonishing observation from those who have endured so much to acquire the outer variety. The fact remains that what they are doing "for themselves" is conforming to certain cultural standards, what they are hoping to achieve is an image to present to the world that others, thanks largely to the mass media, have been taught to covet as well as admire. No one suggests that subjects boost their self-confidence by learning to reject the ideal aesthetic standards of their society: rather, they simply hope to meet them more faithfully. In some instances, as in MTV's *I Want a Famous Face*, participants request that they be made to resemble specific media products such as Brad Pitt or Pamela Anderson.[26] The logic is clear and irrefutable: what they seek is an already media-approved appearance with a guaranteed high market value. Others settle for an appearance that *could* make it onto the screen, an image that is media-worthy, but they choose instead to import it back into their real lives.

COMMODIFYING GENDER

Predictably, the majority of those who audition for personal makeovers are female: this reflects the larger society in which, according to the American Society of Plastic Surgeons, 87 percent of their patients in 2004 were women, this included a 26 percent increase in women having plastic surgery from 2000 to 2004.[27] This is hardly surprising given the cultural demands on women to look good above all else and the long tradition of women being culturally positioned as objects of visual pleasure. But in many instances, the makeovers reflect and even amplify the commercial media's proclivity for exaggerating gender differences, a shorthand and eye-catching form of communication long utilized by advertisers. For very often female patients emerge hyperfeminized, femininity being interpreted in the most clichéd fashion as possessing C-cups, a thin waist, long hair, a long dress, high heels and several ounces of makeup. On *The Swan*, this Barbie-esque composite is particularly *de rigueur*. Women who were earlier seen lolling around in jeans and sweaters eventually indicate success by tottering on high heels and exhibiting their new assets with the aid of plunging necklines. Women who earlier had various lengths and styles of hair emerge with practically identical long, curly locks. The way this and other shows churn out people who conform to a narrow range of media ideals brings to mind Adorno's concern regarding the culture industry, which is the push in monopoly capitalism toward standardization. Here homogenized bodies are turned out with an efficiency that would gratify Henry Ford.

On *The Swan*, the ultimate prize for those formerly certified as "ugly ducklings," is being allowed to parade in a beauty pageant, a form of exhibition that has largely faded from prime time, now that many countries consider it unacceptably sexist. But now the patriarchal sport that sparked off protests in Atlantic City in the 1960s has been revived, apparently without so much as a whimper. While millions watch from home, families and friends in the auditorium cheer on the newly sexualized and homogenized bodies of those who now appear with the glazed expressions and practiced movements of twenty-first-century denizens of Stepford. All of this is in tune with similar parades of already approved models of femininity on those other popular Reality franchises, the find-a-rich-husband harem shows where people trade sexual attraction for money, for example, *The Bachelor* and *Joe Millionaire*.[28] *Extreme Makeover* and *The Swan* are more coy. The fact that the new bodies have greater value on the sexual market is more muted than on dating or mating shows where appearances are more openly assessed and traded.

In reality, looks do matter and certain images are a form of capital; for instance, some studies suggest that those who are deemed physically attractive are more likely to be promoted and to achieve other forms of success.[29] So while these shows may be crass, it would be naive to declare them either wrong-headed or perverse for suggesting that appearances affect how others treat you or how you regard yourself. What this form of entertainment does, however, is increase the pressure and raise the standards of what people are expected to do, and to spend, in order to achieve a satisfactory status. They conflate transformation and consumption—much to the delight of those who fund the programming—and, in a form of commercial eugenics, strongly reinforce the link between beauty and wealth.

Home and personal makeovers jointly demonstrate the commercial advantages of conflating person and place, body and building, family and home. Rendering the body into an object that can enter a commodity market makes commercial sense: both to sell the show, the media product, and to sell the goods and services that make the commodification possible. From the other direction, personalizing the place, attaching personal narratives to building projects, is also effective in selling the media product and its featured materials and appliances. Both types of program serve a consumerist economy on a pragmatic and an ideological plane, urging us to seek in commodities solutions to all problems, big and small. They demonstrate the power of both camera and commodity, and the extent to which each transforms those who come under its influence. Each type of makeover foregrounds what television, because of the technical nature of the medium, has done since its inception, which is showcase surface and sight: a prioritization with profound and still evolving cultural ramifications. Hence, this popular form of entertainment can provide an entry point to thinking about how today we construct different types of interiority and selfhood, and how we are encouraged to do so with great expenditure of time and money. The Reality makeover has proven to be a profitable recycling of transformative narratives which are about as old as the idea of American nationhood itself. But they continue the shift away from improvement of character and societal progress toward that of individual image and personal gain.

NOTES

1. Jean Baudrillard introduced the idea of "hyperreality" to describe a postmodern collapse of the distinction between the real and the simulated. His contention was that, although most do not realize it, what we take as reality is now simulated or hyperreal. Signs have replaced the things they are supposed to represent, and any original or authentic reality is obliterated. To follow his discussion of this matter, see Jean Baudrillard, *Simulacra and Simulations* (New York: Semiotext(e), 1983).

2. Certainly recent conservative administrations have promoted both increased surveillance of the populace, and private or privatized forms of giving, charity being preferred to entitlement. For a broader and really incisive discussion of Reality TV's role in an era of surveillance and late capitalism, see Mark Andrejevic, *Reality TV: the Work of Being Watched* (Lanham, MD: Rowman & Littlefield, 2004).

3. Henri Lefebvre, *Everyday Life in the Modern World* (New Brunswick, NJ: Transaction, 1984), p. 63.

4. *This Old House*, directed by David Vos and Russell Morash, host Bob Vila, PBS, 1979–1989.

5. *Trading Spaces*, host Paige Davis, TLC, 2000-present.

6. *Moving Up*, directed by Karen Kunkle, Kyle McCabe, Carolyn Pane, Colin Rothbart, and Nicole Sorrenti., TLC, 2005; *Town Haul*, directed by Mark Ritchie, TLC, 2005; *Clean Sweep*, directed by Laurent Malaquais and Hans van Reit, TLC, 2003-present; *In a Fix*, host Marc Goldberg, TLC, 2004-present; and *While You Were Out*, directed by Boaz Halaban and Dean Slotar, TLC, 2002-present.

7. See thisoldhouse.com (Accessed on May 10, 2005).

8. *Extreme Makeover: Home Edition*, directed by David Dryden and Patrick Higgins, produced by Tom Forman for Endemol USA, ABC, 2004-present.

9. *Queer Eye for the Straight Guy*, created by David Collins and David Metzler, Bravo, 2003-present.

10. *Queen For a Day*, directed by Hep Weyman, NBC, ABC, 1956–1964.

11. *How'd They Do That?*, directed by Patrick Higgins, ABC, 2005.

12. *Extreme Makeover: Home Edition*, episode 20. Broadcast on ABC (WNET, Albany, NY), November 7, 2004.

13. Home Depot went from 340 stores and $12.5 billion in sales in 1994 to 1,8 890 stores and $73 billion in sales in 2004. For details of the company's growth history see http://www.homedepot.com/HDUS/EN_US/corporate/about/timeline.shtml (Accessed on October 12, 2005). Lowes went from $6.4 billion in sales in 1994 to $36.5 billion in 2004: see http://www.shareholder.com/lowes /index2.cfm (Accessed on October 12, 2005).

14. *Extreme Makeover*, producer Tom Forman, ABC, 2002-present. *The Swan*, created by Nely Galan, directed by Kent Weed, Fox, 2004-present.

15. Lynn Tanni received her Ph.D from California Coast University, an unaccredited, for-profit organization that awards degrees for a flat fee without classroom attendance.

16. Jean Baudrillard, *The Ecstasy of Communication* (New York: Semiotext(e), 1988), p. 26.

17. See, for instance, David E. Nye's recent account in *America as Second Creation: Technology and Narratives of New Beginnings* (Boston: MIT Press, 2004).

18. Jameson is one who draws interesting connections between image culture, commercialism, and aesthetics (see, e.g., "Reification and Utopia in Mass Culture," in Fredric Jameson, *Signatures of the Visible* (New York: Routledge, 1992), pp. 9–34.

19. Jameson, *Signatures of the Visible*, pp. 11–12.

20. See abc.go.com/primetime/extrememakeover (Accessed on June 10, 2005).

21. Jean Kilbourne, *Can't Buy My Love* (New York: Touchstone, 1999), p. 153.

22. *Candid Camera*, producer and host Allen Funt, CBS, 1960–1967.

23. Jean Baudrillard, *Consumer Society* (London: Sage, 1998), p. 129.

24. Michel Foucault has presented what must be the most influential discussion of surveillance as discipline and internalized control in *Discipline and Punish: The Birth of the Prison* (New York: Pantheon, 1977).

25. Anthony Giddens, *Modernity and Self-Identity: Self and Society in the Late Modern Age* (Stanford, CA: Stanford University Press, 1991), p. 7.

26. *I Want a Famous Face*, MTV, 2004-present.

27. See http://www.plasticsurgery.org (Accessed on March 20, 2005).

28. *The Bachelor*, created by Mike Fleiss, ABC, 2002-present, *Joe Millionaire*, directed by Bryan O'Donnell, Fox, 2003.

29. See, e.g., Nancy Ectoff, *Survival of the Prettiest* (New York: Doubleday, 1999).

CHAPTER 11

"HELP IS ON THE WAY!": *SUPERNANNY*, *NANNY 911*, AND THE NEOLIBERAL POLITICS OF THE FAMILY

RON BECKER

"PARENTS OF AMERICA, HELP IS ON THE WAY!" Or so claims the opening sequence of Fox's dysfunctional-family makeover show *Nanny 911*. In the 2004–2005 television season, in fact, both Fox and ABC ostensibly brought "help" to the nation's parents in the guise of two nearly identical and thoroughly formulaic reality series in which no-nonsense British nannies help "transform" a different "family in crisis" every week.[1] *Nanny 911* and *Supernanny* seemed to appear just in the nick of time, for in 2004 the American family seemed in danger of falling apart. Or so claimed social conservatives who warned that gay marriage was on the verge of destroying the bedrock of American society. Earlier that spring, Americans watched while thousands of same-sex couples got married in San Francisco, and later that year Massachusetts became the first state to recognize same-sex marriages. George W. Bush apparently believed that gay marriage was a threat to national stability and joined those calling for a constitutional amendment that would define marriage as a relationship only between a man and a woman. "After more than two centuries of American jurisprudence and millennia of human experience," Bush opined, "a few judges and local authorities are presuming to change the most fundamental institution of civilization."[2]

I begin this article by situating *Supernanny* and *Nanny 911* in the context of the gay marriage debate in order to underscore the shows' connection to the highly political nature of the heterosexual nuclear family. Connected as they are to the supposed biological imperative of reproduction, marriage and the heterosexual family, we are tempted to think, are somehow natural and universal—"the most fundamental institution of civilization" rooted in "millennia of human experience." They are not. Although all societies need to organize reproduction, sexuality, childrearing, kinship relations, and emotional ties, historians, sociologists, and anthropologists have demonstrated that different societies have developed vastly different ways to do so and that such arrangements are constantly changing in response to wider social forces.[3] Thus, despite what George W. Bush may say, the institution of marriage and our understanding of the family—what families should look like and what roles they should play in organizing social relations—are not natural but rather social constructs, and the assertion that marriage and the family are somehow in crisis is deeply political. America's families are always having to be made over—made to conform to an idea of family life that is always shaped by political forces and never inclusive of the diversity of human experience.

With their weekly stories about the rehabilitation of families in crisis, *Supernanny* and *Nanny 911* offer viewers specific ways to think about the heterosexual family, the nature of the American family's problems, and the kind of help it needs (and does not need). Amid the deepening neoliberalism of contemporary America, a romanticized notion of the autonomous family helps legitimate the shift to post-welfare-state governance. Stable families, neoliberal common sense insists, should and can step in as the state cuts back on social security, public schooling, and other civic-minded (and civic-minding) programs. Although scenes of out-of-control children and exasperated parents challenge a romantic image of the heterosexual nuclear family, the programs present these families as dysfunctional exceptions that demonstrate the importance of functional "normal" families. Given the profile of the families featured in their first seasons (predominantly white and exclusively heterosexual, two-parented, with children, and nuclear), the shows naturalize a very narrow idea of the American family. They also present familial troubles as always beginning and ending with the family—usually beginning with poor parenting skills. By focusing solely on individual families' dysfunction and renovation, I argue, these programs work to reinforce a neoliberal faith in the transformative power of personal growth and responsibility and obscure the wider social forces and government policies that shape the fate of America's families and individual citizens.

NEOLIBERAL POLITICS OF THE AMERICAN FAMILY MAKEOVER

"Strong families are the foundation of society."[4] Or so claimed Ronald Reagan in 1984, succinctly expressing an ideology that continues to shape how Americans think about the family and the nation. The assertion that strong families, rather than good government or caring communities, are the key to social stability is a highly political move—one that has overburdened the family with tremendous responsibility (both ideological and material). In the process, it reinforces a neoliberal cynicism about the state and public solutions to many social problems. Neoliberalism relies on distinctions between institutions such as the state, the family, civic life, and the economy. In contrast to the state, for example, the free market is posited as endemic to human nature—an assumption then used to criticize state intervention in the natural operations of the economy. The heterosexual family, connected as it is to the biology of sexual difference and reproduction, is similarly understood to be a product of nature and separate from the public world of government action and market forces. For Reagan (and many Americans), however, a strong family is not merely naturally heterosexual, but also narrowly imagined in terms of loving parents and happy kids safely ensconced in their single-family home and self-sufficient lives. Masked as natural, this thoroughly ideological construction of the family comes to serve as a powerful model against which real families are judged and to which people are expected to conform. When the American family is made to shoulder so much symbolic weight, renovating weak families becomes a national priority.

Historians trace this romanticized conception of the autonomous heterosexual family to the expansion of capitalism during the nineteenth century. John D'Emilio, for example, argues that employment opportunities outside of the home and the availability of mass-produced consumer products weakened the economic bonds that had tied men (and later women) to the heterosexual family. While people had once been dependent upon a relatively insulated family unit for so many basic material needs, their welfare was increasingly entangled within the complex web of social, economic, and legal relations produced by complex capitalist democracies. Although certain demands placed on the family eased, other expectations intensified. More so than ever, D'Emilio argues, the family became "enshrined . . . as the source of love, affection, and emotional security, the place where our need for stable, intimate human relationships is satisfied."[5] This new sentimentalized notion of family life affirmed the importance of the heterosexual family by constructing it in opposition to the individualism of the public world. According to Stephanie Coontz, "Liberal politics and capitalist markets expunged particularistic ties, social obligations, and personal dependencies from their general operating principles . . . [and] redefined these behaviors as *family* functions and relocated them in love relations."[6]

Romanticizing the family as a bulwark against the heartlessness of the public world masks the real material conditions that link families to that public world. In the case of childrearing, for example, D'Emilio asserts that even as the work of raising children has become increasingly socialized (e.g., public schooling, the media, professionalized healthcare), a capitalist ideology "maintains that reproduction and childrearing are private tasks, that children 'belong' to parents, who exercise the right of ownership."[7] Similarly, Coontz points out that the new sentimentalized family was predicated upon a gendered division of labor and class privilege that assumed women were at home creating nurturing environments where healthy children could be raised and to which hardworking fathers could return. The private family emerged as an ideological response to the needs of liberal capitalism, not independent of it.

By the 1950s, the notion that the nuclear family should be the elemental force organizing people's lives became hegemonic. After the economic deprivations and social upheavals of the Depression and World War II, a sentimental notion of a stable, self-sufficient family life held the seductive promise of transformation—a promise seemingly fulfilled by a postwar economy and government policies that enabled many people "to try to live out the romanticized dream of a private family, happily ensconced in their nest" for the first time.[8] Marriage rates, birth rates, and single-family-home construction boomed. Americans seemed eager to make themselves over in line with a narrow family ideal—the harmonious, hermetically sealed nuclear family whose breadwinner father and stay-at-home mother were seemingly capable of meeting all of the family's needs and solving all of its problems. Advice literature, for example, stressed the importance of nuclear-family bonding, encouraging heterosexual couples to prioritize their relationship with each other at the expense of same-sex friendships and community ties. Meanwhile, parents (especially mothers), who had previously relied on the help of extended families and neighbors, were expected to raise their children on their own.

This romanticized ideology of the autonomous family remains powerful. According to Coontz, our contemporary culture's reverence for marriage and its fixation on the relationship between husbands and wives are actually greater now than ever.[9] The importance placed on parenting, especially on mothers' responsibilities, has never been greater either. Susan Douglas and Meredith Michaels, for example, examine what they call "new momism"—a set of expectations that tells women "that to be a remotely decent mother, a woman has to devote her entire physical, psychological, emotion, and intellectual being, 24/7, to her children."[10] More than just "impossible ideals about childrearing," new momism "redefines all women, first and foremost, through their relationships to children. Thus, being a citizen, a worker, a governor, an actress, a First Lady, all are supposed to take a backseat to motherhood."[11]

There is certainly debate over what it takes to be a strong family today. Social conservatives, for example, remain firmly wedded to the belief that families should reflect an Ozzie-and-Harriet ideal, while many people believe that self-fulfilled working mothers raise healthier children. Yet fewer people question the idea that one's expected life progression is to find a soul mate, get married, have children, and raise them in a home of one's own. Few people question the idea that one's relationships with one's spouse and children are or should be based on love, or that those relationships should be the most important in one's life, existing on a more fundamental level than others. Most people assume that family should dictate one's life decisions in ways that one's relationship with friends or neighbors never would. It *seems* natural to move cross-country when one's spouse gets transferred, for example, but odd to do so if one's best friend does. It *seems* natural to spend Christmas morning with one's family, not with one's coworkers or neighbors.

Cultural conceptions about the natural primacy and autonomy of the family serve those eager to dismantle the welfare state. Once the nuclear family was firmly established as the only place one *needed* to look for support, its has taken little effort to assert that it is the only place one *should* look for support. Within this neoliberal logic, government efforts to help struggling families (e.g., Aid to Families with Dependent Children, Medicaid, food stamps, Section 8 Housing Payment Assistance Program, Head Start) become inappropriate. In fact, if ensuring family member welfare is under-stood as the raison d'etre of the family, such government programs actually undermine those they are supposed to help—as stories about welfare queens and cycles of dependency attest. Welfare reform legislation under Clinton and Bush has cut financial assistance to families in need in the name of familial revitalization.

Cutting such welfare programs is only one step in what might be called the neoliberal makeover of the American family. New programs have been introduced to promote "strong" families, defined in terms of stable, married heterosexual family units. Bush's "Healthy Marriage Initiative," for example, proposed spending $1.6 million on a propaganda campaign (promarriage billboards, calendars, and posters) and reeducation programs (premarriage training for highschoolers, single adults, and unmarried couples).[12] Although expensive, such government efforts get framed not as state interference in the private world of families but rather as the government helping people help themselves by encouraging them to get into the marriage system where they will then reap the benefits of famlihood. Such programs are part of a wider promarriage movement fighting for such changes as covenant marriages (legally binding contracts that require couples to attend counseling before separating and drastically limit grounds for divorce). Though spearheaded by religious conservatives and a biblically rooted moral mission, the agenda has also been framed in neoliberal terms. Arkansas Governor Mike Huckabee, who renewed his vows with his wife of 31 years in a covenant marriage ceremony in 2005, framed the covenant marriage movement as fiscally responsible governmental policy: "If you start adding up the costs—the costs of child-support enforcement, additional costs in human services, how many kids will go on food stamps—it all adds up."[13] Behind such efforts, of course, is the naive, neoliberal utopian vision of a society in which healthy, stable, families raise healthy, stable kids who produce a healthy stable society that obviates the need for government.

What gets left strikingly masked by this romanticized ideology of the autonomous family is the fact that, as Stephanie Coontz succinctly puts it, "The strong nuclear family is in large measure a creation of the strong state."[14] While it may seem as though our laws about the family (e.g., marriage, custody, inheritance) merely codify natural familial relationships, such laws actively shape how we think about what a family is. In the nineteenth century, for example, court rulings helped construct the nuclear family by overturning colonial-era laws that had made it difficult for couples to marry without the consent of extended kin or community and by enacting new laws that heightened parental obligations to and liability for their children. Progressive-era child labor laws redefined the role of children in working-class families, strengthening the emerging romantic ideal of the family as a shelter from the outside world. And the demand that Utah make polygamy illegal in order to gain statehood in 1896 reveals the state's role in defining marriage as between two people. Far from natural, the American family has been defined and redefined through state intervention, and American families get repeatedly made over in the image of each new ideal.

Our contemporary ways of thinking about the autonomous family also mask the fact that all families, especially "strong" families, are supported by the state. As D'Emilio argues, capitalist ideology constructed the "private" family even as the family's dependency on wider social institutions deepened. Public schooling, which provides socialized day care and de facto job training, is perhaps the most obvious example of such support. Social Security and Medicare ease families' financial burdens by providing retirement income and health insurance for the elderly who might otherwise be dependent upon their children. (In the process, these programs have also helped carve the nuclear family out of the multigenerational family unit.) The growth of suburban homeownership in the 1950s, long the symbol of nuclear family independence, was subsidized by enormous government programs such as the Interstate Highway Act, the GI Bill, and the Federal Housing Authority. Such government subsidies are often invisible as subsidies because they seem universal, but in reality, the benefits of many such programs get distributed unequally. Funding public schools through local taxes, for example, creates a tremendous disparity in the value of public schooling to different families (usually along class lines). Similarly, FHA redlining policies in the 1950s explicitly blocked federal loans to black communities—a racist policy that kept millions of African American families from the enormous and long-lasting benefits of government-subsidized homeownership.

Given the recent gay marriage debate, marriage laws may be the most prominent examples of such discriminatory government support for families. As numerous articles on the battle for same-sex marriage reported, a marriage license automatically gives heterosexual couples access to over 1000 government-created rights and benefits.[15] Married people, for example, have the right to adopt their spouse's children, inherit their property free of tax, and live together in a nursing home. They have automatic hospital visitation rights and the power to make medical decisions for each other. The Family and Medical Leave Act allows them to take time off work to care for an ailing spouse. A husband receives a portion of his wife's Social Security benefits after her death, or vice versa. While some employers offer healthcare benefits to same-sex couples, the federal government taxes that benefit; it does not do so in the case of married heterosexual couples. Marriage laws (as well as other programs) work to facilitate the stability of certain family forms over others, while the ideology of the family works to obscure this constitutive labor. If two-parent, home-owning, heterosexual families are stronger than other family forms—if they do help create more supportive and stable lives for their members—a good deal of that strength comes from specific government policies that privilege those family structures and disadvantage others.

The gay marriage debate—or more specifically, the intense resistance to it—brings the complex relationship between today's deepening neoliberal politics and the ideology of the family into graphic relief. Of course, as the promarriage movement indicates, the prospect of gay marriage is only the most visible example of the significant changes in marriage and family structures that have taken place in recent decades. Pointing to "the emergence of striking permutations in the family structure," child and family researcher Marc H. Bornstein asserts that the "family generally, and parenthood specifically, are in agitated states of question, flux, and redefinition."[16] A variety of interrelated social forces (e.g., the legalization of contraception and no-fault divorce, greater economic opportunities for women, the gay rights movement, innovations in reproductive technology, extended life expectancies, domestic partnership benefits) have helped erode the power of marriage "to organize sexual behavior, living arrangements, and child rearing."[17] The family unit of two married heterosexual parents and their children, for example, is no longer the dominant household form. While married couples constituted 80 percent of all U.S. households in the 1950s, by 2000, less than 51 percent of households were married couples, and married couples with kids comprised only 25 percent of households—a smaller percentage than single-person households.[18] Between 1990 and 2000, the number of cohabiting couples increased 72 percent.[19] A smaller percentage of America's households look like *Ozzie and Harriet* as more households resemble *Seinfeld, King of Queens, Kate and Allie, The Golden Girls,* and *Friends.* As Lisa Duggan and Richard Kim point out, "Household diversity is a fact of American life rooted not just in the 'cultural' revolutions of feminism and gay liberation but in long-term changes in aging, housing, childcare and labor."[20]

This widening gap between our culture's ideology of the family and the changing realities of how people live has ironically come at a time when America's intensifying neoliberalism is trying to shift ever more responsibility from the state to families. Bush's plan to reform social security, for example, epitomizes this privatization agenda, as does the government's anemic response to the growing problems faced by public schools that, despite the empty promises of "No Child Left Behind," has led many parents to send their children to private schools (at least many of those who can afford it). Families are increasingly left to fend for themselves as the government continues to weaken regulations on a wide range of industries. While the FTC and FCC had once helped parents protect children from marketing messages and adult content, for example, new procorporate regulations place the onus squarely on parents. Such efforts to redefine the proper role of the state in ensuring the welfare of its citizens are enabled by a culture where strong families, rather than good governments, are understood as the foundation of society.

Lisa Duggan and Richard Kim brilliantly connect America's deepening neoliberalism, its ideology of the autonomous family, the perceived marriage crisis, and voter opposition to gay marriage.

> The net effect of the neoliberal economic policies imposed in recent decades has been to push the economic and social responsibility away from employers and government and onto private households. The stress on households is intensifying, as people try to do more with less. Care for children and the elderly, for the ill and disabled, has been shifted toward unpaid women at home or to low-paid, privately employed female domestic workers. In this context, household stability becomes a life-and-death issue. On whom would we depend when we can't take care of ourselves? If Social Security shrinks or disappears and your company sheds your pension fund, what happens to you when you can no longer work? In more and more cases, the sole resource is the cooperative, mutually supporting household or kinship network. But if marriage is the symbolic and legal anchor for households and kinship networks, and marriage is increasingly unstable, how reliable will that source of support be?[21]

According to Duggan and Kim, this larger context helps put the resounding success of anti-gay-marriage initiatives in 2004 in perspective. Calls "to 'preserve' marriage might have produced a referendum vote on the desire for household security," they suggest, "with the damage to gay equality caught up in its wake."[22] Nevertheless, gays and lesbians are certainly convenient scapegoats. Presenting same-sex marriage as the clear and present danger to family stability obscures the economic forces and government policies that are putting families under such stress. Thus, neoliberalism overburdens the heterosexual nuclear family both ideologically and materially.

As the gay marriage debate reveals, our contemporary culture is highly invested in its ideology about the family. It is important to the neoliberal privatization agenda, serving as the rationale for redistributing welfare responsibilities to their proper place: the strong American family. And it is important in the lives of people who have to shoulder the burden of those responsibilities. As deepening neoliberalism helps erode faith in the possibility of good governance, a sense of civic responsibility, and alternative options for finding support, the family seems to be and, in fact, becomes all that one has to depend upon. Thus, it is not surprising that the family unit would be so culturally central today. It is not surprising that our culture's reverence for marriage and its fixation on the relationship between husbands and wives are, as Coontz says, unprecedented. It is not surprising that gays and lesbians would want access to the symbolic and material benefits of marriage, or that, as Douglas and Michaels assert, motherhood is celebrated as the essence of women's identities. And, finally, it is not surprising that primetime television would feature not one but two reality shows devoted to helping make over heterosexual families in crisis.

NANNY TV

Both dysfunctional-family makeover shows have their conceptual roots in Britain, where *Supernanny* first aired on Channel 4 to high ratings in the summer of 2004. Having found a hit with *Extreme Makeover: Home Edition*, ABC fought hard to win the rights to produce the American version of *Supernanny*, which premiered in January 2005. Although outbid by ABC for *Supernanny*, an undaunted Fox announced that not only was it going ahead with its own concept, *Nanny 911*, but that it would also beat ABC to the punch, by debuting its nanny show in November 2004. Immediately, both productions conducted nationwide casting calls for families in crisis. "Are your kids out of control?" Fox asked American parents (with kids two-to-nine). "If so, give yourself a break and contact *Nanny 911*."[23] With only slight difference in set up and tone, the two shows are nearly identical. *Supernanny* stars Jo Frost, a professional nanny from Britain who starred in the original British run. In its only major structural change, *Nanny 911* uses a stable of three British nannies. Each week, an elder states-nanny of sorts (once nanny to the royal family, as her on-screen description informs us) sends out the nanny whose experience makes her somehow particularly suited to solve the case at hand. Both series play up the British angle. Jo Frost pulls up in a traditional London taxi, and the nannies on *Nanny 911* wear hokey British-nanny capes and hats.

Both shows are also exceedingly formulaic, following exactly the same problem-cause-solution-resolution structure in every episode. In the opening, the nannies (and viewers) get a preview of that week's mission. Video highlights show a family in crisis: whining, screaming, violent kids reducing exhausted parents to tears. Knowing a domestic emergency when they see one, the nannies race to the rescue. Once at the house, stage one—problem observation—begins. The nannies spend the first day observing the family going about its normal routine. Of course things quickly devolve. The nanny watches as the children run out-of-control or have emotional meltdowns. Sometimes they hit their siblings, throw their toys, or scream at the top of their lungs. In other cases, they run loose in the street or at the grocery store. In others, they kick and curse their parents. Meanwhile, the parents come off no better. Under the nanny's watchful, disapproving, and often shocked gaze, parents either go about their business ignoring the chaos around them or crumble in the face of their children's behavior. The parents often have their own emotional meltdowns—frequently amid the domestic minefields of dinner and bedtimes.

At the end of day one, the nanny sits down with the parents for stage two at which point she identifies the causes of their problems. Regardless of the family, all problems are rooted in incompetent parenting—in the parent's failure to provide consistency, effective discipline, and structure for the children. Watching families week after week, it becomes clear that screaming kids are modeling the example set by their screaming parents, that tension between husbands and wives invariably spreads to the rest of the family, that busy parents' strategic shortcuts short change their children, and that parents' own emotional baggage leads them to make poor parenting choices. The majority of each episode, however, is devoted to stage three, problem solution, in which the nanny teaches the parents effective techniques that, if done properly, will produce harmony. A daily schedule helps parents maintain a consistent routine for the children and ensures that parents block off important quality time. A rigid series of steps (warning, punishment, apology) helps parents develop an effective means of disciplining bad behavior. And a "feelings box" can facilitate communication between busy parents and overlooked children. Over the course of a week or two, the nanny teaches the parents how to implement these and other behavioral techniques. Although the children often act out under the stress of the changes and the parents always have some problem perfecting their new skills, the nanny eventually succeeds in making the family over by the end of her stay. With the end of the episode comes a positive resolution as scenes of family chaos are replaced with images of family bliss—happy, well-adjusted children and their parents playing in the backyard, going on a picnic, or reading bedtime stories.

As one might expect, *Supernanny* and *Nanny 911* serve as sites where cultural anxieties about the status of the American family overburdened by expectations get negotiated. In many ways, the shows reflect and reinforce the romanticized ideology about the autonomous American family unit essential to the privatization agenda. With only one exception, for example, all of the families featured on both shows in season one were traditional, middle-class, two-parent, heterosexual family units—the very household form that remains ideologically central even as it becomes demographically marginal. Perhaps even more striking is just how unconnected these families are to any outside support system. They are as detached from their communities as the single-family homes they seem sequestered in; there are no grandparents, neighborhood friends, church groups, or daycare centers to be found. The parents may go off to work and the kids may leave for school, but the cameras never take us there. When the family does take a trip to a store or a park, the cameras focus on the chaos the unruly kids cause to the strangers around them. The point is clear: these parents alone are responsible for raising their kids. There is no village to help them. By marginalizing the diversity of family structures in which people increasingly live and presenting families as leading entirely self-contained lives, the shows naturalize a narrow understanding of the family.

Yet the fundamental premise of the show is that these families do need help. If neoliberalism relies on the ability (or faith in the ability) of the family to shoulder more responsibility, *Supernanny* and *Nanny 911*'s tendency to revel in familial dysfunction could erode confidence in the family, especially in the supposedly self-sufficient nuclear family, as an adequate social institution for ensuring people's welfare. After all, these families clearly require professional help, literally, and the need for an outside childcare expert does not dovetail smoothly with an ideology that romanticizes the innate ability of the heterosexual couple to raise kids without outside support.[24]

In the end, however, *Supernanny* and *Nanny 911* expose these struggling families' problems in order to recuperate them. For skeptical viewers, the final few shots of domestic harmony may not adequately offset the almost-hour-long expose of discord. And given the depth of their dysfunction, the family's quick recovery might make their transformation appear unconvincing. Nevertheless, the ideological power of these weekly makeover narratives cannot be dismissed—primarily because they create their own internal logic about what needs to be changed in order to make these families better. The problem plaguing these American families is bad parenting and the solution is parents' taking responsibility to learn and employ techniques such as the "naughty chair" and "daily schedule." Many children (and adults) do suffer from the effects of overstressed and ill-prepared parents, but practical solutions could include the promotion of multigenerational or multifamily households, community subsidized day care programs, abuse intervention programs, family-friendly labor laws, and the like. Furthermore, American families face a long list of external problems (e.g., failing public schools, no access to health care, rising housing costs, environmental pollution, rising levels of debt) that demand complex changes involving not just personal responsibility but also community cooperation and government intervention. And other kinds of families (e.g., single-parent families, gay-and-lesbian families, poor families) require far more than learning the "naughty chair" technique to solve the unique problems that they face.

By framing the American family, its problems, and its solutions as they do, *Supernanny* and *Nanny 911* work to reinforce the ideological notion that families—at least these two-parent, heterosexual families—can be self-sufficient. Like Bush's "Healthy Marriage Initiative," the nannies merely provide temporary (not structural) help and viewers are encouraged to believe that after their two-week renovation these families will take care of themselves and serve as the kind of strong family upon which a stable society rests. Furthermore, as a privatized rather than socialized form of assistance, nannies represent a kind of external intervention that does not fundamentally undermine the autonomy of the family, at least according to a neoliberal logic. The nannies' British-ness also helps in this regard. Not surprisingly, critics often related the programs to *Mary Poppins*, the widely popular 1964 Disney film that starred Julie Andrews as a mysterious, stern, yet friendly British nanny who uses magic and song to transform a cold Victorian-era London household into a warm and child-friendly family. Framed as modern-day Mary Poppins, these supernannies become supernatural helpers of sorts. As such, their intrusion into the nuclear family can seem less threatening to nuclear-family independence. In contrast, a prime-time series entitled *Superssocialworker* or *Child Protective Services 911* would hardly seem possible on prime-time American television, underscoring how engrained suspicion about state involvement in the private family has become.

Although examining viewers' readings of the programs is beyond the scope of this chapter, popular press reviews suggest ways in which such representations of family dysfunction and recuperation could work to support a privatization agenda. Often framing the show as a guilty pleasure, several critics tried to explain what they (and to predict what others) got out of watching the programs. Two reading positions emerge—one derived from the pleasure of relief and the other from the pleasure of recognition. In the first, watching such intensely dysfunctional families made one feel better about one's own. Alessandra Stanley in the *New York Times* claims that " 'Supernanny' allows viewers to wallow in the smug assurance that compared to the Jeanses or the Orms their own households are flawlessly run."[25] Other critics, however, acknowledge that they could see themselves in these out-of-control parents and that watching the show was actually instructive. "I tuned in thinking I'd get some perverse pleasure from watching these people—so clueless they actually asked to be on the show, to let the whole world see how dysfunctional they are," the *San Diego Union-Tribune*'s Jane Clifford admits. "Well after about five minutes of this week's episode on 'Nanny 911', I wasn't so smug anymore. It's like 'Scared Straight' for parents."[26] Although different, both responses dovetail well with the neoliberal politics of the family. The first works to reaffirm viewers' confidence in their own families. The latter encourages them to find ways to improve their families along the lines suggested in the show. In neither, do viewers ask whether out-of-control kids are the most serious problem facing America's families right now nor whether implementing a daily schedule and giving their kids a feelings box are the best solutions for struggling families.

Although the shows themselves suggest that America's families need only themselves (and a two-week visit from Mary Poppins), the commercials aired during the show add their own take on what American families need.[27] A fundamental advertising strategy, after all, is to offer consumers solutions to their problems (often ones they do not know they have). Thus, the seemingly unrelated ads for cell phones, SUVs, and appliances provide solutions to a whole range of domestic problems and work together to define the successful, happy American family in consumerist terms. While this connection is often subtle, an Applebee ad promoting its carside-to-go service that appeared on an episode of *Nanny 911* ("McKelvain Family," April 11, 2005) seemed scripted just for that episode. Like many of the families on *Supernanny* and *Nanny 911*, part of the McKelvain's problem was the father's refusal to help out with domestic labor.[28] Providing for his family by working all day, he felt, was his proper role. Nanny Yvonne's mission was to convince Mr. McKelvain that he needed to be more involved in raising his kids if his family was to be successful. To that end, Nanny Yvonne gave mom the evening off and made dad take care of dinner and bedtime. When the kids misbehaved, however, Mr. McKelvain lost his patience and spanked his son—a parenting technique none of the nannies approve of. Stepping in, Nanny Yvonne takes Mr. McKelvain outside for an intense chat about why spanking is not good parenting. As the scene ends, we cut to the Applebee's commercial in which a man on a construction site receives a call from home. His wife, swamped with overexcited kids pestering her for attention, asks him to arrange dinner. Unlike Mr. McKelvain, this dad happily agrees to help. Will it be an onerous task? No. A quick call to Applebee's solves the problem. On his way home, dad swings by the neighborhood restaurant and a smiling server runs his family's meal out to his car. He returns home like the conquering hero, as his family rushes out to greet him. While his happy kids sit around the diner table relishing their meal, his wife leans over and gives him a kiss. The message could not be clearer: Applebee's can help you make your family functional.

CONCLUSION

Supernanny and *Nanny 911* promise to rescue America's parents, yet the kind of help these makeover narratives offer may ironically work to increase the burden on those parents even more. These struggling families get renovated only to find themselves recast in the image of the strong (self-sufficient, nuclear, heterosexual) American family in whose name neoliberalism continues to roll back government support for families—especially struggling families. Our romanticized notions about the autonomous, heterosexual, nuclear family as a haven from the messy politics of the public world help explain our culture's fixation on the importance of the family. After all, we live in a culture where preserving the sanctity of heterosexual marriage has led to an Act of Congress and where parenting is expected to be the basis of one's identity. But this ideology also masks the reality of the complex relationship between the state and family life, forecloses practical and productive options for helping real families, and limits our ability to imagine ways for creating a society that can better ensure the welfare of all of its citizens.

How else can or should we think about the problems facing America's families? As if responding directly to *Supernanny* and *Nanny 911*, family development expert James Garbarino argues that, "Viewing parents only in terms of individual and interpersonal dynamics precludes an understanding of the many other avenues of influence that might be open to policy or program intervention."[29] When considering children's welfare, Garbarino urges us to consider not only the impact of toxic parenting but also the "socially toxic environment" within which many parents and children must live—an environment broadly understood as the result of government and community policies on clean air protection, gun control, labor laws, and other such areas. Stephanie Coontz, frustrated by the simplistic moralism of conservative rhetoric about the evils of single-parent families, also challenges us to envision the relationship between the family and society differently: "good parenting has always required *more* than two parents. If there is any pattern to be found in the variety of families that have succeeded and failed over the course of history, it is that children do best in societies where childrearing is considered too important to be left entirely to parents."[30] As such, critics point out that, despite what we may think, raising children is a public activity that involves parents, communities, and the government. Acknowledging that fact, rather than continuing to invest in a romantic notion about the sanctity of family life, will enable us to raise children better.

And more profoundly, how else can we consider what a family actually looks like? Our culture constructs the heterosexual nuclear family as the natural place where human welfare is best ensured. As the gay marriage debate and the increasing changes in household structures reveal, however, the heterosexual nuclear family form is far from universal and natural. Nevertheless, a panoply of rights and privileges are distributed through the institution of marriage, creating a system that discriminates against those people living in households or emotional-support networks that do not or can not conform to the government's narrow definition of a family. Tax advantages, joint-parenting responsibilities, medical decisions, and health care benefits do not have to be linked to the conjugal family. People can and do create relationships of support and dependency outside of the traditional heterosexual family. How might new policies that distribute the symbolic, legal, and material benefits that are now solely linked to heterosexual marriages help us think more democratically about the family in radically new ways and actually create greater social stability by make a wider range of family forms work better?

Supernanny and *Nanny 911* do not encourage us to ask these questions. They encourage us to imagine the American family, to understand its problems, and to envision possible solutions in very narrow terms—a highly political move. *Supernanny* and *Nanny 911*, of course, represent only one site where such ideological work takes place, as Jennifer Gillan's essay on *Extreme Makeover: Home Edition* in this volume aptly demonstrates. For a politics of privatization, American families and their single-family homes must at least *seem* strong enough to carry the growing burden of post-welfare-state responsibilities.

NOTES

1. Quoted words and phrases taken from opening credit sequences and promotional spots for *Nanny 911* and *Supernanny*.
2. Quoted in Richard Lacayo, Perry Bacon Jr., and John F. Dickerson, "For Better Or For Worse?" *Time*, March 8, 2004, p. 26.
3. See Christopher Lasch, *Women and The Common Life: Love, Marriage, and Feminism*, ed. Elisabeth Lasch-Quinn (New York: W.W. Norton & Company, 1997); Christopher Lasch, *Haven in a Heartless World: The Family Besieged* (New York: Basic Books, 1977); Wally Seccombe, *A Millennium of Family Change: Feudalism to Capitalism in Northwestern Europe* (London: Verso, 1992); Andre Burguiere, Christiane Klapisch-Zuber, Martin Segalen, and Francoise Zonabend, ed., *A History of the Family Volumes I and II* (Cambridge, U.K.: Polity, 1996).
4. Quoted in Stephanie Coontz, *The Way We Never Were: American Families and the Nostalgia Trap* (New York: Basic Books, 1992), p. 94.
5. John D'Emilio, "Capitalism and Gay Identity," in *The Lesbian and Gay Studies Reader*, ed. Henry Abelove, Michele Aina Barale, and David M. Halperin (New York: Routledge, 1993), p. 473.

6. Coontz, *The Way We Never Were*, p. 55.

7. D'Emilio, "Capitalism and Gay Identity," p. 473.

8. Coontz, *Marriage, a History*, p. 231.

9. Ibid., pp. 2–3.

10. Susan J. Douglas and Meredith W. Michaels, *The Mommy Myth: The Idealization of Motherhood and How It Has Undermined Women* (New York: Free Press, 2004), p. 4.

11. Ibid., p. 22.

12. Sharon Lerner, "Marriage on the Mind: The Bush Administration's Misguided Poverty Cure," *Nation*, July 5, 2004, p. 40.

13. Quoted in Rick Lyman, "Trying to Strengthen an 'I Do' With a More Binding Legal Tie," *New York Times*, February 15, 2005. Available from Lexis-Nexis.

14. Coontz, *The Way We Never Were*, p. 145.

15. See John Cloud et al., "The Battle Over Gay Marriage," *Time*, February 16, 2004, pp. 56–63; Angie Cannon, "A Legal Maze—And More to Come," *U.S. News & World Report*, March 8, 2004, pp. 30–31; Ron Mackey, "Don't Grant Gays Benefits Meant to Bolster Traditional Marriage," *USA Today*, March 25, 2004, A14; Dan Gilgoff, "The Rise of the Gay Family," *U.S. News & World Report*, May 24, 2004, pp. 40–46.

16. Marc C. Bornstein, "Refocusing on Parenthood," in *Parenthood in America: Under Valued, Under Paid, Under Siege*, ed. Jack C. Westman (Madison: University of Wisconsin Press, 2001), p. 5.

17. Coontz, *Marriage, a History*, p. 262.

18. Ibid., p. 276.

19. Lisa Duggan and Richard Kim, "Beyond Gay Marriage," *Nation*, July 18–25, 2005, p. 25.

20. Ibid.

21. Ibid.

22. Ibid., p. 26.

23. Quoted in Charles Goldsmith, "TV's New Nanny Show Is No 'Mary Poppins'," *Wall Street Journal*, September 30, 2004, eastern edition. Available from ProQuest.

24. At a time when conservatives use the supposed unnaturalness of same-sex parenting as an argument against gay marriages, images of traditional families gone awry could be used to argue that no family unit it inherently perfect. Of course, they could also be used to argue for an even more vigilant reinforcement of the heterosexual nuclear family.

25. Alessandra Stanley, "All Unhappy Families Need Mary Poppins," *New York Times*, January 17, 2005, p. 46.

26. Jane Clifford, "Reality TV Hold Up a Mirror To Our Mess," *San Diego Union-Tribune*, January 15, 2005. Available from Lexis-Nexis.

27. The final two episodes of *Supernanny*'s first season also included ads sponsored by Focus on the Family, the James-Dobson-led conservative Christian organization. The 30-second ads encouraged viewers to visit a Web site that offered "family advice and a faith-based perspective." *Supernanny*'s

images of families in crisis provided Dobson an opportunity to promote his philosophy about proper parenting. In books such as *Dare to Discipline*, Dobson blames such domestic chaos on permissive parents afraid to discipline their children. Much like the nannies, Dobson focuses on getting parents back in control. Unlike the supernannies, however, Dobson believes spanking is an important parenting technique. As Ellen Goodman points out, Dobson's anxiety about permissive parents and out-of-control children mirrors the conservative anxiety about the a permissive liberal governance that encourages individualism, no-fault divorce, abortion, birth control, and gay rights and, as a result, has produced domestic chaos on a national level. Although *Supernanny* and *Nanny 911* argue against spanking and do not explicitly promote the conservative family politics Dobson and the promarriage movement advocate, the shows do not challenge them and, in fact, could be read as tacitly supporting such conservative politics. Divorce, e.g., is almost never an option on either show. The nannies' British-ness could play an important role here as well. Although many Americans may be anxious about the stability of the family at a time when neoliberal politics are placing more responsibility on them, few would likely support stricter divorce laws, illegalization of birth control, or even the kind of Old Testament discipline Dobson endorses. The supernannies' British accents, taxis, caps, and capes link the shows' pro-discipline message to the Mary-Poppins-inspired stereotype of the proper British nanny (and an American deference for posh British sophistication) rather than to strident Christian fundamentalism and its spare-the-rod-spoil-the-nation political agenda. In this way, British nannies may help make the conservative-family-agenda medicine go down more easily. Ellen Goodman, "Learning from Dobson's Discipline," *Baltimore Sun*, May 16, 2005. Available from LexisNexis.

28. In general, the shows' gender politics are relatively progressive. Unlike the ideology of new momism that Douglas and Michaels identify, *Supernanny* and *Nanny 911* do not particularly frame parenting roles in traditionally gendered ways. Their techniques, e.g., are gender neutral, and the nannies insist that both parents need to participate in parenting equally. Although families with stay-at-home moms are more common on the shows, most of the families have two working parents. Given the home-bound nature of the shows, however, one parent almost always works from home. Nevertheless, the series still operate in a world where parenting and marriage remain highly gendered. The nannies, e.g., are all women, and the brunt of the domestic labor usually falls on the mothers' shoulders. In line with Douglas and Michaels' argument, ABC ran a *Supernanny* marathon on the Family Channel for Mother's Day; it did not do this on Father's Day.

29. James Garbarino, "Supporting Parents in a Socially Toxic Environment," in *Parenthood in America: Under Valued, Under Paid, Under Siege*, ed. Jack C. Westman (Madison: University of Wisconsin Press, 2001), p. 220.

30. Coontz, *The Way We Never Were*, p. 230.

CHAPTER 12

EXTREME MAKEOVER HOMELAND SECURITY EDITION

JENNIFER GILLAN

THE UNITED STATES, A SELF-INTERESTED SUPERPOWER, began reinventing itself as a disinterested good neighbor with its early twentieth-century foreign policy aimed at maintaining stability in the Americas through cooperation and trade rather than through military force. Describing this "Good Neighbor Policy" in a speech in Honduras, President Hoover assured, "We have a desire to maintain not only the cordial relations of governments with each other but also the relations of good neighbors." Franklin Delano Roosevelt concurred, at least rhetorically: "In the field of world policy I would dedicate this nation to the policy of the good neighbor—the neighbor who resolutely respects himself and, because he does so, respects the rights of others—the neighbor who respects his obligations and respects the sanctity of his agreements in and within a world of neighbors."[1]

This emphasis on neighborliness in U.S. foreign policy has led Americans to conceive of U.S. intervention in the internal affairs of other nations as a form of benevolent aid. Andrew J. Bacevich, Walter Russell Mead, Samantha Power, and Walter McDougall, among others, have commented upon this "abiding preference for averting our eyes from the unflagging self-interest and large ambitions underlying all U.S. policy."[2] In matters of foreign policy, the United States pledges to promote and respect independence and self-government, but it will not hesitate to intervene in a sovereign state in the name of helping its less fortunate "neighbors" reach a level of self-governing independence. Whether the United States is viewed as a philanthropic neighbor or self-interested intervener in relation to those it has offered aid (e.g., American Indians, Filipinos, Vietnamese, Iraqis) depends on the evaluator. The critical citizen's Century of Dishonor, to borrow the title from Helen Hunt Jackson's 1880 denunciation of U.S. Indian Policy,[3] is the enthusiastic patriot's Century of Progress, the name of the early-twentieth-century World's Fair aimed at countering such charges of dishonor by reinventing the United States as the progressive nation of the future. That fair, like its more famous predecessor, the 1893 World's Columbia Exposition,[4] offered displays that "visualized the course of American progress."[5] When William "Buffalo Bill" Cody located his Wild West encampment on the outskirts of the 1893 fair, he offered a live version of the "course of American progress" whose landscape was a "mythic space in which past and present, fiction and reality, could coexist: a space in which history, translated into myth, was re-enacted as ritual."[6]

It is in the mythic space of the Wild West in which *Extreme Makeover Home Edition* (EMHE) located its deeply moving Season Two finale, in which the TV program's design team partnered with rescued POW Jessica Lynch to fulfill her personal promise to care for the family of her fallen fellow solider Lori Piestewa. The way the Piestewa episode writes the history of the War in Iraq and of U.S.-Indian relations might be characterized in the same way that Richard Slotkin describes Cody's Wild West: "despite its battery of authentications, the Wild West wrote 'history' by conflating it with mythology. The re-enactments were not recreations but reductions of complex events into 'typical scenes' based on the formulas of popular literary mythology."[7] As Gioia Woods notes, it is no accident that the May 2005 episode is filled with shots straight out of western films, as the editors of EMHE employ the Myth of the Frontier throughout the episode to translate the War in Iraq and the Piestewas' participation in it into mythic terms of what Slotkin calls "regeneration through violence."[8] Indeed, her argument is that EMHE builds on Slotkin's theory that "the mass media provide the broadest-based and most pervasive means for canvassing the world of events and the spectrum of public concerns, for recalling historical precedents, and for translating them into various story-genres that constitute a public mythology."[9]

Slotkin's and other core American Studies texts are central to this chapter's reading of EMHE as a media text that models for Americans how they should relate to the world and conceive of American aid and their own citizenship. Grounding itself as well in television studies, this essay focuses more particularly on the ways in which the shot sequences in EMHE demonstrate for the audience not political or economic, but personal and emotional, neighborly ways to "support our troops." In so doing, EMHE points to a larger trend of imagining American citizenship culturally in terms of what John Hartley calls "semiotic self-determination," rather than in terms of political or civic identity. In cultural citizenship "semiotic self-determination is 'claimed' as a 'right' and 'taught' as a mode of civility or neighbourliness by those within its purview."[10] In addition, Hartley explains, "citizens of media are presumably 'subject' to some institution which is doubtless seeking to lead them, to take power in their name, to mobilize them in one cause or another."[11] In the case of the Piestewa episode, the cause is for Americans to "support our troops," and "our president" through their willingness to "stay the course." Positioned as empathetic supporters and encouraged to enact neighborliness in their own lives, EMHE viewers are "collectivized as citizens"[12] of the commendable nation.

The plots of EMHE pivot on the idea of a neighborliness that is broadly defined. The show offers evidence that, in general, the United States is characterized by a commendable culture of neighborliness. Through this emphasis, EMHE makes over the image of post–9/11 American culture as well as of its television programming. It does so by distancing itself from the humiliation-based tactics associated with talk shows as well as with the tactics of the Abu Ghraib prison guards. In EMHE's United States, a commendable American POW replaces the contemptible abuser of Iraqi POWs, compassionate and benevolent CEOs replace callous and corrupt corporate leaders, and decent, deserving families replace undeserving gamedoc winners and depraved talk show guests. EMHE offers its viewers a United States reconstituted as "the utopian symbolic 'nation' " of American mythology,[13] a homeland secure in its borders as well as its identity. Such a utopian idea of the nation "offers safe haven and warmth in a cold, menacing world" in which "risk and insecurity are pervasive," Sylvio Waisbord explains.[14]

HOMELAND SECURITY CULTURE

Since the 2001 terrorist attacks, Americans have been living in a constant state of insecurity. Though the climate is one of generalized fear, often that fear hinges on a mistrust of one's neighbors—or more precisely of enemies posing as neighbors, of the seemingly innocuous people living in American neighborhoods or sitting across the aisle on subways, buses, and airplanes. Viewing it as "the catalyst of a shift from a moment of security to a moment of vulnerability," Waisbord describes September 11 as "a 'break-in' through the protective shield of postwar American national identity."[15] No longer could Americans conceive of their homeland as Fortress America, a nation securely positioned between two oceans, far from sites of global conflict. The Department of Homeland Security was created to address heightened awareness of homeland vulnerability. Today's Homeland Security (antiterrorism) policy functions in the way Alan Nadel claims that Containment (anticommunism) policy did in the postwar period: as a national security policy that became part of the U.S. cultural agenda and a source of meaning for its citizens. This Homeland Security Culture is both a makeover of, and a return to, 1950s style Containment Culture that divides the world into two camps, fetishizes national security, and establishes uncritical support as a value unto itself, and makes "personal behavior part of a global strategy."[16] Homeland Security involves the containment of threatening intranational populations and subversive political energies (liberals, protestors, critics). It directs Americans away from active citizenship and toward sentimental and patriotic identification with the utopian symbolic nation. EMHE encourages sentimental sympathy that renders invisible power relations and bypasses the question of "why some individuals are politically and economically empowered and others are not."[17] "As a particular code of identification," Lori Merish explains, "sentimental sympathy can be seen to neutralize the relations of political inequality it upholds."[18]

This focus on political sentimentality, providing evidence of an abundance of emotional support to American troops and their families, distracts from problems of political practicality and the lack of government aid and support for fighting and returning troops (e.g., access to proper body armor during the war and health care thereafter). It turns the complexities of the War in Iraq and the situation of the soldiers involved into a simple catch phrase "support our troops." Emptied of actual political, economic, and social meaning, the phrase becomes a way for Americans to voice emotional support for soldiers without having to confront the complicated national policy or history (this is especially ironic given the phrase's association with the cultural crises and national policy failures of the Vietnam era). Pivoting on the concept of honor, "The Piestewa Family" episode shows Americans how to "support our troops." It suggests that the best way to do so is to affirm the honor of their mission, commend the honor of their self-sacrificing service, and honor their memories should they offer "the ultimate sacrifice."

TRAILER OF TEARS

The episode's intended focus on ways to honor American troops is particularly evident in the sequence of shots during the "before" segment. The medium and long shots of the design team entering the Piestewa trailer and marveling at how all the available wall space is covered with Lori memorabilia affirms the appropriateness of such an emotional outpouring. When Paul DiMeo (carpentry) and Preston Sharp (exterior design) tour the trailer, they point out all of the "tribute" "that people have sent to honor Lori." The segment emphasizes how much Americans have already remembered Lori, but it cannot foreclose an alternative reading of the Piestewas as representatives of the troubling class and racial issues embedded in the U.S. volunteer military policy. Terry reveals that military service is generational for the Piestewas; while the fact is continually characterized as a signifier of their patriotism, it might just as well be read as evidence of the inadequacies of the government's support for returning troops or of the economic alternatives for the American working poor.

When Lori's parents express their grief and push their responses toward a call for political, social, or civic action, the designers contextualize the comments so that they can be interpreted in terms of a discourse of "national sentimentality where complex political conditions are reduced or refined into the discourses of dignity and the authority of feeling."[19] For example, when Percy breaks down while discussing the loss of her daughter, she says, "It's tough and it's never going to go away." After a two-shot of lead designer Ty Pennington comforting Percy, the editors use a jump cut to introduce an interview segment with Eduardo Xol (landscaping). He explains, "Percy and Terry were extremely proud of Lori and Lori's service in the military. Lori comes from a family that has served for the military for a few generations." For evidence, insert shots of Piestewa family military photographs are shown. As the camera lingers over a picture of Terry as a young solider, we hear his voice explaining that he was drafted during the Vietnam War. Once on camera, he says, "Lori, she joined the military to help her family [pause] support her family." To downplay the full ramifications of Terry's statement, the editor inserts an interview with Jessica in which she talks about Lori not as a fellow solider or a working poor American looking to the military for economic opportunity, but as her "best friend and sister." The shot sequence ends with Terry reiterating Jessica's gratitude toward EMHE for helping to fulfill "Lori's dream" of providing for her family: "I tell you, you people are completing the dream for her." Within the montage, in other words, each time an alternate, less honorable reading surfaces of the American history that Lori represents (or of her death in the War in Iraq), the editor adds another interview to reaffirm the message about honorable service, meaningful sacrifice, and commendable culture.

Within this sequence, as well as in the others that follow, the designers reiterate that Lori and her family are Americans deserving of the empathy and aid of EMHE (and viewers) because they made "the ultimate sacrifice." Bert Selva, who, along with Peter Shea, runs Shea Homes and was recruited by EMHE for the Piestewa project, reminds his team of volunteers that the Piestewas "gave the ultimate sacrifice; they lost their daughter and their mother. And we want to do the very best thing that we can for this family because they're giving up their retirement years to raise their two grandkids. Who's in?" The cheering he receives in response exemplifies for viewers the proper reaction of neighborly Americans. The cheering might also be for Shea Homes as a representative of the compassionate corporation. This idea is conveyed in the introduction to "Peter and Bert" as compassionate CEOs via an insert shot of the Shea Homes banner (*Caring since 1881*) and a sound bridge to an explanation by Constance Ramos (building/planning) that Shea is a "family-owned, family-run," all-American business. Once on camera, she adds, "They built the Hoover Dam. They built the Golden Gate Bridge!"

Similarly, commentary by other designers encourages Terry, Percy, and Jessica to represent themselves in terms of personal compassion rather than concerned citizenship. EMHE continually defines them as Americans who fulfill personal promises. In turn, the three often repeat the same narrative espoused by the designers, suggesting that they are aware of the performance environment in the same way that Annette Hill and Laura Grindstaff claim that Reality TV contestants and talk show guests are aware of producer expectations for their "performance."[20] When, for example, Terry says, "It's been two years now and it still hurts quite a bit," he quickly adds, "and I think it's because my grandkids are going to grow up without a mother." The addition moves his comments away from those of a critical citizen and toward those of a compassionate grandparent. Percy has a harder time playing her part. When she says, "We lost our daughter, but we only hope that our families and our friends didn't have to deal with what we did [. . .] because it's hard," she treads close to a common war protestor's lament: how many other people's children have to die before this war ends. She struggles to articulate her thought: "And it's tough, It's tough, but [. . .]" Before she can say anymore, she is forced to pause and respond to Carla's offscreen cry: "Grandma!" Percy turns toward the indirect sound, asking, "What sweetie?" After Carla enters the frame, Percy says, "My, baby girl." Then the editor cuts to the bus where the design team is watching the application tape. The repositioning of Percy is achieved during and after her comments. As Percy speaks, we sometimes see the designers' reactions as they watch the tape. Inserted as well are several group shots of the designers looking empathetic and closeups of a teary-eyed Connie, a crying Jessica, and an emotional Paige Hemmis (carpentry). As Percy finishes, Paige steps across the aisle to comfort Jessica. Connie then explains, "It was moving to experience this with Jessica." The next shot is of Jessica, who, after getting her tears in check, explains her loss of emotional control: "It's just tough losing your best friend." As she says the final word, the camera switches to teary-eyed Paige, suggesting her empathetic agreement. EMHE assures viewers that Jessica's request for aid does not come from her position as a returning solider or a concerned citizen (as from either position she might join others who are critiquing the many ways the American government continues to fail to "support our troops"). Rather, as Michael Moloney (interior design) explains for her, Jessica has come forward as a loyal friend trying to find a way to keep her promise to the "sister" she lost: "You guys had a pact. You're holding up your end of the deal." Jessica and several of the designers nod in assent.

EMHE devotes much of its airtime to these sorts of shot-countershot sequences that establish the emotional interplay between Lori's "family" and the appropriately empathetic designers. The kind of emotional closeup on which the sequences rely can be called the "money shot," a term Grindstaff uses to describe the camerawork on talk shows that captures emotions "expressed in visible, bodily terms."[21] EMHE features several money shots of Lynch and the Piestewas trying not to cry, wiping away tears, and then composing themselves. These sequences are intended to offer the viewer visual signs of their emotional trauma and their courageous recovery. As noted earlier, these sequences are sometimes intercut with the taped commentary with individual designers contextualizing the reactions of Lori's "family" as emblematic of their willingness to persevere despite their losses. The money shot, in these interviews, is of the choked up or teary-eyed designers, as they function as stand-ins for the desired audience position of the empathetic American.

THE CHALLENGE: MAKING OVER TRASH TV

The extratextual interviews with designers also provide occasions for reinforcing and making explicit the show's message about deserving people, especially given that clips from these interviews are shown prior to commercial breaks as coming attractions for the next segment. Although borrowing from the gamedoc's "housemate interview" convention, EMHE uses its praise-filled designer interviews to offer a twist on the usual trash talk and gossip-centered interviews in which individual gamedoc or docusoap contestants reveal negative things about each other.

Through its makeover of such "trashy" programming, EMHE works to calm fears about social decay by assuring its audience that most Americans are deserving, kind-hearted people and solid citizens. The label "trash TV" most often refers to the sensational or tabloid style of programming in which guests "always predominantly female but [since the mid-1990s] increasingly black, queer, and working class—[are] encouraged to abandon politeness and restraint for more raucous, carnivalesque performances."[22] Often the goal of trash TV programs is to humiliate the ordinary people who appear on them or reprimand them for their willingness to expose themselves and their degeneracy, selfishness, or talentlessness. Seemingly about displaying social deviance, this kind of show actually reinforces notions of social normalcy and national civility. It is usually structured to offer an object lesson via uncivil behavior of the guests/contestants who display sexual deviance, bare their bodies, and/or degrade themselves. As a result, they become the targets of ridicule by and reprimand from the audience or other contestants/guests. Hartley describes this behavior as cultural citizenship on display, explaining that the conflict in the programs and their amusing ruptures "can only work for the audience on a prior presumption of neighbourliness and civility in personal, social and domestic comportment."[23] The audience functions as the voice and face of disapproval and reprimand central to the reinforcement of nuclear family normalcy. According to Jane Shattuc both trashy and classy talk shows "depend on the nuclear family as their mainstay, contrary to their reputation as a spectacle of deviants. Almost every show plays on the fear of loss and the triumph of the return of the nuclear family."[24] EMHE shares its image repertoire (teary-eyed guest and host), narrative pattern (crisis and resolution), and thematic concerns (family crisis and intervention) with the talk show genre. Despite its origins in lifestyle and do-it-yourself programming, EMHE does not situate viewers as apprentices to TV experts, but rather positions them more like talk show audiences, except that they always commend rather than reprimand the featured families.

The home makeover show is also a response to the reprimand the *Extreme Makeover* producers received for the first program in their franchise, the one that offered radical plastic surgery makeovers for self-proclaimed ugly ducklings. The show outraged many people who complained that it was complicit with the shallow beauty and youth cultures that had taken hold of the United States. Charges of shallowness as well as mean-spiritedness also were levied against many other forms of Reality TV programming, including less radical makeover shows and gamedocs in which the contestants were encouraged to humiliate themselves and trash talk each other. In order to make over the talk show and the humiliation-based ensemble reality gamedoc, EMHE substitutes a deserving family for the deviants in the former and the turncoats and troublemakers in the latter. It is not surprising that EMHE reworks the television genres most often associated with an unruly American culture, substituting the emphasis in most trash TV on sensationalism and shock with its own on melodrama and sympathy. Cutthroat competitors and unscrupulous producers willing to humiliate guests for higher ratings are replaced with compassionate designers, producers, and corporate leaders working together to aid deserving families. In short, EMHE represents a commendable American culture and character in which CEOs, workers, families, TV home design/construction experts, producers, sponsors, and the media join forces to make America a better place, one family at a time.

By replacing humiliation-based television with altruism-based television, EMHE reestablishes the homeland as a securely moral space, assuring its viewers that the United States still has a solid foundation and just needs some superficial work. With its representation of a nation comprised of nuclear family–oriented citizens and corporations, the show works to stabilize a core national image that has been employed to characterize the United States as "intimate and secure."[25] It tries to reestablish the home (and the homeland) as a safe space, "a zone of protected value."[26] It must do so to maintain the concept of the desirability and exportability of the American way of life. EMHE taps into ready-made discourses about a morally centered, neighborly American culture representative of "human solidarity, tolerant integration, an ethos of compassion and service, and the respect of democratic values."[27]

THE CRISIS: MISSION ACCOMPLISHED?

EMHE pays tribute to Jessica Lynch as a symbol of neighborliness as well as of the nation's promise to rescue the captured, to commemorate the dead, and to care for and support the survivors. The excess of tears Jessica sheds and inspires might associate her with melodrama, a genre Linda Williams contends is characterized by emotional excess,[28] but the program cannot foreclose her connection with the more troubling issue of personal (as well as national) posttraumatic stress syndrome. Unfortunately, the producers' interpretation of Jessica Lynch as a sentimental symbol rather than a traumatic one cannot contain the textual excess—the ruptures in her transformation into a national symbol that point to the histories of national dishonor. For some, the media spectacle that became known as "Saving Private Jessica" is also a signifier of the dishonorable aspects of American history. The way that Jessica's fellow female soldiers disappeared from the coverage makes "recognizable that America does have hierarchy of life, with pretty blondes at the top."[29] The media offered a racially triangulated narrative: Jessica as the symbolic imperiled white woman, Lori Piestewa as the safely vanished Indian, and Shoshana Johnson, wounded and rescued along with Lynch, as the African American who takes a back seat in the representation of symbolic national events. Shoshana needs to be forgotten in the present because as an African American she also has the potential to symbolize the United States' dishonorable slave-holding past, the specter that still haunts American culture.[30]

With the revelation that the endless tape loop of video and images associated with "Saving Private Jessica" may have had more staging than reality to it, the rescue, instead of representing America's purity of motive ended up representing its knowing compromises. Several news reports cast doubt not only on the authenticity of the images, but also on the purity of U.S. foreign policy motives. Acknowledgment that Jessica's rescue was staged or that, despite her supposedly successful rescue, her trauma is ongoing or her injuries are permanent has the potential to destabilize the categorization of *Operation Iraqi Freedom* as a successful rescue mission.

To avoid these troubling details, the EMHE episode focuses on a specific crisis to be resolved—how to help Jessica honor Lori and other Native American veterans. Within this narrative, the Piestewas are represented as signifiers of honor, both in their family's service to the nation and to their grandchildren and in their commendable response to trauma and loss. With this emphasis on honor, the episode's secondary design project—the construction of a Veteran's Center on the Navajo Reservation—tries (and for some viewers fails) to distance itself from the United States' dishonorable dealings with indigenous peoples. Although intended as another example of the United States' orientation toward neighborly aid, this secondary project cannot foreclose the fact that the absence of such a center is indicative of the United States' neighborly failures. Framed patriotically in terms of national honor—the honor of Navajo code talkers and other servicemen as well as of the current American society that wants to commend and commemorate their service—the Veteran's Center also makes visible the dishonorable past, especially the way U.S. Indian Policies (e.g., Removal, Reservation, and Allotment) represented political and territorial dispossession as rescue.[31]

Together the episode's two design projects point to the intricacy of tribal relations in the United States and highlight the complexity of the Piestewas social, economic, and cultural position. Bypassing the history of the U.S. attempt to "rescue" indigenous Americans from tribalism and to transform them into landholders and consumers, EMHE provides the Piestewas a homestead of their own "in the middle of nowhere," relocating them from the Navajo reservation on which they had been living. Terry is actually Hopi and the five acres in the Flagstaff area on which EMHE builds the new house is land that belongs to the San Manuel, a band of Mission Indians now located in California. To acquire the parcel, Ty contacted Tex Hall of the National Congress of American Indians who, in turn, arranged for the land to be gifted by Derron Marquez, the San Manuel tribal chairman. These intricate territorial rights issues only hint at the convoluted history of territorial battles among indigenous tribes as well as between tribes and the U.S. government. Woods claims that EMHE tries to bypass these complexities, but the introduction of a variety of tribal representatives nevertheless destabilizes the program's fairly simple representation of what it monolithically describes as "the Native American culture."

Despite the emphasis in the episode on charitable corporations and individuals, its big "Reveal" is that tribal cultures—characterized in U.S. Indian policy documents as backward for their lack of interest in individual property ownership and consumerism—have supported and continue to support Lori's parents and her children in ways that the U.S. government has failed to do. In short, despite its attempt to represent honorable American culture, the episode offers evidence that not much has changed in the century since Jackson published her book. Ed Sanders (Construction) acknowledges the failure of the United States to recognize the service of American Indian veterans: "they've had a bum deal out of it; they've had a real bum deal . . . it's our job to take care of these people." His statement is mild compared to the way Jackson reprimanded the United States for its "repeated violations of faith with the Indians." She declared that such dishonorable conduct "convicts us, as a nation . . . of having outraged the principles of justice, which are the basis of international law." In this way, she argued, the United States "laid [itself] open to accusations both of cruelty and perfidy," and, thus, was liable "to arbitrary punishments at the hands of any civilized nation who might see fit to call us to account."[32] The description is similar to the criticisms of the justification for the 2002 U.S. attack on Saddam Hussein's Iraq. If the United States is to stay on the side of the reprimanding civilized nations, rather than drift to that of the infringers of codes of civility and breakers of international law, it needs to compensate for the well-known dishonorable aspects of its own history.

The structure of EMHE works both to affirm the idea of national honor in its current mission and to elide the fact that when the episode aired, it was becoming clear that the administration's declaration of "Mission Accomplished" was premature. With its corner textbox time and day stamp, EMHE plays on fears about a mission that cannot be accomplished, a task that cannot be completed in an allotted amount of time. The show reassures audiences because, after displaying such a crisis, it demonstrates that through teamwork and ingenuity, missions can be completed and order can be restored. Produced during an era of heightened national insecurity and anxiety, EMHE appeals to audiences, at least in part, because of its promise of resolution within a prescribed time frame.

EMHE condenses and articulates cultural concerns about the war in which the United States was still embroiled, four years after a bullhorn wielding President Bush declared from atop a burnt out fire truck at Ground Zero that the United States heard the cries of those in need and would respond. In addition to aid and consolation for victims and their families, he assured that the United States would respond to the attacks and locate and bring to justice the responsible evildoers and make the world safe again. All this was achieved, he proclaimed, when he declared, "Mission Accomplished," from the deck of the USS Lincoln in May 2003, exchanging his September 13 bullhorn for a press conference podium.[33]

Both moments are subtly referenced in "The Piestewa Family" episode after the introduction of the Shea Homes compassionate CEOs. After their speeches to their "troops," Ty Pennington, who often uses a bullhorn to address the other designers and each week's new crop of building volunteers, steps in and explains to the on-site crowd of volunteer workers and the at-home audience that, as there is no original house to demolish, the design team has taken on the secondary project. As a transition and introduction to the crosscutting between the Flagstaff and the Tuba City building sites that will characterize the rest of the episode, Ty says, "do me a favor . . . look over there," at which point there is a jump cut to the Tuba City site.

This creative cutting between the two scenes also symbolically invites viewers to look at the United States through the same heroic lens offered by the president's aircraft carrier press conference. The flight deck landing is visually referenced earlier when, after shots of advancing columns of hard-hat-wearing workers and construction vehicles, the editor inserts a sequence in which Ty and the Shea CEOs dramatically arrive on site via helicopter and are greeted by a cheering crowd of designers and workers. At the end of episode, following the pattern of crisis, solution, minicrises, solutions, catharsis, and closure, the designers can indeed assert "Mission Accomplished" and allay the anxieties of an American public (or at least the 15.8 million season two viewers), many of whom had come to the conclusion that the War in Iraq was not only entered into under false pretenses, but that it was also one from which the United States would be unlikely to extricate itself in the foreseeable future. While the president was premature in his proclamation of "Mission Accomplished," EMHE assures Americans that the mission will indeed be accomplished if they are willing "to stay the course." By representing as instructive the Piestewa family's steadfastness in the face of crisis, EMHE acts as a mobilizer of patriotic national identity, one that is "constructed and reinforced [. . .] vis-à-vis the attacks."[34] It offers the same sentiment that asserts that Americans are the kind of people who are battered but will not bend, a sentiment that the media often express about 9/11 survivors and rescue workers. As a response to the trauma that destabilized the sense of a self-evident national self, it reflects "the need" after a trauma "to reinstate a sense of order."[35] EMHE works to makeover the image of the United States as a posttraumatic culture in the midst of an identity crisis to a solidly grounded culture well on the way to a full recovery.

The episode follows the standard EMHE tripartite structure: melodramatic introduction (to the family and its life and housing crises), renovation (with its midpoint crisis and its final segment resolution), and "the Reveal" (starting with the "move that bus" revelation of the newly renovated home and including the "moral" that the designers garnered from their interaction with the family, one that they want the episode to reveal to the audience). At the start of the renovation portion of the episode, the design team discusses overall ideas and plans and each member specifies his/her personal project, usually one tailored toward an individual family member. While the family is away on an all-expenses-paid vacation at Disney (ABC's parent company), the designers work to a finish within a week a project that would normally take a minimum of four months. Usually, all goes well until the midpoint of the episode. A bullhorn-wielding Ty Pennington, alone or along with one or more of the other designers, theatricalizes the anxiety that the mission/task seems impossible to complete. Then the remainder of the renovation section of the program is left to dramatize the successful completion of the team's mission despite those fears about insurmountable obstacles.

With an implied united declaration of "Mission Accomplished," the design team prepares for the family's arrival on a bus that blocks their view of the house until Ty proclaims, "Move that Bus!" Ty's cry is echoed not only by the family members, but also by the "studio audience," the hundreds of curious onlookers who gather to watch the *Extreme Makeover* team in action and to join in the show's signature chant. In order to capture their unified cheering, the camera pans the crowd, evidencing how EMHE offers a mass-mediated sense of intimacy and a form of public catharsis.[36]

THE "REVEAL": DIY CITIZENSHIP

Although the Piestewa episode attempts to recast the world in comforting ways, its resolution of domestic crises is still as ambivalent as that of the international crisis of the still-ongoing War in Iraq. In short, the show works to suture ideological wounds but cannot completely do so. The residual trauma is made overt in the presence of Jessica's cane, indicative of her still-wounded body. For Lynch, other returning soldiers, the Piestewas, and other families in need, the war, trauma, and personal and national recovery are ongoing as are their education, housing, and healthcare crises.

The Piestewas, along with most of the featured families on episodes of EMHE, are representative of the millions of Americans who are in need of broad-based societal aid programs. Like the EMHE featured homes—many of which are so inadequate or beyond repair that the designers tear them down and start again—American health care and education programs are also far beyond the minor improvements stage. While education and health coverage used to be seen as central components of social citizenship rights, rising costs have put them out of reach for many Americans. Representing individuals and not the government as the most appropriate source of aid to Americans in need, EMHE participates in the current attempt to make over the Great Society federal aid polices. The message is ambivalent, however, as all EMHE's showcased families, often strong proponents of the pull-oneself-up-by-the-bootstraps approach, need the design team's help because they are experiencing the very health care, education, and housing crises that the Great Society policies were intended to alleviate. Although EMHE teaches Americans that the burden of care is a private matter, the province of families, friends, communities, charitable organizations, and charity-minded businesses, it undercuts its own message, as it is obvious that a fairy godmother is more effective than any personal, local, or community-based aid could ever be. In directing attention toward the idea of charitable giving and personal contribution and away from the idea of governmental responsibility for citizens, EMHE also highlights the other problem it works to elide—that of inadequate government support for returning soldiers and for the survivors of those soldiers who do not—because Ty has to secure sponsors to step in to support the Piestweas and the veterans in the absence of actual national structures of economic, social, or political support. With all its focus on individual honor and emotional support, the show tries to efface the need for collective action in relation to the inadequate government support.

EMHE advances a form of what Hartley calls DIY [Do it Yourself] Citizenship, a sort of self-fashioning through consumerism in which citizenship is not enacted through abstractions of protesting, voting, and debating, but merely by becoming visible to others as a self-styled individual consumer.[37] In this version of U.S. culture, citizenship and political debate is reduced to opposing consumer choices as expressed by "support our team"-style political bumper stickers and graphic t-shirts. While TV in general offers viewers models for building their own identities, homebuilding and remodeling shows take it a step further, modeling rooms and lifestyles and offering advice on the weekly shows as well as on their dedicated Web site. EMHE provides a case in point as its Web site offers links to sponsors' sites that offer purchasing and charitable giving opportunities and trumpet the commendable behavior of American corporations, communities, and individuals. The kind of empowerment offered by the show (and by Sears' "Ty Pennington Style" and its "As Seen On" section of the EMHE Web site)[38] is in the realm of individual style and, therefore, it represents the privileging of cultural citizenship over political and social citizenship.

On its Web site, EMHE disseminates the concept of citizenship as expressed through consumerism and style choices. With these links, EMHE shares similarities with the kinds of TV programming that offer viewers what Will Brooker describes as "an immersive, participatory experience" that goes beyond watching the weekly TV show.[39] By visiting the program's dedicated Web site, a viewer can "meet" (1) the designers and take their advice, (2) the families and contribute to a related charity, (3) the sponsors and learn about their products as well as about their commitment to corporate charity. The weekly program promotes the Web site that, in turn, promotes future shows as well as the program's sponsors and affiliated charitable organizations and their dedicated Web sites. EMHE periodically reminds viewers, via the "breaking news" text box in the corner of the screen, to "share your reactions while you watch. Log on now to Enhanced TV at abc.com." Given the standardized "Signature American Style" these linked Web sites offer, EMHE teaches viewers more about "how to monitor their behavior within the prescribed norms of American culture than about how to empower themselves."[40]

EMHE models for its viewers a citizenship based on participatory fandom and consumer expression rather than as participatory democracy and political expression. The show works to mobilize Americans as supportive consumers and individually empathetic neighbors rather than as rallying protestors and collectively critical citizens. That is not to say that EMHE's commendation-based programming does not offer a welcome change from the humiliation-based television programming that had begun to saturate the networks. The show does seem to be motivated by a genuine utopian impulse. Indeed, the neighborliness depicted on many EMHE episodes is inspiring: the former cancer patient who wants to go back and makeover the hospital cancer ward in which she spent most of her young life; or the man who renovated all of his neighbors' homes while his own fell into disrepair. Theirs is the kind of neighborly behavior that experienced a renaissance after 9/11. While the change proved temporary, it revealed the potential for a radical overhaul of the way Americans behave toward each other. The general response to the national identity crisis precipitated by the 9/11 terrorist attacks—the revelation to many Americans of the disconnect between the way they perceive themselves and the way the world perceives them—remains problematic. Those interested in soul-searching and social change seem to be outnumbered by those desiring to buttress the utopian symbolic nation. In the end, the United States has made cosmetic changes instead of undertaking a thorough investigation of the foundational cultural and policy weaknesses exposed by 9/11.

Despite its attempts to transform the Piestewa episode into the Homeland Security Edition of its program, the *Extreme Makeover* "Reveal" exposes more insecurities than it allays: the "support our troops" policy is inadequate as it does not have an economic component, only an emotional one; extended family is a necessary support system even though American TV and culture has represented relatives as meddlesome, and tribal structures as backward, in its attempts to privilege the consumerist nuclear family. Most troubling of all, despite all the efforts of the design team and of the architects of Homeland Security Culture, EMHE reveals that there is no safe haven. The United States has problems that will not be remedied by Americans barricading themselves in their home compounds. Fortress America has cracks in its foundation that cannot be fixed with a simple patch job. A structural overhaul is necessary. Without one, the cracks will become chasms and the structure will eventually topple.

NOTES

1. For excerpts from Hoover's and Roosevelt's speeches, see Eric Foner and John A. Garraty, ed., *The Reader's Companion to American History* (Boston: Houghton Mifflin, 1991), sv. "good neighbor policy."
2. Andrew J. Bacevich, *American Empire: The Realities and Consequences of U.S. Diplomacy* (Cambridge: Harvard University Press, 2002), p. 4.

3. Helen Hunt Jackson, *A Century of Dishonor: A Sketch of the U.S. Government Dealings with Some of the Indian Tribes* (Boston: Little, Brown, and Company, 1903). For a more contemporary rendering of the same issues, see Dee Brown, *Bury My Heart at Wounded Knee: An Indian History of the American West* (New York: Henry Holt, 1970) and D'Arcy McNickle, *Native American Tribalism: Indian Survivals and Renewals* (New York: Oxford University Press, 1973).

4. For information on the American Expositions, see Robert Rydell, *All the World's a Fair: Visions of Empire at American International Expositions, 1876–1916* (Chicago: University of Chicago Press, 1984).

5. Richard Slotkin, *Gunfighter Nation: The Myth of the Frontier in Twentieth-Century America* (New York: Harper Perennial, 1993), p. 63.

6. Ibid., p. 69.

7. Ibid.

8. Gioia Woods, "Cowboys, Indians, and Iraq," unpublished essay, 2005.

9. Slotkin, *Gunfighter Nation*, p. 9.

10. John Hartley, "Democratainment," in *The Television Studies Reader*, ed. Robert C. Allen and Annette Hill (New York and London: Routledge, 2004), p. 529.

11. Ibid., p. 528.

12. Ibid., p. 529.

13. Lauren Berlant, *The Queen of America Goes to Washington City: Essays on Sex and Citizenship* (Durham: Duke University Press, 1997), p. 3.

14. Sylvio Waisbord, "Journalism, Risk, and Patriotism," in *Journalism after September 11*, ed. Barbie Zelizer and Stuart Allen (New York and London: Routledge, 2002), p. 215.

15. Ibid., p. 205.

16. Alan Nadel, *Containment Culture: American Narratives, Postmodernism, and the Atomic Age* (Durham: Duke University Press, 1995), pp. 3, xi.

17. Lori Merish, *Sentimental Materialism: Gender, Commodity Culture, and Nineteenth-Century American Literature* (Durham: Duke University Press, 2000), p. 4.

18. Ibid., pp. 3–4.

19. Berlant, *The Queen of America*, p. 100.

20. Annette Hill, "*Big Brother*: the Real Audience," *Television & New Media* 3, no. 3 (August 2002): 323–340 and Laura Grindstaff, *The Money Shot: Trash, Class, and the Making of TV Talk Shows* (Chicago: University of Chicago Press, 2002), pp. 164–168.

21. Grindstaff, *The Money Shot*, p. 19.

22. Ibid., p. 21.

23. Hartley, "Democratainment," p. 528.

24. Jane M. Shattuc, *The Talking Cure: TV Talk Shows and Women* (New York and London: Routledge, 1997), p. 45.

25. Berlant, *The Queen of America*, p. 175.

26. Ibid., p. 4.

27. Waisbord, "Journalism, Risk, and Patriotism," p. 215.

28. Linda Williams, "Film Bodies: Gender, Genre, and Excess," *Film Quarterly* 44, no. 4 (Summer 1991): 2–13.

29. See Deborah Orr, "Even in battle, blondes get all the attention," *The Independent*, April 4, 2003, Available at: <http://comment.independent. co.uk/columnists_m_z/deborah_orr/article113603.ece> (December 15, 2005).

30. See Toni Morrison, *Playing in the Dark: Whiteness and the Literary Imagination* (Cambridge, MA: Harvard University Press, 1992).

31. For more information on federal Indian policies, see Francis Paul Prucha, *Documents in United States Indian Policy*, 2nd edition (Lincoln: University of Nebraska Press, 1990) and *The Great Father: The United States Government and the American Indians* (Lincoln: University of Nebraska Press, 1984).

32. Jackson, p. 29.

33. See "Commander in Chief lands on USS Lincoln," May 2, 2003, Available at: <http://cnn.com/2003/ALLPOLITICS/05/01/bush.carrier.landing> (Accessed on 15 August 2005).

34. Waisbord, "Journalism, Risk, and Patriotism," p. 206.

35. Ibid., p. 205.

36. Berlant, *The Queen of America*, p. 179.

37. Hartley, "Democratainment," pp. 526–530.

38. See *Extreme Makeover Home Edition* Home Page, Available at: <http:// abc.go.com/primetime/ xtremehome/?ad = EMHE> (December 15, 2005).

39. Will Brooker, "Living on *Dawson's Creek*: Teen Viewers, Cultural Convergence, and Television Overflow," in Allen and Hill, p. 570.

40. Shattuc, *The Talking Cure*, p. 10.

CHANGING PROPERTIES: THE MAKEOVER SHOW CROSSES THE ATLANTIC

MISHA KAVKA

BY 2003 IT WAS FAST BECOMING CLEAR THAT makeover logic was the driving force of U.S. reality television, with the promise of "total transformation" providing an effective bridge between the ordinary faces and the extraordinary frameworks that make up the recipe of reality TV. In a sense, the makeover is a recognizable format in a country where the dream of self-invention has narrativized new-world colonization since the seventeenth century, where literature from Twain to Dreiser to Fitzgerald has been consumed with the heady rise and sometimes spectacular fall of American Dreamers, and where the "before-and-after" sales pitch of popular magazines is forever paired in the cultural imaginary with a sand-covered, beached weakling badly in need of a chest-expander. Seen from the perspective of a shorter, television-specific history, however, many of the makeover shows that began appearing on U.S. cable channels in the early 2000s were initially direct British imports and later formats purchased from the United Kingdom where "lifestyle" programming met property consciousness in the mid-1990s and produced shows such as *Home Front* and the greatly popular *Changing Rooms*.[1] As this imported form went native in the United States, moving from cable to network channels, it underwent a shift in the object to be made over: from making over property to making over people, or from the material wares of lifestyle to the intimate wares of selfhood. Despite the existence of some crossover programs—notably *Extreme Makeover: Home Edition* in the United States and

What Not to Wear in the United Kingdom[2]—this culturally differentiated trend has largely continued, with Britons on TV gutting and renovating houses/gardens for habitation and resale, and Americans refashioning bodies to meet the stringent criteria of image culture. While the melodramatic arc of both kinds of shows may be the same,[3] leading as they do to a "reveal" that realizes the fantasy of transformation, the differences of object highlight culturally specific notions of self and space, as well as place-based definitions of "property." Whereas the British makeover tends to take up property in terms of real estate, or domestic materiality coded by class, region, race, and gender, American shows catalogue properties of selfhood in terms of the transformable features of the intimate body. As American as the myth of transformation may be, I will argue that an adequate history of makeover logic on U.S. reality TV must take into account such culturally comparative genealogies.

This chapter will thus trace the development of makeover shows from their origins in "lifestyle programming" on British television in the mid-1990s through their migration to and development on American television in the early twenty-first century. My particular focus will be on two highly popular versions of making over property and people: *Changing Rooms* and *Extreme Makeover*, respectively.[4] In emphasizing the difference between real estate as property on British television and the transformable properties of selfhood on American television, I am of course aware that both countries have cable channels devoted to "lifestyle" or "home and garden" programs. What strikes me as important, however, is to differentiate between programs that appear on free-to-air channels and those on cable or satellite channels, for not only is free-to-air programming a measure of majoritarian audiences—hence serving as a kind of cultural barometer—but it also needs to be read for its productive collectivizing force, since these shows come within the purview of anyone with a television set and are more readily picked up by secondary media such as magazines and newspapers. In the United Kingdom, *Changing Rooms* and a rash of copycat and follow-on programs filled both primetime and daytime schedules on state-owned BBC1 and BBC2, several years before the broad digitization of U.K. television. Although *Changing Rooms* is now in hiatus, the free-to-air channels continue to produce and screen various kinds of real-estate programs,[5] many of which are then shown in syndication on digital stations such as UK Style and Discovery Real Time. In the United States, property-renovation programs are produced for and screened only on cable channels, particularly TLC (formerly The Learning Channel) and HGTV (Home and Garden Television), while the shows that can draw the double-digit million viewers required for good network ratings have involved people-focused makeovers, such as *Extreme Makeover* and *The Swan*, or the heady stint of *Queer Eye for the Straight Guy* on NBC (2003).[6] The one apparent exception to this breakdown, the highly rated *Extreme Makeover: Home*

Edition,[7] is in fact no exception, for the houses to be redone are treated as transformable extensions of the inhabitants themselves. Even when an American network program is working with the material wares of lifestyle, the lesson is that only a radical transformation can smooth the vicissitudes of intimate selfhood.

THE MAKEOVER COMES HOME

In simple terms, a makeover show is defined by its form, always bookended by "before" and "after" shots of the transformable object, with the visual and narrative content of the program filled out and shaped by the labor of transformation. Such transformation, as Thomas Sutcliffe has pointed out in *The Independent*, is premised on the assumption that "all change is for the better"[8]; hence the "after" is structurally offered as an improvement on the "before," although judging whether this is truly the case constitutes an important part of viewers', and reviewers', pleasure. Sceptical about the centrality of the transformative process, Charlotte Brunsdon has argued that, in comparison to earlier hobbyist programs on British television, "[t]he emphasis now is on the result, not the process."[9] Against this, Judith Williamson insists that unlike shows "where they used to zip through instructions with the aid of Ones They Prepared Earlier . . . contemporary DIY programmes focus at length on the physical transformation itself."[10] The disagreement between the two critics usefully clarifies the poles between which all makeover shows are strung: the how-to element on one side wars against the spectacle of the "reveal" on the other. Whereas Brunsdon favors the didactic component of DIY television, dismissing the revelation of the "after" shot as a preference for end-result over educational process, Williamson is drawn to the material process of transformation for the sake of what it *shows* rather than what it teaches. On U.S. television, where didactic DIY programs are relatively rare, we can nonetheless draw on the example of *This Old House*[11] as a show that foregrounds how-to didacticism over the spectacle of the reveal, while older-school domestic divas such as Julia Child of the 1970s or Martha Stewart of the 1990s made programs that relied heavily on elaborate objects "prepared earlier" at the expense of showing nitty-gritty process.[12] Makeover television in both countries now marries the how-it's-done element with revelation, engaging with the work of transformation as a televisable spectacle made pertinent to (if not strictly doable by) the viewer through the on-screen inclusion of "ordinary people like us." The use of ordinary people as unscripted *dramatis personae* is the crucial addition that distinguishes makeover television from DIY or expert-advice programs, planting such shows firmly within the genre of reality TV and making an early form such as *Changing Rooms* "a potent mix of aspirational DIY and the psychology of human relations."[13]

As repeated reviews in the broadsheet press make clear, 1997 marked the year of the home makeover show on British television,[14] at a time when the makeover in the United States was still confined largely to magazines and cosmetics counters. The watershed moment came with *Changing Rooms*, the brainchild of Peter Bazalgette for Bazal Productions, a show that was first screened on BBC2 in September 1996. It fell easily, at the time, into the general trend toward increased "lifestyle programming," identified as cooking, fashion, travel, and home decorating shows.[15] This trend, spurred by the deregulation of the television industry and the incursion of satellite programming in the 1980s, was given momentum by the BBC's attempt in the early 1990s to soften the Reithian edict to "inform and educate" citizens in favor of more ratings-garnering programs that could also fulfil the 25 percent rule (namely the requirement, introduced in 1992, that the total output of the BBC include 25 percent independent productions[16]). Bazalgette himself had produced *Food & Drink* for BBC2 as an independent producer in the 1980s and 1990s,[17] before coming up in 1994 with the hugely successful format of *Ready Steady Cook*[18] which squares off two competing chefs who race to make the best meal within 20 minutes from £5 worth of ingredients supplied by studio contestants. The elements of what Bazalgette was beginning to call the "leisure-based game show"[19] came together in *RSC*, where experts joined with ordinary bumblers in a project of positive transformation (from sweet potato to soufflé) under heavily restrictive time and budgetary constraints. Within two years of *Ready Steady Cook*, and no doubt influenced by the success of the upmarket DIY show *Home Front*,[20] Bazal Productions had melded the *Ready Steady Cook* tactics with the ingredients of home décor and, voila, the simple concept of *Changing Rooms* was born: take two sets of neighbors, supply each with a decorator, and give them 48 hours and £500 to remodel one room in each other's houses. Most importantly, edit the resulting footage to lead to a double "reveal," the moment of dramatic intensity when each set of owners takes off the blindfold and sees their "new" room for the first time. Although the visual pleasure of the reveal must have initially depended only on the spectacle of the madeover rooms, it soon became clear to producers and viewers alike that the uncertainty of how owners would react to the often quite elaborate designs also provided another kind of thrill: the dramatic spectacle of participants' reactions.[21] This redoubling of the aesthetic with the dramatic spectacle was to become a crucial part of American makeover shows.

While *Ready Steady Cook* has faded into the echelon of game shows, what is becoming clear in hindsight is the impact of *Changing Rooms*. The first of Bazalgette's shows to occupy a prime-time slot (9 pm), it later moved from BBC2 to BBC1 and survived in production into 2004 (admittedly to the dismay of some critics: "In yesterday's show, the first in a seventeenth series, they managed to find two of the last rooms in the country not to have been changed"[22]). Like *RSC, Changing Rooms* proved highly marketable as a format, selling first to New Zealand, then Scandinavia, China, Brazil, Italy, the United States, and finally France (not until 2004)[23]. Unlike *RSC*, however, this was the first program to combine a competitive structure with the "before and after" essence of the reveal, and hence to incorporate a climactic moment that was not solely dependent on the suspense of time constraints. *Changing Rooms* thus came to define the makeover show, not least because of the powerful conjunction set up between the before/after structure and the *materiality* of transformation. Whereas the beauty makeover born of American cosmetic counters and magazines focused solely on appearance and hence had a visual appeal, it was the combination of the before/after form with the temporality of process and the materiality of real estate that linked the makeover firmly to DIY culture and brought both to the medium of television. As Judith Williamson wrote about *Home Front, Change That*,[24] and *Changing Rooms* in the heady year of 1997, "These programmes are part of a general bias towards things, rather than ideas, as the basis for media features."[25]

Drawing on programs devoted to the "makeover of objects," Williamson frames the importance of this shift in terms of our increasing remoteness from things and how they work. She points out that consumer capitalism, despite its "supposed materialism," has "created a rift between us and the material world,"[26] for we invest things with symbolic, or commodity, value at the expense of appreciating the material value of their accrued parts. Rather than idealizing a preindustrial, pan-artisan past, however, Williamson's point is to gauge the "powerful fascination with things and material processes [that] runs through everyday culture at the moment," as evidenced by the number of programs encouraging viewers to recycle worn-out objects into chandeliers and planters. For my purposes, she provides insight into the importance of *doing* in these programs, particularly of doing as an engagement with material property. In this, she gestures toward the paradoxical ability of television, despite its status as a virtual medium, to transmit a feeling of material engagement, whether by inspiring viewers to do it themselves or, more often, through the haptic identifications entailed in viewing alone. British makeover shows in the mid- to late 1990s—which remake, reuse, and recycle—may not be as didactic as Brunsdon recalls from earlier hobbyist programs, but in comparison to the highly successful American makeover shows to come, a distinction can be made between an emphasis on doing and on being, between madeover objects that constitute material well-being and the madeover self that defines immaterial well-being. Williamson's focus on reinjecting the material world with meaning, though, does not take into consideration the question of why materiality should be particular to the U.K. makeover series. Indeed, the framework of consumer capitalism would suggest that all viewing audiences in developed countries should be more or less similarly prone to the thingness of the makeover show. The fact that this is not the case indicates that cultural inscriptions of materiality need to be factored in.

DÉCOR VOYEURISM MEETS CLASS

What is particular to Britain, I would argue, is the way that making over property intersects with at least three factors: the social and architectural conditions of sub/urban lifestyle, the "heritage" tradition of material culture, and, importantly, the exercise of taste as a marker of class. Laurence Llewellyn-Bowen, who began his makeover-TV career as a decorator on *Home Front* and *Changing Rooms* before becoming a presenter on the latter, has offered his own expert opinion on the importance of property to British makeover TV: "The Englishman's home really is his castle; property ownership is built deep into the national psyche. Mark-making therein is the inevitable next stage."[27] Though this may be proverbially true, it is important to note that specific conditions apply to the mid-1990s surge in this programming. In 1995, as Llewellyn-Bowen points out, the property market tumbled, meaning that "people were going to be staying in their existing homes whether they liked it or not," so doing up one's space became more of a priority.[28] The arrival of Ikea in Britain around the same time gave an impetus to flat-pack DIY, not just for bookcases but for entire living, bedroom, and even kitchen fit-outs, bringing "European design" closer to the grasp of the middle classes. What had up until this era been a British tendency to expect very little in terms of interior living conditions—the thin walls, draughty sashes, and notorious three-bar heater of the average lounge come to mind—suddenly became a ripe zone for functional and aesthetic overhaul in the name of "lifestyle." Whereas the proverb that the Englishman's home is his castle suggests both domestic luxury and satisfied isolation, the architectural conditions of terraced or semi-detached housing in urban and suburban neighborhoods deem otherwise. Rather, the fact that windows are traditionally close to the street as well as to each other provides both opportunity and incentive for neighborly comparisons of interiors. Ann Treneman, writing in appreciation of makeover shows, claims to have "always been a décor voyeur," and quotes *Changing Rooms* designer Linda Barker as saying that "the British are very nosey people. . . . and the programme lets them into people's houses."[29] The home makeover show, in other words, draws on viewers' experience of living in close proximity to others. In the social geography of British towns and cities, ordinary people's houses are glued together and, by extension and habit, so are the people who inhabit them and peek over the fence.

Treating the domestic space, even rhetorically, as an intimate body primed for the voyeuristic gaze adds weight to the pleasure of the reveal offered by makeover TV, but another reading is also suggested by the peculiarly British obsession with redoing, recycling, and reselling the material objects of domesticity. It is not just that décor and real estate can be probed for the secrets of interiority, but also that such objects are bearers of materialized history. Programs such as *Change That*[30] specialize in taking one kind of object, implicitly worthless, and turning it into another kind of object of greater aesthetic and material value; the "thrill" that Williamson recognizes in turning an old bicycle wheel into a chandelier depends in large part on the traces of the old object remaining embedded within the new. In shows such as *Restored to Glory*,[31] a run-down Jacobean farmhouse, for instance, becomes a palette for historical reinscription, overseen by specialists in period architecture. Even on the perennially favorite *Antiques Roadshow*,[32] which has sparked programs that combine visits to "people's houses" with rooting out their sellable items,[33] part of the pleasure of watching what locals have dug out of the attic comes from the valuation expert who reads off the history of the object. As the cultural product of a nation self-admittedly obsessed with its history, the British home makeover is caught up not only with an aspirational future, but also with a national and personal past whose overhaul will itself become the material of heritage for the next generation.

Neither the aspirational, aesthetic, or historical value of the property makeover makes sense, however, outside the context of class structures. What seems to be material value inscribed by style or history always bears the marks of class-based taste. Laurence Llewellyn-Bowen, who became a "phenomenon" on *Changing Rooms* because of his recognizable, even *outré*, style, encapsulates this construction: "On television . . . he scrapes and paints and delivers little historical anecdotes dressed in leather pants and knee-length velvet tunics. His television persona is camp, snooty and dictatorial."[34] In this description one can read the conflation of taste with class, where leather pants and velvet tunics serve as the material vestments of the camp and snooty persona. Although Llewellyn-Bowen became synonymous with extravagant style (especially when his redesigned rooms caused participants to wail in dismay at the reveal), this is not to say that the more extravagant the style, the higher the class; rather, his extravagant sense of style is always framed as a historical reference, indicating a level of education—and implicitly intellect—that in itself serves as a class marker. Thus, Llewellyn-Bowen recalls creating "a complete Aubrey Beardsley room" in an episode of *Changing Rooms* whose function had much less to do with designing what the participants wanted for their neighbors' space than with locating his own taste in terms of the history of design.[35] This connection between taste and class, moreover, is written into the very rhetoric of the British home makeover; one speaks of doing *up* a house, to indicate not only home improvement but also the impulse to rise a few notches in the social hierarchy through the application of good taste.

That unspoken term, the education or class-based knowledge that guarantees the definition of "good taste," is a mobile marker that operates just as effectively for extravagant designers such as Llewellyn-Bowen who quote historical styles, as for the maliciously ironic descriptions of the "after" image that characterize the broadsheet reviews. Reviewers of *Changing Rooms* who delight in cataloguing "retina-damaging" paint combinations[36] or "urinous yellow wall-covering"[37] remind us not only that taste is class-based, but also that it is only ever evoked as a universal standard when the "masses" begin to clamor for its possession.[38]

In this light, where the connubial relation of design and television draws on a taste deemed too common to be any good, it seems curious that these shows are often celebrated for democratizing taste. What had been jealously guarded by trained designers and elitist magazines is made available, according to the democratists, to "ordinary people" through viewing and imitating the work of these programs. As Emma Cook optimistically argues, "Just as popular television skilfully demystified the once esoteric art of haute cuisine, so interior design on the small screen now seems as simple as sticky-back plastic."[39] *Haute cuisine*, it turns out, has a sister operation in *haute chambre*, and is just as prone to demystification by changing rooms on a £500 budget. More recent programs such as *Relocation Relocation, Trading Up* and *Property Ladder*[40] ply much the same aspirations of class mobility through the purchase and renovation of properties. Indeed, after nearly ten years of *Changing Rooms*, Llewellyn-Bowen declared the elitism of taste to be past:

> There used to be a sense in Britain that taste was a class issue. Posh people thought they had it, and the rest of society didn't. But now the boundaries have been blurred. People know it's about intelligence and imagination, not about money or breeding, and we all have access to good taste. But just to make sure, we like to switch on the TV from time to time to observe other people's choices. It's like twitching the net curtains, but with the remote.[41]

Characterizing television as a means of "observing other people's choices" is a turn of phrase that draws on both observational documentary and the democratic potential of "choice," yet what such programs make clear is the way that "choices" of material estate are shot through with markers of class, region, race, and gender. In this electronic form of "twitching the net curtains," décor voyeurism names less a libidinal urge than a wish to see how others work with the material vestments of their social position. Similarly, the ability of property and objects to serve as palimpsests for personal or national heritage is part and parcel of the way that both materiality and history are weighted with class considerations. Ultimately, the property makeover show in Britain survives because it exercises, rather than exorcises, the bugbear of class mobility through the aestheticization of material surroundings. Despite Llewellyn-Bowen's optimism for home-makeover democratization, the class bias remains; change is possible but full-scale transformation is restricted by the way that social possibility is deeply embedded in the very material surroundings one seeks to do up. If the language of "transformation" is missing from the British makeover, this is something the American makeover show, when it comes into its own, will address with a vengeance.

"HOLY TRANSFORMATION, BATMAN!"[42]

Although a relatively recent addition to the national lexicon,[43] the transformative promise of "makeover" fits comfortably into the tradition of the American Dream: the aspirational fantasy of self-(re)invention inscribed on every school kid's heart with the promise that he (sic) could one day grow up to be president. Transformation, or metamorphosis, as such is hardly an American concept—witness the unfortunate discovery made one morning by Gregor Samsa in Kafka's tale[44]—but once metamorphosis becomes positive transformation, especially positive *personal* transformation, we are in familiar cultural territory. The element of the personal in the American makeover draws on a paradoxical combination of self-fulfilment, or being most yourself, and self-reinvention, or casting away a prior self for an improved version. Once the goal of personal improvement is linked with the procedure of transforming the *appearance* (a term central to both the OED and American Heritage Dictionary definitions of makeover), it becomes clear why this version of the American Dream readily found a home in the visual media, first in magazines and then on television. *Changing Rooms* was already airing in the United States on BBC America when Bazal Productions sold the format to American producers in 2000 as *Trading Spaces*,[45] the first of a long line of American home makeover shows. The format of *Trading Spaces*—involving two sets of neighbors, 48 hours, and $1000—is the same as *Changing Rooms*, with the closing "reveal" again doubled not only by showing two redesigned rooms but also by serving the dual function of visual spectacle (the design itself) and dramatic spectacle (the owners' responses). On *Trading Spaces*, too, participants are sometimes deeply unhappy with the results, suspecting that they have been manipulated by designers and producers alike for the sake of "good TV."[46] Unlike the United Kingdom, however, where such programs are produced for free-to-air television and migrate in syndication to lifestyle-specific digital channels, *Trading Spaces* and related home makeover programs (e.g., *While You Were Out, Surprise by Design, Designers' Challenge*[47]) are offered as niche programming on cable channels, such as HGTV, which provide "must-see TV for the home obsessed."[48]

The full-blown makeover aimed at majority audiences came to U.S. network television in late 2002, with the first season of *Extreme Makeover* on ABC. The premise of *EM* is simple even if the enactment requires a high degree of specialized—and very expensive—labor. Aiming to bring the makeover back to its earlier association with personal beauty,[49] the show replaces over-the-counter cosmetics—the DIY version of personal beauty—with cosmetic surgery as the instrument of transformation, thereby updating the concept of "makeover" for the age of surgery-on-demand. In place of renovating real estate, the bodies of each episode's two participants become the material to be radically altered, inviting a panoply of cosmetic surgical procedures to fix what the team of medical consultants euphemistically calls the "problem areas": face lift, brow lift, nose job, chin implants, lip augmentation, breast augmentation, tummy tuck, liposuction, orthodontic reconstruction, and so on. As in all makeover programs, it is taken for granted that change is good, but on *Extreme Makeover* there is no toying with the dramatic possibility of participant disapproval. These changes cannot be ripped out or painted over as readily as on home makeover shows (as proven by the participant on *Trading Spaces* who sold the detritus of her bedroom makeover in a garage sale[50]), so the production and editing go to great lengths to produce a unanimous vision of positive transformation. The reveal on *EM* is carefully choreographed as a public revelation to an intimate audience that includes the viewers; the camera tracks participants from the back as they enter a hall where family and friends are waiting, offering the facial closeup of the transformed person to viewers at the "same" moment as the on-site audience sees it. Almost more important than the revelation of the "after" image in this show are the closeup reaction shots of shocked-but-delighted family and friends, as eyes fill with tears, mouths drop and lips shape "ohmygod, ohmygod" in a disbelieving if happy confirmation of blossomed selfhood that seeks to repress the uncanniness of metamorphosis.[51] Indeed, unwavering belief in positive transformation is the defining affect of the surgery makeover show, because the idea of participants being gravely disappointed with what is in effect a permanent makeover is unthinkable.[52]

Other than the material substitution of bodies for home appurtenances and the excision of anything but positive response to transformation, the notable difference between cosmetic and property makeover shows is the source of the labor that goes into the transformation. Rather than adopting an ethos of "mucking in," which extends the hobbyist tradition of British leisure pursuits, the surgery makeover show highlights the role of the professional and particularly the specialist. There is, after all, nothing DIY about surgery. In place of the DIY rhetoric of home makeover shows, this majoritarian makeover program reflects the professionalism of American commodity culture: consumerism in this late-capitalist age proves to be less about buying object-commodities than about procuring the professional services of specialists. Any task can be done by a specialist and, more importantly, can implicitly be done *better* by someone with the appropriate know-how—provided one can pay the cost. Although it may seem perfectly reasonable to demand ten years' medical training from someone before s/he resculpts your body through invasive surgery, it is notable that on these programs the surgeon is less a site of knowledge-specific labor than part of an extensive discourse of specialization that includes the cosmetic surgeon, the therapist, the personal trainer, the life coach, and even the TV host. As on *Queer Eye for the Straight Guy*, where each of the Fab Five is characterized by their expert knowledge (e.g., Thom/interiors, Ted/food & wine, etc.), the self to be made over can only undergo transformation by first being fragmented and classified according to the specializations offered by professionals. Even on the crossover program *Extreme Makeover: Home Edition*, where the actual specialized labor is performed by a horde of faceless tradesmen led by a well-advertised contractor, the "design team" is nonetheless presented according to their specializations: Preston—exterior/big ideas, Paige—carpentry/creativity, Paul—carpentry/nuts and bolts, and so on.

What this shift away from a DIY, hobbyist ethos also means for the makeover is that the implicit democratization attendant on the cheapening of products and services has shifted terrain. No longer can one get "the look" by the judicious application of concealer or sticky-back plastic based on information transmitted by televisual didactics. Unlike home makeover shows such as *Trading Spaces*, which costs some $30,000 per episode,[53] there is nothing cheap about *EM*, which throws a minimum of five invasive surgical procedures at each of two participants and films them during several months' convalescence for the sake of 53 minutes of final footage (this is one of the reasons why *EM* appears on a major network, with deeper pockets than specialist cable channels). Given these economics, the anyone-can-do-it democracy of earlier makeover television is replaced by the lottery of application videos, privileging a lucky winner who promises "good TV." DIY democratization, as I suggested earlier, is necessarily a double-edged sword, bringing taste and beauty within the reach of "ordinary people" but simultaneously resuscitating the restrictive aesthetic standard that is evoked every time the means are placed in the hands of the masses. Rather than offering to democratize beauty on a budget for all, then, the surgery makeover shows offer expensive professional services to "ordinary" people who can prove their worthiness based on *need*. And neediness, in the case of this American makeover myth, is defined not simply in financial terms (the usual definition of "need-based") or aesthetic terms (e.g., the "fashion-crime" perpetrator) or on merit (e.g., the makeover as reward), but in terms of devalued selfhood, marked by the failure of self-belief and experienced as a lack of appropriate social and intimate interactions. This becomes the defining premise on *Extreme Makeover: Home Edition*; in place of "before" shots we see excerpts from the participants' application video, in which neediness is defined as a disfiguration of family relations brought on by a traumatic experience (usually the illness or death of a family member) and exacerbated by economic hardship.

Applicants who most successfully invoke pathos for the sad state of their selfhood will thus find themselves on programs that offer to remedy failures of intimate or familial relations with a remodelling of image. When a participant on *The Swan* shyly notes in her "before" video that she has "been intimate [with her boyfriend] only seven or eight times over the last three or four years," this sets the stage for a surgical alteration of ugliness into beauty that will raise self-confidence and hence "correct" the said failures of intimate interaction. Because makeover TV uses neediness to discriminate but also offers a surgically altered ideal as universal remedy, the result is curiously, if perversely, democratizing. Television is selling not the cheap version of prohibitively expensive surgery to the masses, but rather the idea that such expense is *worth it* to everyone with flagging self-confidence. And indeed, cosmetic surgery, while not necessarily becoming cheaper, is certainly becoming more widespread, a phenomenon increasingly put down to the message of the media. The president of the American Society of Plastic Surgeons, Dr. Rod Rohrich, has put it succinctly: "With all these reality shows, the interest [in plastic surgery] has sky-rocketed. I think they've increased the awareness that plastic surgery isn't just for the wealthy and for the famous—it can be for everybody, for anybody that wants it if they save for it."[54] The democracy of beauty comes at a price, but one that is worth saving (or going into debt) for.

In an article that presaged the syndication of *Extreme Makeover* in Britain (on digital channel Living TV), Gaby Wood darkly compared the program to *Home Front*, calling *EM* a "kind of interior design programme. Dilapidated women and men are knocked through and rebuilt before receiving finishing touches that depersonalise them and increase their apparent market value."[55] Wood's economic model of a human marketplace suggests that men and women are "depersonalised" so as to meet a common, measurable market standard: this person is worth the equivalent of that person in terms of wrinkle-free skin, breast size, full head of hair, and other such enhancements. And indeed, watching a number of episodes of *EM* or *The Swan* does make it worryingly clear how much the cosmetic surgical consultants work to rote, always fixing the same problem areas with the same set of procedures to produce men and especially women in a typified aesthetic mode, no matter what their original aura. (One striking moment on *Extreme Makeover* involved an African American woman who rejected the recommendation of nose reconstruction on the grounds that she wanted to retain her racially marked features; as I recall, she ended up capitulating to a mild nose job, if there is such a thing.) The concern here, of course, is with the cultural prescription of this image, one for men and one for women, that sits without any apparent contradiction alongside American individualism. Ultimately, the collective image that we are asked to share in shores up our *self*-confidence, a confidence that in turn supports the economic, social, and intimate worth of the individual.

In this schizophrenia of the extreme makeover, where body parts are disposable and dissociated from the self, we find another disturbing similarity with the home whose walls can be removed without taking anything away from its status as "my" house. Indeed, later seasons of *Extreme Makeover: Home Edition* positively delight in razing the house to the ground, so as to be able to make everything anew without undermining its claim to being the same home. This program treats each house transformation like the intimate bodies of participants on surgical makeovers, with the designs drawn directly from, and equated to, the participants' hobbies, memories, and familial relations. The houses raised on *EM: HE* are thus built upon an immaterial idea of selfhood—who the participants "really" are—that the participants in turn instantiate as they are introduced into spectacular new rooms that reveal not the expense per se but the cost of bringing out the inhabitants' inner being. From a British perspective Wood may see this as depersonalization arising from the "me/not me" schizophrenia of cosmetic surgery, but from an American perspective it can be read in terms of the radical personal extensiveness of selfhood, which sees every material aspect of/around the person as a transformable property of an immaterial self.

The figure of Jay Gatsby, for instance, that great mythic expression of the logic of American metamorphosis, makes it clear that by the twentieth century to *re*make oneself is simultaneously to become *most* oneself, to fulfil one's potential. Where earlier versions of the new-world dream had focused on American self-invention, Fitzgerald's cultural touchstone marks the point at which self-invention turns to self-*re*invention, the casting off of one self so that another can be grafted in its place, not unlike the house that is razed so that "my house" can be raised from its shadowy footprint. The American makeover thus highlights the heady potential encapsulated in the "re" of invention, however groundless it may seem. If anything, the decades since Fitzgerald's novel have moved us even further away from a suspicion that reinvention might be charlatanism, a confidence trick; on the contrary, such grafting/refilling/overlaying is the means by which "true" self-confidence is secured, the point at which the personal outside (those transformable properties of body and home) is brought in line with the personal inside (the self I know I can become). When the presenter of *The Swan* asks Kathy, who has just seen herself in the mirror for the first time, "what is it about yourself that has changed most, do you think?" Kathy answers, "I feel comfortable in my skin." The once misaligned self, in other words, has now become one with its outer casing, both remedied and revealed by a raft of radical procedures.

The extreme makeover, I am arguing, is in equal amounts both discrimination and democratization, not because beauty is accessible to all, but because the *fantasy* of such beauty, and the remedied self to which it gives rise, is accessible to all. Not only can money be turned into image, but the image already *is* capital. Jim Holt, as quoted by Gaby Wood, points out the equivalence of wealth and beauty in this national culture: "The distribution of beauty in America is as imbalanced as the distribution of wealth. Americans don't mind the inequitable distribution of wealth very much because they all feel that it's possible to become rich here."[56] Holt recognizes "something of the same logic" at work in the culture of personal image: just as, on the capitalist model, an investment is needed if one hopes to reap wealth, so here an (equally financial) investment is needed if one hopes to reap beauty. This is why beauty on makeover programs is a culturally normative substance; like money, beauty must be exchangeable, available to everyone alike, and hence it must work according to a standard. Although the capitalist model suggests that investing money to gain beauty in turn leads to greater wealth,[57] the greatest wealth of all, according to the internal logic of the American makeover shows, is the radically revised but finally coherent subject.

THE RIGHT (TO) BEAUTY

Not all makeover shows in the United Kingdom are about property, just as not all makeover shows in the United States are about people. Genre- and interest-specific cable channels try to make a clean distinction that is impossible in this era of global media networks and user-chooses technology, while network programs such as *Extreme Makeover: Home Edition* in the United States and the fashion makeover show *What Not to Wear*[58] in the United Kingdom indicate that crossover models can garner high ratings and popularity in each country. Nonetheless, a notable difference between the two television makeover cultures does exist, a difference that Gaby Wood has put down to the distinction between the United States as "a country founded on the pursuit of happiness" and Britain as "a country wedded—rhetorically at least—to its failings."[59] Rather than parsing this difference in terms of hope versus misery—since the makeover, by definition, is hopeful of positive change—I have attempted to understand it in terms of the culturally specific object of making over, with object meaning both transformable property and the degree of expected transformation. The experience of a new country, after all, both demands and incites change, so survival requires embracing change as good (we might think of this as the settler, or even creole, attitude); even making the decision to move from an old to a new country requires a temporal readjustment, from a historical past that secures the ground on which one stands to a utopian future that begins from, and is sustained by, the moment of change. The American celebration of "total transformation" thus goes right through the self, as the makeover programs show, whereas selfhood in Britain, where materialized identities are so embedded in class, is far more impenetrable. In Britain, one paints a wall or swaps a house in the hope of perhaps going up a class; in America, one gives over as many properties of the body as possible to transformation, in the hopes of doffing material embeddedness for the sake of immaterial self-fulfillment. Perhaps not so oddly, even on the crossover programs mentioned above the same distinctions apply. *EM: Home Edition* destroys the old house entirely, in all its materiality, so as to erect an immaterial dream of family identity and unity. *What Not to Wear*, in the original British form, turns the body being styled into a material landscape of curves, edges, proportions, and geometries, draping and tucking the participant's physical body according to "rules" of clothing choice in the same way that one might improve a room by adding a more suitable curtain rod.

This is not to say that Americans are without class, in either sense of the term, but that class itself is possessed as a potentially transformable property, measured not in the "after" image of the makeover but precisely in the differential between "before" and "after." In the historical narrative of self-(re)making that is the American Dream, capital and image have become tightly interwoven; the initial absence of one (capital) can be compensated for, and even created by, the labor of/on the other (the immaterial image). As extreme makeover shows make explicit, the capital and the labor are someone else's (the TV production company paying the style professionals), but the American self-transformation, and the class thus generated, by rights belongs to *you*. Indeed, it comes across precisely as a question of rights: in the United States, whose founding documents guarantee the right to pursue happiness and seem thus to guarantee the right to happiness itself, it is increasingly hard to distinguish happiness from having the body and house beautiful. Makeover TV in the United States points to this latest configuration of democracy and image culture: when beauty is deemed synonymous with happiness, then (all) people have a right to beauty. The aspirational quality of the American makeover is thus a principle of right in these programs in a way that does not hold true for the United Kingdom (where, arguably, people do not assume they have a right to happiness).

Whereas property on British makeover shows is a set of material possessions in which class, regional, racial, and gendered identities are embedded, American programs catalogue the material properties of selfhood—hairstyle, clothing, family homes, and breasts, thighs, and chins—so as to prove how readily they can be transformed into the immaterial supports of idealized identity. If property is a condition of "belonging to," then the reinvented image on *Extreme Makeover* or *The Swan* is synonymous with self-possession, where self-possession is experienced as a match between the body-turned-image and the cultural economy of beauty. Between self-erasure and self-fulfillment the important element is the ground traversed, that material difference that can be transformed into the promise of beauty for the next American Dreamer. It is here that the democracy of the American makeover resides, less in a false hope peddled equally to everyone than as a working fiction, a kind of suspension of disbelief in the ideological bias of the beauty image in which we are all invited to share. While Andy Medhurst has argued about British lifestyle programs that "our dreamscapes have become domesticated," one could make the opposite claim about American makeover shows: in the United States our most domestic and intimate properties have become waking dreamscapes.[60] Or as Nelly Galan, life coach on *The Swan*, put it about the winner of one of the episodes, "Rachel wins because she surrendered to transformation in the most incredible way."

NOTES

1. *Home Front*, BBC, 1994– ; *Changing Rooms*, BBC, 1996–2004.
2. *Extreme Makeover: Home Edition*, ABC, 2003– ; *What Not to Wear*, BBC, 2002– .
3. See Charlotte Brunsdon, "Lifestyling Britain: The 8–9 Slot on British Television," in *Television after TV: Essays on a Medium in Transition*, ed. Lynn Spigel and Jan Olsson, 89 (Durham, NC: Duke University Press, 2004).
4. *Changing Rooms*, BBC, 1996–2004; *Extreme Makeover*, ABC, 2002–2005.
5. A week's overview of current British makeover/do-up programs in November 2005 included the prime time shows *How to Rescue a House* (BBC2, Tues. 7:00–7:30), *Property Ladder* (Channel 4, Tues. 8:00–9:00), *What Not to Wear* (BBC1, Wed. 8:00–9:00), *Grand Designs* (Channel 4, Wed. 9:00–10:00), and *Restored to Glory* (BBC2 Thurs. 8:00–9:00). Regular daytime programs included *To Buy or Not to Buy* (BBC1 9:15–10:00) and *House Detectives* (BBC2 1:00–1:30), as well as the auction and boot sale programs *Car Booty* (BBC1 11:30–12:00) and *Cash in the Attic* (BBC1 12:00–1:00).
6. *The Swan*, Fox, 2004– ; *Queer Eye for the Straight Guy*, Bravo/NBC, 2003– .
7. *Extreme Makeover: Home Edition*, ABC, 2003– .
8. Thomas Sutcliffe, "Television Review," *The Independent*, April 10, 1997, Newsbank database, British Library.
9. Brunsdon, "Lifestyling Britain," p. 80.
10. Judith Williamson, "This Life: The Thrill of Thrift," *The Guardian*, May 10, 1997, Newsbank database, British Library.
11. *This Old House*, PBS, 1979– .

12. Both *This Old House* and Martha Stewart programs can still be seen. *This Old House* remains on PBS, while TLC produces *The New Martha* and HGTV airs syndicated episodes of *From Martha's House* and *From Martha's Garden*. In recognition of the importance of *This Old House* to DIY programming, HGTV also shows *This Old House Classics* (for more on HGTV, see Patricia Dan Rogers, "Channeling Home Shows—HGTV, a Network Devoted to View-It-Yourselfers," *Washington Post*, December 5, 2002, sec. H1, Newsbank database, British Library).

13. Sarah Crompton, "True Colours Revealed in *Changing Rooms*," *The Daily Telegraph*, August 23, 1997, sec. Arts, Newsbank database, British Library.

14. Consider, for instance, the opening to an article from early August 1997: "No, there is no escape. Everytime [sic] you turn on the television there's some maniac waving a grouting gun and telling us how we should be buffing up our bathrooms" (John Preston, "Television: Cheery maniacs with grouting guns," *The Sunday Telegraph*, August 3, 1997, Newsbank database, British Library).

15. For more on lifestyle programming, see Brunsdon, "Lifestyling Britain"; and Rachel Moseley, "Makeover Takeover on British Television," *Screen* 41, no. 3 (Autumn 2000): 299–314.

16. Brunsdon, "Lifestyling Britain," p. 78.

17. John Morrish, "Simply Add a Touch of Bazal," *The Daily Telegraph*, August 24, 1997, Telegraph Magazine, Newsbank database, British Library.

18. *Ready Steady Cook*, BBC, 1994– .

19. See Morrish, "Simply Add a Touch of Bazal."

20. Rachel Moseley describes *Home Front* (BBC2, 1994–) as a show that "carefully privilege[s] 'design,' aesthetics and, above all, a universal notion of taste" (Moseley 302).

21. Peter Bazalgette's PA from the first few series of *Changing Rooms* has suggested that there came a moment when production staff decided to encourage the possibility of owners' dramatic negative reactions because it made for good television (Amy Walker, conversation with author, October 31, 2005).

22. Sam Wollaston, "TV Review: Makeover and over again," *The Guardian*, April 20, 2004, sec. G2, Newsbank database, British Library.

23. Laurence Llewellyn Bowen, "What's the French for makeover?" *The Guardian*, April 5, 2004, sec. G2, Newsbank database, British Library.

24. *Change That*, BBC, 1997.

25. Williamson, "The Thrill of Thrift."

26. Ibid.

27. Llewellyn Bowen, "What's the French for makeover?"

28. Ibid.

29. Ann Treneman, Interview with Linda Barker, *The Independent*, November 7, 1997, Newsbank database, Britsh Library.

30. *Change That*, BBC, 1997.

31. *Restored to Glory*, BBC, 2005– .

32. *Antiques Roadshow*, BBC, 1979– .

33. For example, *Cash in the Attic* (BBC, 2002–), where two experts search through people's houses for antiques to take to auction, and *Car Booty* (BBC, 2004–), quite literally the cheaper version, where experts search for items to sell out of the participants' "car boot" on the local market day.

34. Simon Hattenstone, "Handy Dandy," *The Guardian*, October 15, 2001, Newsbank database, British Library.

35. Christopher Middleton, "Life Story," *The Daily Telegraph*, September 5, 1998, Newsbank database, British Library.

36. Thomas Sutcliffe, "Television Review," June 17, 1997, Newsbank database, British Library.

37. Preston, "Cheery Maniacs with Grouting Guns."

38. *Telegraph* reviewer John Preston, for instance, makes no secret of his appeal to a universal standard: "Absolute bad taste does exist and here it was, in full spangled array" (Ibid.).

39. Emma Cook, "Inside *Taste*: The Final Frontier," *The Independent on Sunday*, December 28, 1997, Newsbank database, British Library.

40. *Relocation Relocation* (Channel 4), *Trading Up* (BBC) and *Property Ladder* (Channel 4) are all currently on air in 2005.

41. Hattenstone, "Handy Dandy."

42. Michael Montano, host and stylist, *Ten Years Younger* (TLC, December 9, 2005).

43. The *Oxford English Dictionary* gives "makeover" as being of U.S. origin, although the first mention listed in the OED is the caricatured "Miss Angelica Makeover" in Thackeray's 1860 novel *Vanity Fair*. The present use of the term denoting a transformation of appearance (OED, *n.*, "a complete transformation or remodelling, esp. a thorough refashioning of a person's appearance by beauty treatment") begins to be found in American magazines from the 1970s.

44. Franz Kafka, "The Metamorphosis," trans. Willa and Edwin Muir (Harmondsworth: Penguin, 1961).

45. *Trading Spaces*, TLC, 2000–. While the British title, *Changing Rooms*, puns both on the makeover atmosphere of the retailer's dressing room and the social camaraderie of the locker room, the American title draws out the aspirational potential of the show by punning on the 1983 film *Trading Places* (in which Eddie Murphy plays a bum who switches places with a financier and begins to live the high life [directed by John Landis, produced by Paramount]).

46. Consider the following comment from a *Trading Spaces* participant: " 'One of the producers told me they want two bad reveals for every 10 shows,' says Kasey Downing, who so disliked the flimsy partitions, enormous padded headboard and mirror above it in the December 2001 redo of her Seattle bedroom that she sold '99 percent of it' at a garage sale" (Annie Groer, "Trading in Trading Spaces," *Washington Post*, May 29, 2003, sec. H1, Newsbank database, British Library).

47. *While You Were Out*, TLC, 2000– ; *Surprise by Design*, Discovery Channel, 2002– ; *Designers' Challenge*, HGTV, 2000– .

48. Patricia Dan Rogers, "Channeling Home Shows."

49. In tracing the provenance of "makeover," the *Oxford English Dictionary* gestures to the crucial link between make-up, makeovers and homemaking in the title of a 1969 article in *Hairdo*: "Make-up Make-over for a Busy Homemaker."

50. Annie Groer, "Trading in Trading Spaces."

51. Of course, the uncanniness of radical metamorphosis, where "I" am still "me" but different, cannot be fully forced out of the frame. In *Extreme Makeover*, it is sometimes caught in the reaction shots of the partners and the children of the transformed person. Small children in particular look simultaneously confused and terrified at being presented with a monstrously same-but-different mommy.

52. This does not hold true for spin-off programs that combine the surgical makeover with the shock-umentary style of clip TV (e.g., *When Good Pets Go Bad*). The British program *Cosmetic Surgery Live* (Channel 5, 2004–), for instance, combines the shock of graphic surgery with the impulse to differentiate between the normality of viewers and the abnormality of those who volunteer for surgical procedures. A double prurience drives programs such as this: the will to see into the body, as well as to see what kind of "freaks" would demand such procedures.

53. Hank Stuever, "The Panic Rooms—TV's Home-Makeover Show 'Trading Spaces' Papers Over a Lot," *The Washington Post*, April 7, 2002, sec. F1, Newsbank database, British Library.

54. Gaby Wood, "Meet Marnie," *The Observer*, July 18, 2004, sec. Review, 2.

55. Ibid., p. 1.

56. Jim Holt, quoted in Wood, "Meet Marnie," p. 2.

57. It is striking how often newspaper articles about the increase in cosmetic surgery mention "studies" that claim attractive people make more money than less attractive people (e.g., Wood; and Decca Aikenhead, "Most British woman now expect to have cosmetic surgery in their lifetime," *The Guardian*, September 14, 2005, sec. G2, Newsbank database, British Library).

58. *What Not to Wear*, BBC, 2002–.

59. Wood, "Meet Marnie," p. 2.

60. Andy Medhurst quoted in Brunsdon, p. 82.

CHAPTER 14

AFTER: WARHOL'S "REVEAL"

LYNN SPIGEL

IN 1960 ANDY WARHOL MADE THE FIRST IN A SERIES of paintings he called *Before and After*. Based on an ad for nose jobs, and rendered on canvas with polymer paints, the painting portrays a woman's face, pre- and post-surgery. On the left side of the painting the woman is pictured with a large hooked nose. On the right side, her post-surgery double has a small turned up one. Is the image a comment on Andy's own nose, which he had already surgically improved by the time of the painting? Is it a critique of consumer beauty culture? Is it one of Warhol's art jokes told for the benefit of those who might appreciate the ironic convergences between art and kitsch? Or is the painting just a copy of a pleasing graphic design?

However you look at it, *Before and After* is a makeover, an aesthetic and commodity logic that Warhol pursued throughout his career. At the time he made *Before and After* Warhol was in fact making himself over, gradually leaving his career as a successful commercial artist to become a renowned Pop painter. Then in the mid-1960s, after proclaiming that painting was too hard, he made himself over as a filmmaker. Noting this and other career shifts (including his stints as a magazine publisher, TV soap opera producer, celebrity model, collector and archivist, and patron/artist for the Velvet Underground), Peter Wollen has called Warhol a modern "Renaissance Man."[1] Speaking specifically of *Before and After*, Donna de Salvo suggests that the painting provides insights into Warhol's own shift from the working-class, Polish Andy Warhola to the renowned Pop artist with a smaller, more assimilated American nose.[2] Nevertheless, throughout his life Warhol whined about his looks, donning a series of fashion poses and famous silver wigs.

In addition to his personal makeovers, Warhol was also a makeover artist, the first "queer eye" to craft fabulous "superstars" out of drag queens, fashion models, and fading box-office idols. In his *Thirteen Most Wanted Men*, Warhol turned criminal mug shots into a famously censored pin-up mural at the 1964 New York World's Fair. A devout Catholic, Warhol, toward the end of his life even remade *The Last Supper* in monumental Pop silkscreens that level out the difference between religious art and billboards.[3] In fact, from his nose jobs to his wigs to his superstars to his crime pinups and da Vinci remakes—especially because of his remarkable talent for turning art into money (or, as his *Dollar Sign* paintings suggest, money into art)—Warhol encapsulates nearly all the themes of the makeover mythos as it runs through American popular culture and through this book.

As the various authors in this book suggest, makeovers have been central to the history of U.S. popular culture. Yet, at least since Pop, makeovers have also become a central fascination for artists (e.g., think of Cindy Sherman's dress-up photos of herself as a fictional film star or the various manifestations of self-reflexive dress-up and drag in video, body, and performance art). Warhol's intervention is key here because his work (whether he intended it or not) provides a metacritique on the makeover mythos itself. For example, Warhol slightly alters the image in the first *Before and After* when making the subsequent versions in the series, and the very act of serialization complicates the promise of redemption that makeovers offer.[4] In other words, by painting more than one *Before and After* Warhol negates the makeover's happy ending. There is no "After," just a menu of stylish choices. In Warhol's hands, serialization frustrates narrative closure. The makeover wish is not fulfilled; instead it is figured as a repetition compulsion—a compulsion that Michael Jackson and the Barbie Doll Twins would later confirm.

In its original exhibition context, *Before and After* performed a metacritique on the relationship among fashion, decoration, and fine art. The painting initially functioned as scenic design for Warhol's 1961 window display at the upscale New York City department store Bonwit Teller. Hung without a frame and overlapping against five other paintings (including his 1960 *Superman*), *Before and After* was a decorative backdrop against which five female mannequins stood, each in a stylish springtime dress for purchase inside the store. Purposefully posed in the window, the mannequins appear to be inside a gallery of modern art, even if in a state of distraction (they are not absorbed in aesthetic contemplation, although some are glancing at the paintings). In this way, Warhol reappropriates the nose job ad not just for painterly interests, but also to restage a narrative of consumer desire. As Cecile Whiting argues, the Warhol window asks passersby to look at his paintings as a female shopper might look at clothes.[5]

After Warhol exhibited his soup cans at the Ferus Gallery in Los Angeles in 1962, his makeover from commercial to Pop artist was underway. His subsequent filmmaking career is by now well documented. Much less is known about his work in television, which in many ways anticipates contemporary makeover reality TV.[6] Although his early films look nothing like *Extreme Makeover* or *American Idol* (they were minimally edited; often silent and/or projected in loops, serial installments, or on multiple screens; and some such as *Sleep* and *Empire* went on for five to eight hours with no apparent plot), Warhol's interest in staging real performances (as in his *Screen Tests*), his use of nonactors in nonscripted scenes, and his most famous quip—"In the future everybody will be world-famous for fifteen minutes"—are by now hallmarks of Reality TV. So too, as David Joselit has argued, Warhol thought that TV and life "mutually derealize one another."[7] In *The Philosophy of Andy Warhol,* Warhol writes, "A whole day of life is like a whole day of television. . . . At the end of the day the whole day will be a movie. A movie made for TV."[8]

Not surprisingly in this respect, Warhol was on the scene in 1971 when PBS began filming *An American Family,* a 12-hour serialized documentary aired in 1973 and featuring the Louds, the first family to allow their lives to be filmed as they lived it for television cameras. Widely regarded as an influential Reality TV prototype, the program followed Bill and Pat Loud's divorce and the adventures of their flamboyant son Lance, who whether he intended to or not, became the first person to come out on national television. In one episode Lance and his mother Pat are in New York City where they stay in the Chelsea Hotel. There they meet an assortment of drug addicts, drag queens, and runaways. They also go to the Whitney where the TV cameras capture them looking at a Warhol retrospective of Elvises, flowers, Warhol's 1967 self-portrait, and his 1963 portrait of Ethel Scull. Later in 1986, while giving a talk at the Andy Warhol museum, Lance confessed that when filming *An American Family* he was "totally influenced" by Warhol. "When the cameras were on me, I was really thinking you know *Chelsea Girls, Bike Boy* . . . I felt like I was in *Chelsea Girls* II, the sequel." In 2001, Pat recalled Lance's friendship with Warhol to whom he spoke on the phone, wrote letters every day, and submitted screenplays for movies that Warhol might possibly direct.[9]

Warhol's own productions during the 1960s and through to his death reveal his fascination with television's histrionic efforts to transform the lackluster everyday into the excitement of the "real." In 1964, just before he made *Chelsea Girls,* Warhol codirected *Soap Opera,* an unfinished film project whose title suggests his interest in the most quotidian of broadcast genres.[10] Just as Pop paintings took their subject matter from vernacular products aimed at housewives (soup cans, Brillo boxes, bottles of Coke), *Soap Opera* took up a daytime genre—not to revile it in the typical modernist disdain for all things female or domestic, but rather to rethink its formal operations and its relationship to daydreaming and everyday boredom.

Soap Opera rearticulates the relationship between commercials and narrative time on television. Whereas television soaps are notorious for their stagy dialogue and "cliff-hanger" effects, Warhol's soap scenes have no dialogue and pose no enigmas (other than the major question of what the film is about!). Instead of the typical "Yesterday, on General Hospital" recap, the film begins with a demonstrational commercial for the "Roto Broilette" meat knife. The sequences then alternate between silent scenes of Warhol superstar Baby Jane Holzer and other nonprofessional actors who seem to be improvising everyday acts (fighting on the telephone, unpacking groceries, passionately making out, reading a newspaper article about Frank Sinatra, masturbating, dancing). These scenes are intercut with commercials for Glamerine Wool Rug Cleaner, Seven Day Beauty Set Shampoo, Secret Deodorant, a public service announcement by Jerry Lewis for Multiple Sclerosis, a Pillsbury cake commercial, an ad for a Miracle-edge Knife, and another for a Wonderscope all-in-one microscope/compass. All were actual commercials made by Warhol's friend Lester Persky, who made 60-second spots for national brands as well as longer commercials for mail order products (the film's alternative title is *The Lester Persky Story*).[11]

One of Persky's long-form commercials is an elaborate makeover story that, when recycled and excerpted by Warhol, bears all the "dead seriousness" of Camp. The commercial features "famous model" Rosemary Kelly demonstrating the miraculous new Seven-Day Set Shampoo. Promising that "science has finally captured the secret of taking one single hair setting and making it last seven days," Kelly recalls her stint as the lucky girl chosen to represent the product that holds hair up even under the most challenging conditions. To prove the point, she subjects herself to a "hair torture test" that includes everything from riding in a wind tunnel to standing under a simulated hurricane. As the commercial goes on, Kelly's advertising persona grows increasingly frantic until she literally screeches with joy as she fluffs up her wondrous waves. In line with his penchant for serialization, Warhol repeats the commercial twice in his mock-TV lineup, thereby restaging and yet also disordering television's everyday programming flow. For audiences who were familiar with programs such as *Queen For a Day* or *Glamour Girl*, Warhol's *Soap Opera* defamiliarized the logic of the TV makeover, highlighting its artifice through repetition, duration, and recontextualization.

Warhol's interest in television and makeovers continued in the 1980s with his TV shows on New York City cable stations and MTV. These programs variously level out the difference between haute couture, drag, and fine art by presenting an eclectic mix of interviews with fashion designers, models, artists, and drag queens. A 1979 episode of *Fashion* (his first program aired on

Manhattan Cable) is a simple demonstrational format with makeup artists doing makeovers, and it also features girls holding up their before and after photos and Warhol (as executive producer) introducing the show. Though initially shot in cooperation with the video studios of Bloomingdale's department store, as *Fashion* evolved Warhol left the studio to shoot in drag clubs and other places around town. Aired in 1986 and 1987 on MTV, *Andy Warhol's Fifteen Minutes* mixes fashion and gossip with a more Warholian graphic look (a mix that is seen also in his magazine *Interview*). The first episode features Blondie's Debbie Harry and model Jerry Hall in a variety format of gossip, fashion, and performance (including music videos in which Warhol appeared). The program begins with "anchor" Robin Leech standing outside Warhol's factory asking, "What kind people visit him here at the factory?" Answering the question, Warhol, Hall, and Harry (who is dressed in an outfit meant to coordinate with Warhol's camouflage paintings) introduce drag queens who are shown making up and performing their acts.

Notorious for his deadpan image that he had already cultivated in television interviews, Warhol in his TV programs restages the conventions of television talk to interrogate the boundaries between person and persona. As opposed to the typical TV art documentary in which a commentator would go to the artist's home or studio to reveal something "true" about the man and his method, in his TV appearances Warhol avoided revealing his private self by cleverly playing with *other* people's public images. Warhol was notorious for alternatively flirting with or frustrating his TV interviewers and hosts, answering with a simple "yes" or "no," or "um," asking the interviewer or people in his entourage to answer for him, and in some cases sending a look-alike to do the interview for him.[12] In a segment of *Fifteen Minutes* (Episode 1) titled "Andy's Guest Room," Warhol turns the TV interview into a kind of surrealist game when his various guest stars are given topics to discuss—vegetables, sex, and brothers and sisters—and each star confesses something personal about each topic by directly addressing the camera. The bizarre grouping of subjects defamiliarizes the entire operation of confessional first-person discourse so important to television as a whole and to the makeover genre in particular. Were Warhol's guests sincere or put-ons? Did we ever really learn what kind of people went to Andy's factory, or anything about Warhol himself? In other words, Warhol's interviews anticipate the now-popular game of simulation and dissimulation on reality game and makeover shows, from *Survivor* to *The Biggest Loser*. But rather than a big money prize or a magical transformation from duckling to swan, the climactic "reveal" in Warhol's TV turns out to be a cover—or at least a displacement for something else.

This sense of the displaced reveal is especially apparent on a 1981 episode of *Andy Warhol's TV* (Manhattan Cable) when Warhol talks with his friend and artist Larry Rivers.[13] In this conversation, Warhol turns the artist's interview format inside out. Rather than letting Rivers discuss his paintings (which Rivers at least initially seems to want to do), Warhol derails him by asking him why he does not get a nose job. In fact, the two spend the bulk of the interview talking about beautiful people and judging their own looks. Finally, Rivers winds up confessing that he has recently had an "eye bag job." When considered alongside the other topics they discuss—Rivers's recent revelation that he likes gay sex, his enjoyment of sadomasochistic sex, and his discussion about his prostrate trouble and related fears of diminishing virility—the fact that Rivers got an eye job would seem (at least to the typical TV audience of the 1980s) less shocking than the fact that he was discussing intimate details of his queer sex life on TV. Yet in his characteristic deadpan way, Warhol remains blasé about everything but the eye job, to which he responds with an incredulous gasp (followed by effusive compliments). In this way, as a TV interviewer Warhol reverses the mechanisms of popular scandal and Hollywood gossip that in his time "outed" gay men. Rivers's coming out narrative and frank discussion of his sexual preferences are presented as just one more banal bit of TV talk, while Warhol reacts to the makeover eye job story as the shocking "reveal."[14]

To understand the myth of the makeover and its resonance in contemporary popular culture, we need—as Warhol did—to connect the popular with the Pop. At least since the 1960s, Pop art and Warhol in particular took up an interest in makeovers in the context of a larger fascination with beauty, glamour, and fashion. In so doing, Warhol delineated many of the makeover's defining features: its fascination with celebrity, simulation, masquerade, artifice, faith, sexual ambiguity, privacy, publicity, and fleeting bouts of fifteen-minute fame. As a mythologist, Warhol used the makeover to present a "queer" version of glamour hovering between, and perhaps breaking down, the perceived boundaries between haute couture and drag (and the sexual subjectivities each assumed). In his hands, the makeover became "Camp" at the same time that it continued to fascinate him (and us) by holding out the promise of redemption.

Makeovers may be a national myth, but today they are a self-reflexive myth that people routinely ridicule for their false hopes, humiliating rituals, and manipulative hucksterism. Just as Max Horkheimer and Theodor Adorno ended their famous "Culture Industry" essay by observing that people feel compelled to buy products even when they see through the ads, the makeover myth revolves around that same elusive paradox and still-unanswered enigma.[15] In response to this enigma, Warhol provided a Pop strategy for pleasure—a reading protocol for commodity culture in which desire, fun, depression, and outright disgust, all mingle. As various authors in this book suggest, makeovers ask us to submit to the self-disciplinary demands of commodity culture. There is something terrifying about makeovers.

Warhol knew this. Just as he followed his Pop portraits of nose jobs, soup cans, and stars with his equally beautiful "Disaster" series of suicides, electric chairs, and tuna fish poisonings, Warhol used the makeover genre to reveal the chilling horrors of performative glamour.[16] In a 1981 guest segment on *Saturday Night Live*, Warhol sits looking in a mirror while a makeup artist applies chalky makeup to his already super white face. The credits roll: "Warhol on Makeup." Warhol says: "I don't want to talk about men wearing makeup or perfume. I don't want to talk about New York fairies and hair-dressers. I have something more important and meaningful to say." Then a second set of credits roll announcing: "Andy Warhol on Death." Still framed in the mirror shot, Warhol offers his views on death, concluding:

> Death can really make you like a star. But then it could be all wrong because if your makeup isn't right when you're dead you won't look really right. . . . When [people] go to see an open casket they always say, Did ya see that makeup? I mean isn't it wonderful? God! I mean didn't they do the right thing?

Here, Warhol turns the makeover into its uncanny double, the death mask. With his ghoulish makeup, Warhol suggests makeovers are a prelude to the grave. While perhaps he did not intend this, his hyperbolic whiteness and ghastly glamour also remind us that makeovers have historically been used to whiten-up ethnic features, objectify female bodies, and demarcate sexual norms. When viewed from this point of view, the myth of the "Great American Makeover" is always also a national cover-up for more deadly historical trends.

NOTES

1. Peter Wollen, "Andy Warhol: Renaissance Man," in Colin MacCabe, ed., *Who is Andy Warhol?* (London: British Film Institute, 1997), pp. 11–16.
2. Donna M. de Salvo, " 'Subjects of the Artists': Towards a Painting without Ideals," in Donna M. de Salvo, Paul Schimmel, Russell Ferguson, David Deitcher, eds. *Hand-Painted Pop: American Art in Transition, 1955–1962* (Los Angeles: Museum of Contemporary Art, 1992), p. 89.
3. Warhol made this series in 1986 and it was first exhibited in Milan in 1987. Some of the paintings were forty feet in length. About half were made by silkscreening the image, and the other half by outlining the image as projected on the canvas.
4. A few other graphic details on the face are also minutely different and, as Donna M. de Salvo points out, in the second two paintings in the series, Warhol decided to "erase the telltale brushwork that characterized his first hand-painted version of Before and After," p. 89.
5. Cecile Whiting, *A Taste for Pop: Pop Art, Gender and Consumer Culture* (Cambridge: Cambridge University Press, 1997), pp. 9–21.

6. Although I am focusing on his working for broadcast and cable TV, more has been written about his involvement with video and multi-media presentations for the Exploding Plastic Inevitable. See, e.g., Branden W. Joseph, " 'My Mind Split Open': Andy Warhol's Exploding Plastic Inevitable," *Grey Room* 8 (Summer 2002): 80–107; David Joselit, "Yippie Pop: Abbie Hoffman, Andy Warhol, and Sixties Media Poltiics," *Grey Room* 8 (Summer 2002), pp. 62–79.

7. Joselit, "Yippie Pop," pp. 70–71.

8. Andy Warhol, *The Philosophy of Andy Warhol (From A to B and Back Again)* (New York: Harcourt Brace Javonovich, 1975), p. 5. In the same passage Warhol captured the sense of derealization and disassociation involved in his confrontation with death by likening his life to a TV show: "Right when I was being shot and ever since, I knew that I was watching television. The channel's switch, but its all television." (*The Philosophy of Andy Warhol*, p. 91). Joselit ("Yippie Pop," p. 71) observes the "deadening of affect" and emotional dissociation involved in Warhol's comments about the conflation of media and life. For example, Warhol says, "People sometimes say that the way things happen in the movies is unreal, but actually it's the way things happen to you in life that's unreal. The movies make emotions look so strong and real, whereas when things really do happen to you, it's like watching television—you don't feel anything"(*The Philosophy of Andy Warhol*, p. 91).

9. Lance and Pat's discussions are in *Lance Loud!: A Death in An American Family* (PBS 2001).

10. His codirector was Jerry Benjamin.

11. According to Warhol, this was the first movie Baby Jane Holzer did for him. See Andy Warhol and Pat Hackett, *POPism: The Warhol Sixties* (New York: Harcourt Brace, 1980), p. 60.

12. For an excellent discussion and analysis of Warhol's interviews and strategic presentation of himself in them see Reva Wolf, "Introduction: 'Through the Looking Glass,' " in *I'll Be Your Mirror: The Selected Andy Warhol Interviews*, ed. Kenneth Goldsmith (New York: Caroll & Graf, 2004), pp. xi–xxxi. See also Kelly M. Cresap, *Pop Trickster Fool: Warhol Performs Naiveté* (Urbana: University of Illinois Press, 2004).

13. *Andy Warhol's TV* was alternatively aired on Manhattan Cable and the Madison Square Garden Network.

14. Admittedly, in 1981, it would already be somewhat shocking to see two men talk about their desire for nose and eye jobs because at that point cosmetic surgery had not yet been as mainstreamed as it is now and certainly would have seemed a "queer" conversation between two men.

15. The last line reads, "The triumph of advertising in the culture industry is that consumers feel compelled to buy and use its products even though they see through them." Max Horkheimer and Theodor W. Adorno, "The Culture Industry: Enlightenment as Mass Deception," in *Dialectic of Enlightenment*, trans. John Cumming (New York: Continuum, 1988), p. 167.

16. This fascination was notably registered in a series of "camouflage" portraits taken by Christopher Makos that showed Warhol in various states of ghoulish androgyny with, for example, chalky white makeup, blood-red lips, and women's wigs. See Christopher Makos, *Andy Warhol* (New York: Charta, 2002).

ABOUT THE
CONTRIBUTORS

EDITOR

Dana Heller is professor of English and director of the Humanities Institute and Graduate Program at Old Dominion University in Norfolk, Virginia. Her previous publications include *The Feminization of Quest-Romance: Radical Departures* (Austin, TX: University of Texas Press, 1990), and *Family Plots: The De-Oedipalization of Popular Culture* (Austin, TX: University of Texas Press, 1995). In addition, she is the editor of *Cross Purposes: Lesbians, Feminists and the Limits of Alliance* (Bloomington, IN: Indiana University Press, 1997), *The Selling of 9/11: How a National Tragedy Became a Commodity* (New York: Palgrave Macmillan, 2005), and *Makeover Television: Realities Remodeled* (London: I.B. Tauris, forthcoming in 2007).

CONTRIBUTORS

Ron Becker is an assistant professor of Communication at Miami University. He has published essays on television history and the politics of gay/straight representation in *The Television Studies Reader, Television & New Media, The Velvet Light Trap*, and *The Historical Journal of Film, Radio, and Television*. His book, *Gay TV & Straight America* (Piscataway, NJ: Rutgers University Press, 2006) examines the rise of gay-themed programming on U.S. network television since 1990.

Marsha F. Cassidy teaches media studies in the Departments of English and Communication and in the Honors College at the University of Illinois, Chicago. She is an award-winning teacher and feminist scholar whose essays have appeared in a number of journals and books since 1980. Her book *What Women Watched: Daytime Television in the 1950s* (Austin, TX: University of Texas Press, 2005) offers a critical appraisal of popular women's genres before the prominence of soap opera.

Alisia G. Chase is assistant professor of Art History and Visual Culture in both the Art and Women's Studies Departments at SUNY College, Brockport. Her primary research focuses on women, costuming, transatlantic travel, and the representation of virginity in mid-century American cinema. She is currently finishing a book titled *A Year to Learn the Language: The Cinematic and Cultural History of American Women Abroad, 1950–1965*. Concurrently, she is curating an exhibition, "Diaristic Indulgence: Persistence of Feelings and Renegade Female Artists," that focuses on comics, graphic novels, and zines created by Canadian and American women in the last two decades.

Melissa Crawley teaches media and cultural studies at Lingnan University, Hong Kong. She received her Ph.D. in Media from Macquarie University, Sydney. Her book *Mr. Sorkin Goes to Washington: Shaping the President on Television's* The West Wing (Jefferson, NC: McFarland, 2006) deals with the critical role that television has come to play in American politics.

June Deery is associate professor of Literature and Media Studies at Rensselaer Polytechnic Institute, Troy, New York. She is author of *Aldous Huxley and the Mysticism of Science* (London: Macmillan, 1996; New York , St. Martin's Press, 1996) and has in addition published numerous articles on reality television, including "Trading Faces: the Makeover Show as Prime-time Infomercial," in *Feminist Media Studies* 4, no. 2 (2004), and "Reality TV as Advertainment" in *Popular Communication* 2, no.1 (2004).

Jennifer Gillan is an associate professor of English and Media Studies at Bentley College, in Waltham, Massachusetts. She has published essays on TV, Film, and Native American Studies in *Understanding Reality Television, Cinema Journal, American Literature, Arizona Quarterly*, and in a number of other journals and anthologies. She is working on a book on Reality TV and is the coeditor of several award-winning multicultural anthologies, *Unsettling America, Identity Lessons*, and *Growing Up Ethnic in America* (New York: Penguin, 1994, 1999, 1999) and *Italian American Writers on New Jersey* (Piscataway, NJ: Rutgers University Press, 2003).

Misha Kavka is a senior lecturer in film, television, and media studies at the University of Auckland, New Zealand. She received her Ph.D. from Cornell University. Her research interests include reality television, TV theory, history of Hollywood film, gothic cinema, feminist theory and criticism. She is one of the editors, along with Elisabeth Bronfen, of *Feminist Consequences: Theory for the New Century* (New York: Columbia University Press, 2001) and is currently at work on a monograph entitled, *Reality Matters: Affects of Reality Television*.

Toby Miller is professor of English, Sociology, and Women's Studies and director of the Program in Film & Visual Culture at the University of California, Riverside. His teaching and research cover media, sport, labor, gender, race, citizenship, politics, and cultural policy. Toby is the author and editor of over 20 books and has published essays in more than 30 journals and 50 volumes. His current research covers the success of Hollywood overseas, the links between culture and citizenship, and anti-Americanism. His work has been translated into Chinese, Japanese, Swedish, and Spanish.

Clay Motley is an assistant professor of English and the honors program director at Charleston Southern University, in Charleston, South Carolina. He received a Ph.D. in English from the University of South Carolina, and he conducts research on nineteenth-century American literature, Southern literature, and popular culture, particularly in relation to religious faith and gender.

Claire Pamplin is assistant professor of English at the Borough of Manhattan Community College in New York City, where she teaches writing and journalism courses. She has published essays on Pauline Hopkins and Marilynne Robinson and is currently preparing a book on the numerous popular culture interpretations of Joel Chandler Harris's work.

Lynn Spigel is a professor in the School of Communications at Northwestern University, in Evanston, Illinois. She is author of *Make Room for TV: Television and the Family ideal in Postwar America* (Chicago: Chicago, 1992) and *Welcome to the Dreamhouse: Popular Media and Postwar Suburbs* (Durham, NC: Duke University Press, 2001). She also has edited numerous anthologies on media and culture, including *Television After TV: Essays on a Medium in Transition* (Durham, NC: Duke University Press, 2004).

Zoe Trodd teaches at Harvard University, in the department of History and Literature. Her publications include *Meteor of War: The John Brown Story* (Naugatuck, CT: Brandywine Press, 2004), with John Stauffer, and *American Protest Literature* (Cambridge, MA: Harvard University Press, 2006).

Amber Watts received her MA from the department of Film and Television at University of California, Los Angeles, and is currently a Ph.D. candidate in Radio/Television/Film at Northwestern University, Evanston, Illinois. Her dissertation examines the phenomenon of *schadenfreude* on contemporary television and in celebrity discourse.

INDEX

(Numbers in bold indicate figures within the text)